A Theology of Criticism

ACADEMY SERIES

SERIES EDITOR
Kimberly Rae Connor, University of San Francisco

A Publication Series of
The American Academy of Religion
and
Oxford University Press

GREGORY OF NYSSA AND THE CONCEPT OF DIVINE PERSONS
Lucian Turcescu

GRAHAM GREENE'S CATHOLIC IMAGINATION
Mark Bosco, S.J.

COMING TO THE EDGE OF THE CIRCLE
A Wiccan Initiation Ritual
Nikki Bado-Fralick

THE ETHICS OF ANIMAL EXPERIMENTATION
A Critical Analysis and Constructive Christian Proposal
Donna Yarri

PAUL IN ISRAEL'S STORY
Self and Community at the Cross
John L. Meech

CROSSING THE ETHNIC DIVIDE
The Multiethnic Church on a Mission
Kathleen Garces-Foley

GOD AND THE VICTIM
Traumatic Intrusions on Grace and Freedom
Jennifer Erin Beste

THE CREATIVE SUFFERING OF THE TRIUNE GOD
An Evolutionary Theology
Gloria L. Schaab

A Theology of Criticism

*Balthasar, Postmodernism,
and the Catholic Imagination*

MICHAEL PATRICK MURPHY

UNIVERSITY PRESS

2008

OXFORD
UNIVERSITY PRESS

Oxford University Press, Inc., publishes works that further
Oxford University's objective of excellence
in research, scholarship, and education.

Oxford   New York
Auckland   Cape Town   Dar es Salaam   Hong Kong   Karachi
Kuala Lumpur   Madrid   Melbourne   Mexico City   Nairobi
New Delhi   Shanghai   Taipei   Toronto

With offices in
Argentina   Austria   Brazil   Chile   Czech Republic   France   Greece
Guatemala   Hungary   Italy   Japan   Poland   Portugal   Singapore
South Korea   Switzerland   Thailand   Turkey   Ukraine   Vietnam

Copyright © 2008 by The American Academy of Religion

Published by Oxford University Press, Inc.
198 Madison Avenue, New York, New York 10016

www.oup.com

Oxford is a registered trademark of Oxford University Press

Library of Congress Cataloging-in-Publication Data
Murphy, Michael P.
A theology of criticism : Balthasar, postmodernism, and the Catholic
imagination / Michael P. Murphy.
    p. cm. — (The American Academy of Religion academy series)
Includes bibliographical references and index.
ISBN 978-0-19-533352-7
1. Balthasar, Hans Urs von, 1905–1988.   I. Title.
BX4705.B163M87 2007
230'.2092—dc22   2007018724

9 8 7 6 5 4 3 2 1

Printed in the United States of America
on acid-free paper

The "flesh" of the Word touches our flesh,
and in him God becomes our neighbor.
                    —Hans Urs von Balthasar

Preface

A major theoretical premise of this work is that no person stands alone. I am pleased to report that the writing of this book helped me commune more intimately with this truth—to see its many forms and to witness it in action in countless ways.

As Paul Giles writes, books "are the product of specific times and places." I wrote this book while being employed as a full-time high school teacher, and this fact, professionally speaking, has shaped this experience most consistently and meaningfully. I am honored to be called "teacher," and I am grateful to all the excellent teachers whose influence upon me has made its life-giving mark—whether by the example of their lives, the communication of their wisdom, or the dedication to their craft. Several teachers in particular deserve special acknowledgment. I thank Erasmo Leiva-Merikakis, who set me on the Balthasarian road when I was an undergraduate at the University of San Francisco in the late 1980s. Erasmo's passionate and faithful approach to scholarship inspired me as a young man just as it inspires me today. Thanks also to the director of my master's thesis, Michael Krasny, who encouraged me to pursue doctoral studies (and also recommended that I read David Lodge). Patrick Ford of Harvard University also merits a hearty "thank you," for Pat saw the scholar in me so much that I began to see it vividly in myself. Pat (himself a great patron of teachers) heartily encouraged my turn to interdisciplinarity and began to help me understand the idiosyncratic beauty of academe.

I owe a debt of gratitude to my professors at the Graduate Theological Union, Berkeley. In particular, I thank Alejandro Garcia-Rivera for his refreshing blend of gentle guidance and scholarly rigor; I found our conversations about the significance and application of

Balthasar's theological program both challenging and provocative. My grati-tude also goes to Richard Gula, whose interest in the theological imagination benefited my project immensely. Thanks also to Jerome Baggett for his early guidance and support. Jerome's sense of humor provided a refreshing antidote to the more stodgy approaches to scholarship. I honor the memory of the late Timothy Lull by thanking him here. Tim's delight with these topics and the courage with which he enacted his convictions continues to inspire not only me, but a large, diverse community of other scholars as well. My very special thanks, however, is reserved for Albert Gelpi of Stanford University. Al's en-thusiasm for this project sustained me in my darker hours, and his (very) close readings of all of my drafts helped me keep my "precious prose" under control and focused upon more substantive concerns. From my point of view, Al (along with his wife, Barbara, and his brother, Donald,) exemplifies the very heart of scholarship—by the generosity of his teaching, through his ardent love for learning, and in his warm companionship without which all these other endeavors would be meaningless.

No person stands alone. I am grateful for the large and mysterious web of friends who supported this enterprise. To the community at Carondelet High School—the sisters, my colleagues, the students—I say "thank you." To my friends Matt Luskey and Mark Bosco S.J., I appreciate your collegiality, wit, and wisdom. To Kimberly Rae Connor: another hearty "thank you." How won-derful it is to be shepherded through these pastures by you. To my friend and brother Matt Stensby, I value all the phone calls and the promises of steak dinners. To my pals on the "Search Committee," the folks at 1492, and "The Family," a resounding "Hassah!" What great conversations!

My mother's encouragement has been a constant source of inspiration. She may be surprised to find that, even with all of this formal learning, she is still my favorite theologian. Thanks, mom, for modeling the value of hard work, determination, and joy. To my sister, Suzanne, I say another large "thank you." Suzy, you have the knack of saying the right thing at the right time, and I'm profoundly grateful for a lifetime of steady sisterly support. I thank my father for his sense of humor, his courage, and his regular ad-monishment to "keep it real." I feel his spirit and hear his voice most every day. Pretty nifty, dad; I pray that God continues to rest you in peace.

No person stands alone. I'm pleased to say that I stand with three very special people, my wife, Marjie, and my daughters, Caroline and Elena. Car-oline, an accomplished author in her own right (in the five-year-old set), demonstrated amazing sensitivity and understanding as I worked through this project. When "daddy was working," she gave space; when "daddy was done," she was right there with "a big squeeze," ready to play, or proofread, whichever the situation merited. Elena, whose recent arrival makes this work all the more meaningful, seems to get Balthasar already and is a living ex-ample that "love alone is credible." Marjie deserves credit as spiritual coauthor of this piece. As I worked at my writing, Marjie took care of most every household detail—from bills to baths—and kept our ship afloat. She also helped format the document and offered a series of useful criticisms. Most important, as far as I am concerned, Marjie's selflessness these past years has deepened my understanding of what love is and what love can do. She provided the spiritual and emotional support that kept all of us going. All of this and a fabulous smile to boot. Thank you, sweetheart.

Credits

"O Taste and See" by Denise Levertov. From POEMS 1960–1967. Copyright © 1964 by Denise Levertov. Reprinted by permission of New Directions Publishing Corp.

"On Belief in the Physical Resurrection of Jesus," by Denise Levertov. From SANDS OF THE WELL. Copyright © 1996 by Denise Levertov. Reprinted by permission of New Directions Publishing Corp.

"Archaic Torso of Apollo," translated by Stephen Mitchell. Copyright © 1982 by Stephen Mitchell. From THE SELECTED POETRY OF RAINER MARIA RILKE by Rainer Maria Rilke, translated by Stephen Mitchell. Used by permission of Random House, Inc.

Contents

Table of Abbreviations

Works written by Hans Urs von Balthasar

A Theology of Criticism

I

Locating Difference

Theological Imagination, Narrative Expression,
and Critical Discourse

In degenerate ages, arts are pastimes.

—Holbrook Jackson, 1911

If it's just a symbol, to hell with it.

—Flannery O'Connor, c. 1956

Reason comprehends rationally that He is incomprehensible.

—St. Anselm of Canterbury, c. 1100

Philosophy ends with beauty, theology begins with it.

—Hans Urs von Balthasar, 1984

Theology and Literature: A Continuing Conversation

We cannot know his legendary head
With eyes like ripening fruit. And yet his torso
is still suffused with brilliance from inside,
like a lamp, in which his gaze, now turned low,

gleams in all its power. Otherwise
the curved breast could not dazzle you so, nor could
a smile run through the placid hips and thighs
to that dark center where procreation flared.

Otherwise this stone would seem defaced
Beneath the translucent cascade of the shoulders
And would not glisten like a wild beast's fur:

Would not, from all the borders of itself,
Burst like a star: for here there is no place
that does not see you. You must change your life.
                    —Rainer Maria Rilke, "The Archaic Torso of Apollo"

Theology and literature have long been disciplinary companions, and the "Word" has historically been at home in the warm environs of literary and narrative form. As Graham Ward rightly asserts, "Theology's business has always been the transgression of boundaries,"[1] and the same can be said for the "business" of literary art. Narrative, for example, the central trope of literary art, is itself endowed with so many of the metaphysical and epistemological qualities that are associated with theological activity that it has long served as a prime mode—a prime aesthetic—in everything from inductive making of myths to deductive meditations on divine revelation. Since it would be injudicious to deny the theological possibilities implicit in narrative form (or that literature is a prime model of both thought and consciousness),[2] this book will use the relationship as a guiding premise. However, the presumption also initiates a dilemma, and immediate questions arise: if narrative is theological in character, do we not have an obligation to be specific about what we mean by "theological"? Can we not furnish ourselves with more descriptive epithets, even, than "spiritual" or "religious" (terms, oddly, that tend to domesticate theological inquiry) when we engage in these kinds of discussions? Can we not get beyond, even, "Jewish" or "Christian" distinctions, for that matter, especially since we are finally disposed to viewing these specific religious distinctions more expansively? Conversely, as serious critics—and as serious theologians—do we not owe it to ourselves, to the literary art we engage (as well as the mysteries they purport to illuminate) to follow the text where it leads even if it leads to the politically dicey regions of specific denominational doctrine and dogma?

  The answer to all these questions is *yes*. We must follow the clues where they lead. Unfortunately, the tendency today is to shy away from making such hard theological distinctions. There are many reasons for this, of course, ranging from the political to the theological to the cultural, and some reasons are more valid others. Many in the academy, for example, are accountable to several disciplines (or other institutional commitments) and are therefore more prone to protecting cultural diversity and less disposed to promulgating divisive opinions that often accompany truth claims. Similarly, the reticence to claim theological uniqueness can arise from patently ideological reasons: many scholars, for fear of making snags in the fragile garment of intellectual pluralism, relegate serious theological discussion to the extreme margins of academic discourse. These scholars have become reticent about using any other epithets beyond *religious* or *spiritual* or, worse, *ideological* when it comes to assessing arts and literatures, for example, that convey theological themes. These developments, of course, are understandable, especially given the volume of one-dimensional fundamentalist interpretations that often encroach upon more nuanced and careful readings. However, the wholesale flight from making specific theological distinctions ultimately does a disservice to any valid notion of scholarship in the same way it curtails the freedom of thought upon which good scholarship is rooted. The need to reclaim narrative as a prime model of theological inquiry, then, is revealed. The time is ripe to reestablish the promise of astute religious criticism for what it is: a meticulous and imaginative epistemology. A theological imagination in the narrative arts is no mere window dressing, but rather an element that inspires and constitutes its very expression. Religious criticism, then, remains a valid option against the more nihilistic and restricting versions of criticism, versions that hold considerable sway in certain quarters of current scholarship.

A Catholic Imagination (A): Elucidating a Hypothesis

The main purpose of this study, then, is to suggest creative and credible options for religious critics. As a Catholic reader of fiction, poetry, and film, I am interested specifically in how a theological imagination is "worked out" in some contemporary fictions and how these fictions might merit the qualifying adjective of "Catholic." Since Catholicism is a *kath holon*, a seeking "after the whole," this kind of project demands that one venture outside the threshold of one's own native intellectual discipline (which, in my case, is English and American Literature) and into the larger arena of interdisciplinary study. Indeed, it can be speculated that the intrinsic interdisciplinarity of Catholicism, the fact that Catholicism, for better or worse, proposes a holistic and interdependent ontology, is precisely what is behind the historical tendency of literary writers and critics alike to jettison the myopia of their own narrow disciplines and foray into a more expansive and more interdisciplinary mode of scholarship. This development has sparked a renewal in the scholarly consideration of the theological imagination. The Catholic imagination has become, perhaps in a spirit of déjà vu, one such "school"—in aesthetics and in religious criticism—a distinct expression within the boundless parameters of what I'll refer to, broadly, as the "theological imagination."[3]

However, the notion of a *Catholic imagination*, as a category of aesthetics, lacks specific thematic and theological coherence. It functions at this time as a deeply felt intuition about the nature of an organic connection among theological insights, cultural background, and literary expression. Part of the problem in articulating this intuition is the difficult interdisciplinary borders that must be crossed between theology and literature. For example, even though in the latter half of the twentieth century (and on into the twenty-first century) a fair amount of work has been done by literary scholars and cultural critics in interdisciplinary "border-crossings"—in articulating the various ways that Catholicism, for example, can have a literary or cultural aesthetic—a relatively scant amount of space has been devoted to a serious examination of the *theological aesthetic* upon which these other "aesthetics" might hinge. Another part of the problem in articulating this intuition, as I suggested, is political. The term *Catholic imagination* incites a variety of strong reactions. On one side of this particular polemic, the prospect of a *Catholic imagination* is perceived by some as imperialist and hegemonic, which entails a rank exclusivity; on the other side, the high regard for pluralism and ecumenism inherent in other perceptions of Catholicism implies that such an imagination ought to be inclusivist, even to the point at which this imagination may lose any of its cultural or intellectual distinctiveness. As we will see, one of the main tendencies of a Catholic imagination is to negotiate such wide "opposites," so as to reveal the mysterious harmonies that often dwell in such tensions.

Along with Thomas Aquinas, Jacques Maritain, William Lynch, and Michel de Certeau (and, of course, with Hans Urs von Balthasar, with whom we will be very well acquainted in short order), I recognize the primacy of the *complexio oppositorum* that resides at the heart of any theological imagination. Moreover, I assert that intuition is an indispensable human sense that helps locate the paradoxical logic that is revealed by the coincidence of opposites I propose. "Intuition," according to classical Thomism, "brings a person in touch with the real"[4] and fertilizes the imagination. This discussion admits intuition as a foundational faculty of personhood and asserts that intuition, contrary to rationalist Cartesianism, precedes *ratio* and provides, as Maritain posits, a fundamental approach to God.[5] Balthasar, for his part, specifically links intuition to imagination and upholds this relationship as a theophanic site:

> The essence of worldly things consists so truly in their imagining God, and this image itself is so transparent, that God seems to shine forth immediately [*immediate*] from it. There is then, a form of 'intuition' specific to symbolic cognition, which consists in a psychologically immediate transcendence of the ontological sign [medium quo], though without removing it at any time.[6]

In this study, then, I seek not only to interrogate the notion of a Catholic imagination but also to add depth—specifically theological depth—to the term *Catholic imagination*. In this sense, its uniqueness may be admitted as a bona fide category in literary criticism, a context of Catholic Studies, and an aspect of a larger theological imagination.

Upon serious examination, then, we find that the Catholic imagination is not merely a cultural or sociological distinction, as so many have recently posited. Quite the contrary: it is fundamentally a way of figuring the world. "Imagination," to borrow from William Lynch's definition, constitutes "all the resources of man, all his faculties, his whole history, his whole life, and his whole heritage, all brought to bear upon the concrete world inside and outside of himself, to form images of the world, and thus to find it, cope with it, shape it, and even to make it."[7] The imagination, according to Lynch (1908–1987), a Catholic literary critic, is a borderless and holistic faculty. It is, to employ a Catholic taxonomy, a sacrament, a palpable manifestation of what is apprehended by the intuition, a sensible manifestation of the real. As an aesthetic operation, the Catholic imagination seeks to describe the peculiar dynamism that exists between religious and artistic experience and to hold this mix up as an ontological and aesthetic category. It is an imagination, theologically speaking, that sees Christ as the revelatory key to the cosmos and figures aesthetics in terms of the Incarnation as axial miracle of history, as existential, as continually eucharistic, and as locus of (and reason for) community.

In my view, the challenge of interrogating and elucidating a Catholic imagination seems particularly timely, and our current academic and intellectual context provides a perfect occasion in which to engage the argument. To this end, my effort becomes a discourse within a burgeoning intellectual community, Catholic Studies, just as it is a discourse in narrative criticism. Part of my goal, then, is to interrogate the credibility of a *Catholic imagination* as a valid aesthetic category for religious and literary critics alike.

Seeing the Form, Forming a Thesis: Christ in Ten Thousand Places

The key to my approach in articulating the Catholic imagination lies in the interdisciplinary style of the Swiss theologian Hans Urs von Balthasar (1905–1988). I will argue that the theological work of Hans Urs von Balthasar provides a model, content, and a lens for interpreting and demonstrating the Catholic imagination as it is depicted in selected narrative arts. In his monumental seven-volume series, *The Glory of the Lord*, Balthasar meditates upon the significance of first approaching the unity of God through the transcendental attribute of beauty rather than through the other transcendentals, truth or goodness, the ways more traditionally associated with engaging in theological studies. A textured consideration of beauty aids in developing a theological imagination that is more comprehensive and perceptive: it helps one *see the form* of God's revelation. For Balthasar, the fruit of this concentration on the beautiful results in a theological aesthetics that locates "the form of God's self-revelation" and then constructs an analogical theory "about the incarnation of God's glory and the consequent elevation of man to participate in that glory."[8] Balthasar's other major works—particularly his *Theo-Drama* and his *Theo-Logic*—enhance and activate his aesthetics in order to further provide, among other things: (1) A Theology of Time—an approach that locates the divine *logos* not merely as speculative but as historically incarnated and identified with Jesus of Nazareth; (2) A Theodramatic Aesthetics—a theology that, because it sees all existence as endowed with a theatrical structure, consequently sees all existence as revelatory and eschatological. In this schema, Jesus is not merely an iconographic expression of the beautiful but rather a "central actor" in creation; and (3) A Trinitarian Logic—a logic that sees human persons as free players/agents who respond to and participate in, because of God's *incarnation* and *kenosis*, the dynamics of an inner-trinitarian dialogue. The theological perspectives that Balthasar promulgates in all of these instances implies that our responses to beauty—our "action" or "in-action" upon encountering (theological) art, our various responses to both "The Word" and, analogically, to other words, and so on—are immediate, ethical, relational, transformative, and, therefore, profoundly theological acts in nature.

This book looks favorably upon Balthasar's theology. However, I will examine and employ Balthasar's work also as an epistemological model for critics of literature, poetry, and film who possess broader theological sensibilities. While I'll affirm that a turn to Balthasar will show that reading narrative art through his theological optic (because Balthasar is a Catholic theologian) will point to the validity of a Catholic imagination, my discussion is not meant to be exclusive. Quite the contrary: while parts of this study will certainly tend to the "Balthasar as lens" approach, this study is not a Frankensteinian grafting of Balthasarian theology upon a host of narrative art in order to provide a sustained apologia for Catholic Christianity in literature. Rather, it is meant to be a study of: (1) how the concept of a Catholic imagination gains distinct credibility when considered against Balthasar's interdisciplinary theological program, (2) how the proposition of a Catholic imagination in narrative arts gains unique intelligibility when viewed in the light of Balthasar's aesthetics, (3) how some representative "Catholic" fictions, when conceived under a Balthasarian light, transmit both cultural and theological relevance, and (4) the Catholic imagination as but one expression of a transformative theological imagination. Of course, most of us will allow that art can be transformative; but Balthasar will persuade us that art is transformative precisely because it is a theological enterprise. Just as Rilke's "The Archaic Torso of Apollo" demands that, upon encountering beauty, we must *Change Our Lives*, so, too, does encountering Balthasar's theological program.

While Balthasar articulates the depth and breadth of his theological imagination in a unique way, his work is not esoteric. His voice harmonizes with an eclectic group—artists, philosophers, theologians—who speak in a common theological tongue. Balthasar takes as premise the traditional theological doctrine of logocentrism that much current scholarship, especially since 1945, has questioned. A postulate to his approach is that the "word" is a theological aesthetic, a sensible and historical manifestation of the spiritual. The word is at the service of the transcendentals—Truth, Goodness, and Beauty—which, again, as, properties of God, illuminate the unity of *being* and, in Catholic intellectual tradition, "regulate reality."[9] The word, to put it directly, transcends. It has both a sacramental and teleological quality about it that some thousands of years of logocentric theology has sought to comprehend and that some current modes of scholarship seek to critique, supplant, or annihilate.

This development, however, presents a beautiful irony: while Balthasar joins his voice with others who share in his sacramental imagination, I will also show how his sustained critique of the dry logic of enlightenment certainty can be seen in league, however obliquely, with many of the concerns raised by the very postmodern theorists who would otherwise critique his logocentric imagination as naïve and provincial. His work, therefore, goes a long way in aiding both the critic and the theologian who inhabit postmodern spaces. The tools that Balthasar (as theologian) offers may give new interpretive options to the literary critic; the tools that Balthasar (as critic) offers demonstrate the many ways that a facility with literary sources can aid the theologian in conveying deep insights about meaning. We see once again the beauty of intellectual pluralism—of interdisciplinarity—and recognize it as a viable interpretive option that might address the current "crisis in meaning." If theology is to remain instructive as a prime interlocutor of meaning, it must come to grips with the deconstructive interpretive milieu that postmodernity proposes. However, this need not be a cause for alarm, as the challenge also discloses yet another oblique complementarity: I will suggest that any cleavage between the theological imagination and postmodernity boils down to faith, which, in turn, is largely a matter of grammar. As Balthasar describes, faith is a vision and an imagination. Faith persuades us to its vision based largely on "subjective evidence,"[10] and issues in "subjectivity" also preoccupy postmodernist criticism. In the interest, then, of demonstrating another indirect kinship between postmodernism and theological investigation, my approach is a traditional *fides quaerens intellectum* and proceeds, largely, along those normative lines. Faith, in this way, may be seen as a prime ingredient that facilitates the reconstruction of texts, an impulse that works through the more nihilistic tendencies that lie at the heart of deconstruction. In fairness, postmodernist critics have rightly insisted that the appropriate social function of the imagination operating through the arts (especially narrative art) is to submit to destruction the standing assumptions of the day; but faithful vision demands that we redeem that destruction through a process of rebuilding and reimagining.

I will now turn to issues in methodology in order to elucidate my approach further. Drawing on tools employed by literary critics and by employing Balthasar's own methods, I will continue examining the issue of logocentrism. As a kind of demonstration, my brief foray into this topic will serve as an exemplum that indicates how I plan to make use of several disciplines in my general examination. I will then round out the chapter by offering additional remarks on methodology, several "contexts for criticism," a short reflection on the significance of this work, and a note on chapter sequence.

Theology and Interdisciplinarity (A): A Methodological Exemplum

Balthasar makes prudent and judicious use of a vast array of sources. For example, he recovers Augustine not only for Augustine's theological credibility but also for Augustine's relevance as a resource for aesthetic and rhetorical commentary. As one of the earliest logocentrists in Western history, Augustine exemplified and fostered a characteristically Latin attention to language, rhetorical forms, and expression. While Greek Christianity tended to prize visual representations and looked to liturgical praxis for the development of doctrine, Latin theological reflection explored a multilevel textual hermeneutic in which metaphor, parable, and other narrative forms are seen as vehicles of revelation.[11] In keeping with his exaltation of auditory art, Augustine's *De Ordine* (particularly the first twenty chapters) outlines how grammar and literature—how forms of the word—participate dialectically in the revelation of God. Such a focus anticipates the twentieth-century concern with language and transmission of meaning, not so much in the obsessive, self-loathing, and fetishistic aspects that linguistic concern has taken on, but rather with language as a primary and pluriform host for meaning. Language, for most deconstructionists, has taken on a contradictory and convoluted character. It is, oddly, the locus of everything and nothing at the same time; it is the essential vehicle that illuminates the important idea that nothing, after all, is essential or meaningful. Language, to quote Rene Girard's critique on the matter, gives "to airy nothing a local habitation and name,"[12] which is to say that language, for strict deconstructionists, is, ironically, a location for conveying the fact that there are no locations. We will interrogate this intriguing notion more deliberately in short order and find that deconstructionism, among its other attributes, shares a buoyant affinity with mystical theology (and other "negative" forms of theology), at least as far as language is concerned.

In *De Musica*, Augustine's sustained meditation on beauty, Augustine anticipates the postmodern suspicion of language and culminates his project by establishing the link between the divine animation of beauty—specifically in the creative and visual arts and in spoken word—in the conversionary effects of the Eucharist. Balthasar will develop such connections into a theological aesthetics and endorse the prime value of "seeing the form." Augustine writes, "I find 'O taste and see that the Lord is good *suauis*' (Ps 34)...If so be ye have tasted that the Lord is gracious (1 Peter 2)."[13] The poet Denise Levertov (1923–1997) is instructive here. Her poem "O Taste and See" (1964) dwells on this deep mystery: the mystery of presence in the Eucharist. With its wider span and its attention to the subtleties of sacramental vision, it extends Augustine's theology. Therefore, it is a good example of a theological aesthetic—postmodern in era, certainly, but not in ultimate effect:

> The world is
> not with us enough.
> O taste and see
> The subway Bible poster said,
> meaning The Lord, meaning
> if anything all that lives
> to the imagination's tongue,
> grief, mercy, language,
> tangerine, weather, to
> breathe them, bite,
> savor, chew, swallow, transform
> into our flesh our
> deaths, crossing the street, plum, quince,
> living in the orchard and being
> hungry, and plucking
> the fruit.[14]

As I've mentioned, Balthasar's aesthetics, following Augustine, is concerned primarily with "seeing the form"—with meditating on a local expression, on a concrete universal. Levertov's poem provides one such "form." She uni-fies thought and thing by faithful vision, by imagination itself, and then by linguistic/poetic affirmation, "imagination's tongue." While this poem was written before her formal return to Christian belief, she illuminates this fe-cundating negotiation by adorning her poem with a sacramental scaffolding, by an implicit (if buried) reference to the eucharistic event of Christ: "O taste and see . . . meaning The Lord." The astounding revelation of the Lord is con-veyed, beautifully, in the blasé setting of a subway through a reproduced ar-tifact of two-bit advertising, a "Bible poster." Next, Levertov casts a variegated range of lush moments, so that eucharistic presence bursts out from this underground experience and blooms in a panoply of effect. She tastes and sees the Lord in actions ("to breathe them"), in objects ("tangerine," "orchard"), in emotions ("grief"), in primal human need ("being hungry"), to categorize just a few. We work to center of the poem, toward an in-the-flesh oriented plea to taste and see. We are confronted with a compelling invitation to conversion that recalls the Augustinian exhortation: "bite, savor, chew, swallow, transform into our flesh our deaths," invited so that Christ may *Easter* in us, that we may "cross the street," banally, as if to the post office, to a holy encounter.

Clearly, Levertov's Tuesday morning subway ride is a revelatory event, and her meditation on tasting and seeing the Lord is both intimate and expansive. Her poem, furthermore, identifies a core issue of philosophical aesthetics: that of language and (real) presence. It renders some aspect of the mystery of the Eucharist without dogmatic qualification and without a systematic commen-tary. It's a good way station on our road toward understanding how Balthasar negotiates the difference between theological aesthetics and "conventional" theological reflection. For example, theologian Catherine Pickstock, who is also concerned with the sacramental beauty of the Eucharist, expounds philo-sophically on what is occurring in poetically in Levertov's piece:

> So whereas, for Marion, the Eucharist is something extra-linguistic that makes up or compensates for the deathliness of language, it is on the contrary the case that the Eucharist situates us more in side lan-guage than ever. So much so, in fact, that it is the Body as word which will be given to eat, since the word alone renders that the given in the mode of sign, as bread and wine. Yet not only is language that which administers the sacrament to us, but conversely, the Eucharist un-derlies all language, since in carrying the secrecy, uncertainty, dis-continuity which characterize every sign to an extreme (no body ap-pears in the bread), it also delivers a final disclosure, certainty, and continuity (the bread is the Body) which alone makes it possible now to trust every sign. In consequence we are no longer uncertainly distanced from "the original event" by language, but rather we are concelebrants of that event in every word we speak (the event as transcendental category, whose transcendality is now revealed to be the giving of the Body and Blood of Christ). The words of Consecra-tion "This is my body" therefore, far from being problematic in their

meaning, are the only words which certainly have meaning and lend meaning to all other words. This is because they fulfill the contradictory conditions of the beneficent secrecy of every sign (certain/uncertain, continuous/discontinuous, iconic, arbitrary, present/absent) to such a degree of oppositional tension that the inhering of bread and Body is not a relation of signification (as for a Zwinglian view), but more like a condition of possibility for all signification.[15]

Pickstock asserts in prose what Levertov renders in poetry. The eucharistic moment is never at a distance: Christ is on a subway; Christ is frying fish in olive oil on the shores of the Sea of Galilee a week or so after his death; Christ is somehow present both in quince and in handshakes of strangers. Clearly, this kind of distinction—between prosaic/systematic and aesthetic theology—is a central question in this study and will be addressed in the second half of this book. My hope is that such an articulation will result in more clarity about theological aesthetics and the contours of the theological imagination.

In any case, Pickstock's point is striking: transubstantiation in the Eucharist uniquely validates the possibility for human meaning. Balthasar agrees:

> We cannot separate his word from his existence: it possesses his truth only in the context of his life, that is, in the giving of himself for the truth and love of the Father even unto the death on the Cross. Without the Cross, which means equally without the Eucharist, his word would not be true ... it would not be the two-in-one christological world which reveals life in the three-in-one ... it is he, in his presence here and now, who is the fulfillment of all the past, and by fulfilling it makes his own past and the past of the Kingdom present. The "words" that he treats here as present ... are a continual reconversion to the reality of the Gospel.[16]

For his part, Augustine is likewise "aesthetically optimistic" in regards to linking language with reality.[17] In any case, my brief consideration of the vitality of a Catholic imagination reveals a curious point: the imagination I propose develops a list of theological tendencies, but the list is not exclusive, dogmatic, or ultimately final. Augustine was certainly Catholic, but not in the way that reverberates with current versions of Catholicism; Levertov, to reiterate, wrote "O Taste and See" before her formal return to the church; Pickstock is Anglo-Catholic. The Catholic imagination herein proposed, then, derives more from theological intuition than it does from institutional affiliation. The common focus on sacramentality and transcendence, on Incarnation and Eucharist, links these thinkers, and the broad chasm that would seem to divide them is made narrow by their common imagination. This relationship bears ripe fruit today for those who read and view not only literary narrative but also all the vast universe of language and sign with theological sensibilities.

Theology and Interdisciplinarity (B): Further
Remarks on Methodology

Balthasar demonstrates the variety of ways that we can consider theology or,
rather, the variety of ways in which theology demands consideration. As we will
observe more systematically next chapter, Balthasar was a vastly integrated
person, the "most cultivated man in Europe."[18] Balthasar was a theologian; an
expert on culture, philosophy, and literature; a publisher and editor; and
would-be cardinal. The deep respect Balthasar pays to interdisciplinarity, in
turn, reveals and models a central facet of the Catholic imagination that I
propose. As a Catholic, Balthasar, again, "seeks after the whole"; he seeks to
negotiate a variety of conflicting elements in order to integrate them into an
intelligible theological system. Balthasar commentator Aidan Nichols observes
well:

> What the reader who comes to the trilogy from a background in hu-
> man letters will marvel at is the range of reference which can integrate
> into the dramatics a myriad dramatic constructions suggested by ac-
> tual plays, and into the aesthetics rich raids on the mythopoeic, the
> common fund of images understood (or at any rate understandable)
> by members of the race. But Balthasar is no Chateaubriand, seeking to
> impress the secular critic with the genius of Christianity via his own.
> The entire trilogy is controlled by a deep feeling of docility.[19]

Balthasar makes judicious use of the complexities of narrative art to interrogate
theological mystery. Therefore, just as Balthasar integrates a broad range of
work by narrative artists and commentators to clarify his vision, so will I. In
this regard, my methodology is deliberately mimetic. Moreover, while the book
focuses on Balthasar's contribution to religious criticism, Balthasar is not always in the foreground. As a writer, Balthasar is particularly astute in that he
discerns the moments when texts and topics ascend on their own merit and
can stand alone without comment. In the following discussion, there are
sections in which a text or topic will stand alone without qualification against
Balthasarian commentary; in other sections, I will refer to Balthasar in order to
add specific depth to the issue at hand. At minimum, this approach seeks to
emulate Balthasar's methodology so as to endorse both the textual uniqueness
of theological expression and the wide scope of theological imagination.

    Narrative then, as Balthasar illustrates, is fundamentally a theological act.
By examining some exemplary instances of narrative art, this study will put
forward the ways that Balthasar's work reveals that "doing theology" is as
much an artistic enterprise as anything else. Balthasar, who earned his first
doctorate in German literature, formulated his theology through the lens of
many "literary" artists, from John of the Cross to Georges Bernanos to John
Steinbeck. While, curiously, he never referred to himself as a "theologian," his

theology is unique in that it looks to literature, drama, and poetry (and music, which only sweetens the mixture) to "see the form." Literary texts, in his view, are incarnational tapestries *par excellence*—living canvases that play host to the great theological questions. Because his theology dwells upon and makes use of the rhetorical power of narrative art, it provides a model by which other literary forms can be theologically interpreted.

Another method has to do with the musicality of presentation. Balthasar's trilogy meanders, arcs, and crests like a great symphony; and readers will find no surprise in this fact since Balthasar, from his youth, was an accomplished musician. He perceived the world largely through the prism of music and tracked the intelligibility of the world—the nature of being, history, and revelation—in musical terms:

> The world is like a vast orchestra tuning up: each player plays to himself, while the audience takes their seats and the conductor has not yet arrived. All the same, someone has struck up an A on the piano, and a certain unity of atmosphere is established around it; they are tuning up for a common endeavor.... In his revelation, God performs a symphony, and it is impossible to say which is richer: the seamless genius of his composition or the polyphonous orchestra of creation that he has prepared to play it.[20]

The works selected in each of the following chapters mimic and illuminate the various stages of Balthasar's theological excursion. However, while the architecture of my remarks relies on the organizing principle by which Balthasar guides his trilogy, we must note that Balthasar is also relatively asystematic in his approach. As we will see shortly, his is a *concentric* vision; he repeats and deepens theological themes, often in a nonlinear order. To an extent, I will follow suit: the general structure of my discussion moves from the aesthetics to dramatics to logic, but I will amplify and circulate around several select themes that I see as important in the reconstruction of a valid religious criticism. My choices, I hope, will make sense on the other side of the journey. As Balthasar astutely proposes in his *Theo-logic*:

> What does a Mozart symphony mean? To answer this question, one must begin by listening to the piece over and over again and by taking in its fullness of meaning through sympathetic understanding. Only afterward can we talk about the symphony, and only with those who have opened themselves to the same tonal image.[21]

While it would be a traditional approach to select one author and engage in a Balthasarian reading of his or her work, ultimately such an approach would not do justice to large scale of Balthasar's concern. Therefore, since "transmission" in literary art has been so important in current discourses, I offer several different narrative and poetic voices that "transmit" a Catholic imagination. For the last thirty years, literary studies have been preoccupied not so much with authors or meaning but with how authors transmit meaning. Balthasar is likewise concerned with aesthetic and linguistic transmission, but mainly as a means and mediator of transcendental truth:

> Everything that exists is allusive, is a pointer and a reminder, and any conceptual clarification or univocal definition of these infinite signi- fications would appear to him as an impoverishment, perhaps even profanation. [The knower] understands *that* things 'signify'; they do it so intensely that one simply should not ask *what* they signify. It is enough if they regard us with their deep, inscrutable eye.[22]

In my view, postmodernism's diminishment of the "transcendental signified" has been a negative development and thrown otherwise well-intentioned critics off the scent. In this sense I develop a discussion of how Balthasar's thought offers practical ways in which meaning (and transmission of the meaningful) can be retrieved and reconciled and suggest options for postmodern critics who have finally become exhausted by deconstructing music videos or by writing about the other ephemera of pop culture.

Balthasar the Humanist: Contexts for Criticism (A)

It is fair to say that Balthasar's work sits at the nucleus of the current move- ment to revitalize aesthetics. He also sits at the center of discussions in the- ology and art, which are rapidly gaining in popularity and scope. The philo- sophical consideration of aesthetics, though, like theories of religion and literature, did not emerge as a distinct discipline in the West until the eigh- teenth century. Widespread enthusiasm for disciplinary categorization in scholarship was at least one by-product of the Enlightenment; and aesthetics was one of the earliest examples of a discrete "self-conscious discipline" in the modern/secular age.[23] As Balthasar notes, "In the age of German idealism, an attempt had to be made to bring together the theory of beauty, which by now had become self conscious, with Christian revelation, and beyond this, to identify the two, if at all possible."[24] Balthasar recognizes that the task of these Enlightenment idealists seems noble enough: to offer a sustained and sys- tematic account of what beauty is and what beauty can "do," especially as an attribute of God. However, upon closer inspection, the undertaking of these early modern "aestheticians" can also be construed as an exercise in a philo- sophical pacification of beauty, a sterile, abstracted, and ultrahygienic "tam- ing" of something constitutive in the universe, something that *is* the universe, "the love," according to Dante, "that moves the sun and the other stars."[25]

How we view beauty (and the arts of the beautiful) has changed so radically over the last three thousand years that it is striking in itself to pause and take stock. The modern notion of a museum, for example, to take one repository of "beauty," would be an idea totally repugnant to Plato or Augustine and would strike them as an inordinate use of community space. The ultimate conse- quence of Kant's aesthetic, to take the apex of Enlightenment aesthetics, is a disinterested (and decontextualized) stroll through this museum. Our encounter with beauty, in this scenario, comes off merely as a project in artifice, one task in *aestheticism*, three or four removes, at best, from beauty's intimacy. Even our critical observation of the figurative gallery-goer is itself a kind of remove, a *watching* of the *watcher* of beauty, an apparition *par excellence* of the alienation between "art" and its organic roots, its grounding in the artist and the community. In Ralph Waldo Emerson's words, "if eyes were made for seeing, then Beauty has its own excuse for being," and we need to be very careful when we speak of beauty and endeavor to make beautiful things. If Nadine Gordimer is on to something when she says, "truth isn't always beauty, but the hunger for it is," we need to be mindful that beauty touches the very heart of our desire, the very heart of what it means to be uniquely human. And if Jean Anouilh is right when he proposes, "beauty is one of the rare things that do not lead to doubt in God," we need to remember that discussions about beauty are essentially holy and sacred events. And Balthasar knows this well: even though he can traffic in the language of Enlightenment-generated philosophical aesthetics, his is a "discourse from the knees,"[26] a contemplation, really, that, in its radical adoration of God, honors the wholeness of human experience.

Balthasar's work models the vitality of engaging historical concepts, such as aesthetics. Moreover, his work explicitly endorses a continuing dialog with history, but it is also a hermeneutic critical of the historical-critical method spawned in the Enlightenment. Balthasar seeks to monitor the complicated mystery of salvation history and underscores the validity of our personal and communal *via*, the unfolding of our narrative as human persons in relationship with God. As G. K. Chesterton reminds us, such an engagement is essentially pluralistic and cross-cultural: "Tradition means giving votes to the most obscure of all classes, our ancestors. It is the democracy of the dead. Tradition refuses to submit to that arrogant oligarchy who merely happen to be walking around."[27] Balthasar shares this conviction; and his instrumental role in *ressourcement*, the mid-twentieth-century movement of a group of European theologians, demonstrates how a responsible consideration of historical sources can aid scholarship and inform current problems in a variety of disciplines in humanistic study. A chief goal of the *ressourcement* group was to rein in errant epistemologies by reengaging thoughtfully with historical sources. A by-product, of course, was that the recovery of antecedent texts and sources became, ironically, new elucidations on modern thought, which, in turn, provided a foil against the monolithic excesses of Enlightenment rationalism. In Balthasar's case, the experience with *ressourcement* discloses two apparently competing attitudes: (1) *ressourcement*, as I mentioned, honors history and serves as a corrective to the excesses of the Enlightenment; (2) *ressourcement* contextualizes Balthasar and establishes his rightful place as a major figure in postmodernist thought. Moreover, since a fuller understanding of theological aesthetics resides in more democratic and pluralistic modes of interpretation, we must include active consideration with the past in our study. After all, as Charles Péguy is purported to have said, "One has to go to the bottom of the well to retrieve the freshest water." Marxian literary and cultural critic Terry Eagleton's recent work (with its attention fixed squarely upon Augustine and Aquinas) attests that there really is nowhere else left to look. Balthasar and his colleagues knew they must converse with history in order to be theologically credible. Jacques Derrida, who writes from the generation that immediately succeeds Balthasar, also knows that he cannot avoid history, even in his attempt to be ahistorical. History becomes but one discourse in Derrida, but it nevertheless serves as a constant challenge to him as he engages Plato, Denys, and Eckhart. Even though Balthasar and Derrida end up with two distinctly opposed views on the value of history in thought, the whole of their work relies precisely on history.

The implications of Balthasar's high regard for both aesthetics and history disclose, perhaps, an even deeper value: the theological nature of dramatic art. Balthasar's theology gains particular relevance as a theology of drama, and he employs a vast array of work—from Aeschylus to Shakespeare to Eugene O'Neill—in his theological program. Following Aristotle's aesthetic theory, Balthasar's strong insinuation is that resolution in a drama itself can have what amounts to liturgical and sacramental effects, that is, *transformative* effects that stem from a simple encounter with dramatic art. Indeed, it may be said that Aristotle realized the innate potential, specifically in the arts of tragedy, for the natural development of religious media as well as the possibility for a theological aesthetics. He saw that art, particularly when it seeks to negotiate and explore the ambiguities and paradoxes of life (as it does in tragedy), can fill "gaps" in nature and can account for a unique indeterminacy of human activity that doesn't register on the radar of idealism, whatever its historical manifestation. In short, Aristotle provides for the key component of "mystery" in narrative art, which, in turn, becomes the cardinal hinge in theological aesthetics. In many ways, the acknowledgment of these "gaps," which breaks the rigid hegemony of Plato's ideal forms, provides the starting point in Balthasar's schema. The acknowledgment also highlights the locus of affinity that Balthasar's project (via Aristotle and the Cappadocians) shares with postmodernity: the primacy of *aporia*, of *Khora*, of gap, or, as Balthasar observes (on how theology can confront and heal the dehumanizing mechanization of the modern world), "When everything is blocked off, one must live in the interstices."[28] Balthasar will dwell on this phenomenon in his work and explore how "empty places" reveal dynamic truth in the very same motion that they conceal it.

Balthasar endorses the Aristotelian respect for narrative aesthetics precisely because of its healthy approach to drama. Like Plato, Balthasar's aesthetic begins formally: God, as "form of forms," can be imagined and perceived as monolithic and otherworldly, as iconic and static; but this conception of form on our part is ultimately an esoteric misapprehension and does not provide for the "action" of trinitarian revelation that, once and for all, provides content for human activity. Only in one aspect of our perception can Christ be held in a kind of iconographical stasis: the part that seeks to stop time in the aesthetic/artistic moment of representation (which itself is a paradoxical notion that later iconographers will fiercely refute, for icons, even in their stillness, reveal divine fluidity). As far as God is concerned, that is, from a cosmological perspective, God has chosen to be in motion, has chosen to "traffic" with humanity, and has endowed and animated humanity to be disposed to such "trafficking." Balthasar's massive trilogy provides precisely for this central attribute in its emphasis on the vibrant inclusivity of all creation in the "household" of God, in the Economic Trinity. God, while self-sufficient and eternal, chooses relationship out of love and thus is ever and always pouring out; Christ is ever and always in "action;" and the Spirit is precisely the "action" of this unfolding, this Theodrama. From at least the second angle, the English poet-priest Gerard Manley Hopkins puts it particularly well in the sestet of his oft-cited "Kingfishers" sonnet:

> Í say móre: the just man justices;
> Kéeps gráce: thát keeps all his goings graces;
> Acts in God's eye what in God's eye he is—
> Chríst—for Christ plays in ten thousand places,
> Lovely in limbs, and lovely in eyes not his
> To the Father through the features of men's faces.[29]

As Hopkins meditates, all truth is grounded in and negotiated through Christ. It is revealed thus precisely by human action, by human participation in the great drama of existence, the "grace" of which, according to Balthasar, is *impression*, "the stress of God in man" that plays, incarnates, and *expresses* in ten thousand places. In this regard, the frozen moment is illusory, an aesthetic concept, as we will see later, that cinematic art negotiates so persuasively. Hopkins writes of his own poem: "It is as a man said 'That is Christ playing at me and me playing at Christ, only that it is no play but truth; that is Christ being me and me being Christ.'"[30] In this regard, both Hopkins and Balthasar extend the implication inchoate in Aristotle and elucidated by Balthasar: that of aesthetic linkage between the visible and invisible aspects of our experience. Christ is historical yet *supratemporal*; Christ is paragon of pluralism yet *supracultural*, "the unique phenomenon Christ is not wedded to any 'culture,'" writes Balthasar, but "Jesus remains the fulfiller of the Old Covenant for every culture."[31]

A Theoliterary Project: Contexts for Criticism (B)

At first glance, the idea of "Christ as *supracultural*" or of "Christ as center" is one repulsive to "traditional" postmodernism. Postmodernism's suspicion of metanarrative and its aversion to theological (i.e., absolutist) structuralism challenge such claims. Tensions such as these are at heart in this discussion, so we must offer some prefatory remarks. A judicious, if brief, analysis of current trends in philosophy is needed here to make further sense of the movement that loiters behind my commentary, that of postmodernism. We

find that postmodernism is, like all historical movements, a complicated phenomenon. For example, upon sober consideration, it has become increasingly
clear that postmodernism is not as generally atheist as some have proposed.
This is not to say, of course, that atheism is not a major tendency in the
postmodern "system," as I discussed earlier, for it certainly is. Any hesitation
in placing faith in the language of truth claims carries with it the necessary (if
not fully articulated) disposition toward atheism or, at the very least, agnosti-
cism. Yet there is also a refreshing honesty in the position that does not
presume to know the mind of God, the disposition that remains humble before
God (as *Other*, even, of *other*) that does not make absolute claims as we journey
through our lives. Such a hesitation strikes one as apophatic; and *apophaticism*,
in its examination of all that God *is not*, is a profoundly mystical approach to
theology. It becomes very clear that many with a so-called postmodern temperament share this kind of spirituality and are in fact propelled by this kind of
theological imagination. The key response to the whole conundrum, furthermore, relies precisely on the faculty of the imagination: in the willingness and
ability to see the form and follow it where it leads. Balthasar is sensitive to this
where other theologians critical of postmodernity are not. In freedom, Balthasar "allows" truth to do truth's work, to go where truth will go. His theology
is not threatened by other "forms" or by the textured nature of truth. Quite the
contrary: Balthasar embraces the expansion of truth that postmodernism
proposes, embraces the movement beyond the illusion of dualistic structures;
and his theology makes a fundamental provision for the annihilation of such
conventions. Balthasar celebrated the "surplus of meaning" that piques the
interest of deconstructionist critics but also figures the excess of meaning as
an emblem of the "transcendental signified." The key, according to Balthasar,
is to remain "open" to such horizons: "This openness to any truth that might
show itself is an inalienable perfection of every knowing subject, and, as
knowledge increases, it cannot contract but only expand."[32]

The challenge to remain "open," of course, reveals deep tensions that
reside at the heart of narrative criticism. According to Graham Ward, "methods of handling texts function on the basis of presuppositions and prejudices."[33] Ward, who is both theologian (he has written on Balthasar, Pan-
nenberg, and Tracy, among others) and critical theorist (he has written on
Certeau, Derrida, and Kristeva, among others), is profoundly conscious of the
cleavage of perspective that divides theologians from other contemporary intellectuals. He assesses the situation in this manner: "The presupposition of
hermeneutics (i.e., the theological tradition) is that universal meaning exists
independent of, but is accessible through, all local expressions of meaning.
The presupposition of the critical tradition is that meaning is constructed—by
the way we perceive, conceive, and think (Kant), and by our language (Derrida)."[34] Rather than being alarmed by the ravine that apparently separates the
two camps or by the prejudices each interpretive community harbors, Ward
has done well to highlight the ways that critical theory and theological understanding can be of mutual aid to each other. If we approach theology in a
"new key" (a concept that Balthasar the musician would surely appreciate), and

if our theological method makes good use of the innovations of critical theory, Ward concludes that we will be "reenchanted" with the world. It is then perhaps ironic to conclude that postmodern critical theory is not actually the threat to the theological imagination that many fear but can be employed to articulate and demonstrate a more comprehensive and animated approach to religious criticism.

Derrida's Challenge: Contexts for Criticism (C)

No discussion about postmodern theory would be complete without devoting ample space to its major figure: Jacques Derrida (1930–2004). More important, a brief introduction to Derrida's work will go a long way in presenting vital concepts and vocabulary that will instruct many of my subsequent analyses. Not only is Derrida influential as an instigator of one most significant intellectual and cultural movements of the twentieth century, but also he is, perhaps, the most influential negative theologian since Meister Eckhart. Had this title been ascribed to him thirty-five years ago, most scholars (probably along with Derrida himself) would wave it off as a ridiculous proposition. Derrida began as a philosopher and, as often happens in life, ended up elsewhere. Derrida is the father of deconstructionism, a massive intellectual revolution that critiques the whole of Western metaphysics. Deconstructionism has become a source of sustained ambivalence: it has had vast appeal in the academy and has been, at the same time, a prime source for rancorous backlash, viewed by some as a kind of philosophical snake oil. The very word *deconstruction* is divisive. It inspires blind supplication, and it spawns harsh invective; but it also aids theological discourse, a point that serves as yet another critique of the modern tendency that bifurcates and oversimplifies.

Derrida's work has increasingly become the default optic through which various and disparate disciplines—from biblical studies to anthropology to rhetoric to poetry to architecture—are viewed and analyzed. Derrida's influence has shown up even outside the academy and has invaded the mercurial regions of popular culture. However, Derrida's fundamental interest has always been precisely with metaphysics; he has always been preoccupied with the "big questions" in anthropology, philosophy, and theology. His ardent consideration of theological sources attests to this fact. Just prior to his recent death, Derrida became ensconced in the ever-surging wave of theological discourse. He became increasingly preoccupied with the issues that lie beyond the bounds of "trace" elements in human experience, the same elements that he long held constitute the limits what we can "know." Derrida recalibrated his deconstructionism and concluded that some concepts—concepts such as justice, love, and reconciliation—are not, in the end, deconstructible. It seems that, among other things, the case of Derrida's personal journey illuminates a kind of pragmatism of aging: that all roads, whether begrudgingly or not, lead back to questions of theology—even if one denies, as Derrida did, that theology and deconstruction have comparable objects.[35] Derrida's own pathology may illuminate a compelling personal application of *exitus* and *reditus*: a reluctant creature drawn back to God even against the parameters of his own magnificent logic.

Derrida's profound impact on late modern thought began in 1967 with the simultaneous publication of three major works, *La Voix et le phénomène*, *L'Ecriture et la différence*, and *De la Grammatologie*, works that began to articulate his extensive and sweeping critique of Western metaphysics, a critique that draws, in part, from the writings of Nietzsche, Freud, Marx, and Levinas, but most of all from the watershed phenomenology of Husserl enhanced and refined in casks fashioned by Heidegger. Derrida developed a method of identifying types of patterns within the act of writing and called this process "deconstruction." Deconstruction seeks to identify logocentric paradigms (such as binary dichotomies, transcendental correspondences, connected semiotic schema) and show that the possibility of presence within any contextual language is in constant "play" and "differs" continuously in relation to something else, leaving only a "trace" of the subject/object. In its most favorable light, Derrida's deconstructive strategy is not an attempt to remove paradoxes or contradictions or escape them by creating a system of its own. Rather, deconstruction embraces the need to use and sustain the very concepts that it claims are unsustainable. Derrida was looking to open up the generative and creative potential of philosophical discourse, as I mentioned above; but he takes issue with the way in which much of metaphysical thought, according to his experience, had foundered into a series confining polar oppositions such as male/female, good/evil, interior/exterior, essence/appearance, nature/culture, true/false, and life/death, to name a few. It is in this area specifically that Balthasar and Derrida have much to say to each other. They, along with other figures in the theological inquiry of *ressourcement* (Henri de Lubac, Louis Bouyer, Paul Claudel) and in postmodern critical theory (Michel de Certeau, Julia Kristeva), criticize what they saw as the hegemony of dualism in modern approaches to philosophy, theology, and literature. It is precisely on this front that *ressourcement* and postmodernity can unite to assail the idealistic abandon of modernity, on this front that a vibrant theological aesthetic may be further retrieved, revealed, and developed.

As an aesthetic framework, though, deconstruction is as far away from Balthasar's constant call to "see the form" as possible. Derrida's invocation might be to "see the 'trace' of the (indeterminate) form (and then, just as quickly, erase this 'seeing')," as we erase words from a page. Be that as it may, deconstruction, while wary of dualism and dialecticism, still tends to be paradoxical and apophatic: it tends to "propose" truth or meaning by "unsaying" it, which strikes critics of deconstruction as the kind binary maneuver that Derrida's stated aims reject. In any case, Derrida's 1986 essay "How Not to Speak" (the title itself relies on a kind of dialectical irony for emphasis) expatiates on this enterprise of resituating and relocating the "said" (i.e., any aesthetic text, film, list, novel, discourse, etc.) against classically dualistic epistemologies in that it revives the very important Platonic term *khora* to aid his quest for conceptual precision.[36] For Derrida, meaning, as I indicated above, lies in the ever-fluctuating zone of the "trace" that navigates the "spaces" and the "gaps" in between, a pattern that John Guare tries to penetrate when he writes of Cezanne in his play *Six Degrees of Separation*: "Cezanne would leave blank spaces in his canvasses if he couldn't account for the brush stroke, give a reason for the color."[37]

Cezanne grapples, aesthetically, with what is unsayable or, rather, what is uncolorable. There is something beyond the boundary of being (or, in Cezanne's case, beyond the spectrum of color) that has not been thought of but that needs to be valued. This is the "zone" of the *khora*; and this kind of inexpressible dynamic begins to get at what Derrida means by seeking a "religion without religion."

Derrida takes *khora* from Plato's *Timaeus* to recuperate difference at the origin, the possibility of a third logic, one that is in "contrast" to all dialectics. John Caputo notes:

> *Khora* is neither form (idea) nor sensible thing, but the place (*lieu*) in which the demiurge impresses or cuts images of the intelligible paradigms, the place which was already there, which, while radically heterogeneous with the forms, seems to be as old as the forms. Plato has two different languages for relating to the forms and to *khora*. When *khora* is reappropriated by ontology and treated "analogically," in various and famous figures, likely stories to illustrate a philosophical point, "didactic metaphors," then it is described as receptacle (*hypodokhe*), space, or matrix/mother. By being said to participate in *both* the sensible and the supersensible without quite being either, *khora* is given a role interior to philosophy, assigned a proper place inside philosophy, and engenders a long history of philosophemes, as the matrix and mother of offspring like Aristotle's *hyle* and Descartes's *extensio*.
>
> But in the other language, the one that is of greater interest to Derrida, *khora* is an outsider, with no place to lay her/its head, in philosophy or in mythology, for its proper object is neither logos nor mythos. In this more negative trope, the second tropic of negativity, there is there (*il y la*) something that is said, very apophatically, to be neither being nor non-being, neither sensible nor intelligible, that is not analogous to either, and is unable to be hinted at by metaphors. *Khora* is neither present nor absent, neither active nor passive, the Good nor evil, living nor non-living (*Timaeus 50 C*). Neither theomorphic nor anthropomorphic—but rather atheological and non-human—*khora* is not even a receptacle.[38]

Caputo's observation of Derrida's meditation on what is "sayable" (and what is not) reverberates with the Augustinian logic on which Derrida was weaned.[39] Derrida's project, then, to put it succinctly, contributes nothing new to structural (or *deconstructural*) considerations of philosophy, but what he does do is promulgate the importance of grammar in "God talk" and argue that grammatical pluralism and intertextuality are as important as, say, political pluralism and interreligious dialogue. We will see that Balthasar heartily agrees with Derrida on the preeminent need for a "third logic"; but Balthasar will employ an entirely different grammar, a grammar based on the sacramentality of Catholic trinitarian logic. Balthasar will assert the vitality of form, the dynamic of the *apophatic*, the *unformed* and "negative," with the analogical value of the *kataphatic, the formal* and "affirmative." It is not enough to say that, for Balthasar, Christ is Plato's *Khora* and that Mary is the *hypodokhe*, but, as we will see, it's a really close call.[40]

Derrida's work offers a legitimate challenge to Balthasar's theology of *Gestalt*. Derrida demonstrates that there is an important relationship between "discourses" and "forms." However, as Graham Ward observes, the closest that Balthasar comes to an overt discussion of "discourse" is in his section "The Mediation of the Form" in volume 1 of *The Glory of the Lord*: "His form in various ways became intertwined with the interrelated forms of his immediate and more distant historical context and with the given forms of the world of nature and of salvation history."[41]

Ward shows that, while there is a kind of affinity between Derrida and Balthasar (in that Balthasar "affirms a recognition of the intertextual nature of mundane existence"),[42] Balthasar will not dispense with supporting the theological implications inherently proposed by intertextuality. In another turn to analogy, Balthasar asserts that intertextuality is a kind of cosmological model, an invitation to make broader connections in meaning. Ward reaches a similar conclusion: "We have to learn how to read all these forms that constitute the particularity of our existence. We have to learn to see them as forms and not as objects containing a meaning closed within themselves and independent of Christ."[43]

For his part, literary and cultural critic Paul Giles does well to locate the phenomena of postmodernism and deconstruction within the intersection of theology and narrative art. Moreover, he becomes a very significant interlocutor in both articulating and critiquing the notion of a Catholic imagination within this critical setting. Since current critical theory tends to privilege and emphasize the unique character of cultural expression, Giles is a good way station between points of view that see Catholicism as theological truth and those that see Catholicism as cultural or literary text. In his seminal work, *American Catholic Arts and Fictions: Culture, Ideology, and Aesthetics* (1992), Giles examines why it is that looking to François Mauriac, Flannery O'Connor, or Martin Scorsese can "reveal more about the Catholic experience than reading many wearisome issues of *Catholic Digest*."[44] While Giles is particularly interested in this notion because of the aesthetic and sociological implications it delivers to narrative art (the idea of that Catholicism is one textuality among many others, that "theology itself might be seen to function as a fluctuating signifier, a series of fictional constructions,"[45] and so on), one can modulate the register slightly and conceive of Giles's insights in regard to aspects of Catholicism that are theologically mysterious and probably supercultural. For example, mulling over the violence of Walker Percy's *Lancelot* or contemplating the theological intensity of the series of Bess's interior monologues in Lars von Trier's *Breaking the Waves* will tell one as much (or more) about the mysteries of *justification* and *kenosis* as reading Rahner's *Hearer of the Word*. Giles's method, while it hesitates to invest explicitly in theological claims, plots a route for appreciating the aesthetic complexity and theological possibility of a broadly canvassed intertextuality. Giles's insights celebrate cultural similarity and cultural difference. In this manner, his work facilitates the recognition of essential questions in order to challenge and aid the articulation of a *Catholic imagination*.

In the second volume of Balthasar's *Theo-Drama*, Balthasar reminds us that the Greek word *analogia* "implies a mysterious, irreducible 'similarity in dissimilarity.' "[46] We are again struck, then, by the idea that postmodernity and the Catholic imagination have much to say to each other. Seen together, they can offer joint critique of the arid dualism that scaffolds the history of aesthetic theory. Balthasar decries the historical turn to dualism; and we shall witness shortly how he responds to the constraints of the dualistic imagination with an interdisciplinary articulation of an incarnational imagination, one that mitigates duality by reasserting and demonstrating the legitimacy of the trinitarian structure of being. However, Balthasar's endorsement of the triadic structure of the *imago Trinitatis* is not to be read as a dismissal of the value of binary relationships. Balthasar, as a student of the great Polish Jesuit Erich Przywara, was clear about the existence of the "polarity structure" of the universe. More important, he came to see that "polarity structure" and dualism were not the same thing and that Przywara's presentation of the triadic structure of the *analogy of being* makes it clear that mystery and truth reside somewhere in between the polar extremes of any binary proposition and any dualistic relationship. It is a theme, we shall see, that Balthasar returns to time and again. In the first volume of *The-Logic* (*The Truth of the World*), Balthasar writes: "Truth can be found only in the floating middle between the appearance and the thing that appears. It is only in the relation between these two things that the empty mystery becomes a full, perennially self-replenishing mystery. It is only in their relation . . . they can now be interpreted."[47] It is perhaps here that Balthasar and Derrida are most closely approximated: what is present is an absence, an unseen reality whose power is perhaps beyond verbal expression. Paul Fiddes refers to this analogical dynamic as nothing less than the grace of God: "Only the gift of divine grace can create an analogy between human speech signs and the reality of God, between the word and the words."[48]

Serving the Community, Reviving Old Relationships

The significance of my study is threefold, the first being theological. In his revival of the patristic notion of Christ as cosmological center of all space and time, Balthasar vivifies the withered hand of scholasticism and grounds some of more theologically restricting tendencies of modern thought: "We now know that love has been given a form," writes David Schindler of Balthasar's fusion of aesthetics with history, the meaning of which "is forged in Christology, and in turn in the analogy of being which is developed in light of that Christology."[49] Again, Balthasar urges us to "see the form [of Christ]" in all manner of being, whether they be human activities, natural phenomena, or, even, human works of art. "Seeing the form," then, becomes a central inter-disciplinary theological hermeneutic that promises to be fruitful for all sorts of interdisciplinary investigations in which theology is one of the disciplines.

The second level of significance is literary. One of Balthasar's many con-tributions is that he furnishes the contemporary religious critic with the tools to reforge a space for *bona fide* theological discourse in environments that have become indifferent—or even hostile—to such activity. Such a retrieval of this powerful relationship between theology and narrative art—between theologi-cal rhetoric and literary representation—is a main topic of Balthasar's *Theo-Drama*, and a serious study of the implications that his theodramatics entails for literary theory has yet to be done.

In the true spirit of the trinitarian model, the conjugation of the first two levels of significance produces an essential third. Close inspection reveals that Balthasar has practical contributions to make to discourses in critical theory. Like critical theory, Balthasar's work is theological, literary, anthropological, philosophical, psychological, political, and historical, the disciplines that out-line the breadth critical theory's multivalent concern. Like critical theory—and in the spirit of the *ressourcement* theology that shaped him—Balthasar is pri-marily interested in critiquing the idealistic *excesses* of modernity. Balthasar, too, is concerned with issues of language and difference, with *aporia*, with plu-rality, with surplus, and with horizons of meaning, to name a few. The dif-ference between Balthasar and the majority of critical theorists resides in on-tological and theological orientation: it is therefore a difference of imagination and of grammar. This book aims to elaborate on this relationship.

I am now in a position to move to chapter 2, in which I offer both a biography of Balthasar and a protracted bibliography of his work. By this effort, I will introduce a more systematic presentation of the main pillars of Baltha-sar's theological program and begin to convey Balthasar's unique contribution to current discussions about the intersection among theology, history, phi-losophy, and narrative art. In chapter 3, I focus on Balthasar's aesthetics as a call to *vision*; and I cultivate a parallel between seeing the "word" and "seeing the form." I'll develop an aesthetics of the "word" in the first three sections of the chapter and then apply what I glean to a very close reading of Flannery O'Connor's "Revelation," (1964) particularly as a literary embodiment of a Catholic imagination. In chapter 4, my goal is to isolate several essential as-pects of Balthasar's theodramatic theory and to demonstrate how they "play" in and through Lars von Trier's dramatic film *Breaking the Waves* (1996), the first installment of his *Golden Heart* trilogy. It is no coincidence that Balthasar places his theodramatic program precisely between his aesthetics and logic in order to emphasize the spatial centrality of God's dramatic *action* in, with, and through the world. In chapter 5, I offer a reading of David Lodge's novel *Therapy* (1995). Lodge does very well to illustrate that the erasure of God that preoccupies postmodern consciousness significantly affects philosophical conceptions about "subject formation" and theological conceptions about "people in relation." Lodge develops these themes by constructing a narrative that mirrors the existential progression—that is, the aesthetic, ethical, and religious "stages"— identified by the Danish philosopher Soren Kierkegaard. Importantly, a close consideration of Kierkegaard's stages reveals a direct analogy with the transcendentals, which, in turn, illuminates one of the many reasons that Balthasar admired Kierkegaard and that Lodge's novel is a perfect piece to read against Balthasar's *Theo-Logic*. In this sense we can discover again how philosophy and theology work together and discern how God's logic— how human logic—exists in a trinitarian dynamic.

2

Hans Urs von Balthasar

Transmodernist

The modern mind is in complete disarray. Knowledge has stretched
itself to the point where neither the world nor our intelligence can
find any foothold. It is a fact that we are suffering from nihilism.
　　　　　　　　　　　　　　　　　　　—Albert Camus, 1954

Nothing is so dangerous as being too modern; one is apt to grow
old fashioned quite suddenly.
　　　　　　　　　　　　　　　　　　　—Oscar Wilde, 1884

Post-modernism is modernism with the optimism taken out.
　　　　　　　　　　　　　　　　　　　—Robert Hewison, 1978

Initially, they stand or sit next to one another as strangers, in mutual contradiction as it were. Suddenly, as the music begins, they
realize how far they are integrated. Not in unison, but what is far
more beautiful—in symphony.
　　　　　　　　　　　　　　　—Hans Urs von Balthasar, 1972

The Most Cultivated Man of His Time:
Some Biography for Context

The appeal of intellectual interdisciplinarity, now ubiquitous in
the academy, would likely have remained an unrealized and vaporous
proposition had it not been for the Enlightenment. Of course, the
origins run even deeper, and the massive volume of current forays
into interdisciplinarity, along with the widespread formalization of
interdisciplinary studies as a major course of study, solicits a
more complex analysis. Interdisciplinarity is *both* a reaction *and*

a renaissance: a reaction in the sense that it responds to the hyperintense intellectual specialization inaugurated by Enlightenment convention, and a renaissance in the sense that, in its emphasis on seeing something more behind phenomena than linear and syllogistic conclusions, it recovers a more integrated and traditional approach to scholarship. The holistic urge of inter-disciplinarity—that is, the healthy ambition to locate "disciplinary" connec-tions outside of the proverbial "box"—goes a long way in explaining a thinker such as Balthasar, particularly in his role as major intellectual figure of the twentieth century. Without the Enlightenment, Balthasar's contribution to continental philosophy—his ontology, his epistemology, and, most especially, his aesthetic theory—is inconceivable; and without the vast territory of intel-lectual history that precedes the Enlightenment—ancient philosophy, early mediaeval theology, and, most especially, Patrology—Balthasar's contribution *in toto* does not seem imaginable at all. Such a peculiar ambivalence is re-freshing, especially in our present context, and the recognition of it reveals something essential about Balthasar: his *oeuvre*, his mission in life, is a full-gazing two-eyed affair. One eye is fixed upon *ressourcement* and seeks to return to and recover authentic sources in order to right the ship of theological scholarship that was assailed by the storm of the Enlightenment; the other eye gazes imaginatively on what may lie ahead, on what the Spirit may bring as things unfold. In any event, Balthasar's work seeks for the fullness of being, the fullness of God's expression, which itself is a response to our own unique context: his work begins as a counterfriction to the rigid and desiccated myopia that has come to characterize the underbelly of the "Age of Reason," of mo-dernity, and continues as a rich resource for postmodernity, which vigilantly values a plurality of epistemologies and endorses the unreserved mingling between disciplines.

This last point acutely reveals an additional complexity in that Balthasar, who rejects from his core the very *ethos* of modernism, appears in practice to be one of its greatest adherents. For instance, Balthasar excelled in a variety of prototypical Enlightenment institutions, mastered a host of disciplines, and understood disciplinary distinctions. He was an accomplished musician and composer from his youth; he was a polyglot, polymath, and, at times, a Polly-anna. Indeed, Balthasar's peripatetic approach to life and learning would make any eighteenth-century rationalist stand and cheer. However, it would not be long before this very same rationalist would get awkwardly quiet and excuse himself from the room, wondering what purpose all of Balthasar's *Ave Marias* served, a point that illuminates a critical distinction: the difference between Balthasar and this hypothetical rationalist ancestor lies specifically in how the two approach, perceive, and identify ways of knowing and ways of "disciplin-ing." For example, Balthasar did not believe, as the rationalist might, that his various skills, in the end, were purely a result of a personal and Promethean achievement, the faculty of the intellect set free in enlightened circumstances. This simply does not go far enough. Balthasar viewed his prodigious and gen-eral capacity for knowledge as a gift from the spirit, a unique aptitude to be cultivated and communicated for the benefit of all. As a gifted musician, for example, he did not make music his God or view himself, narcissistically, as the high priest of piano; rather, he saw his success in the arts, sciences, and humanities—in the disciplines—as a service of something greater than himself, as an instrument in the great symphony of being and becoming. This manner of orientation and approach fundamentally informs all of Balthasarian thought, a detail not unnoticed by one Balthasar's great mentors, Henri de Lubac, who famously assessed Balthasar in the strongest of terms: "This man is perhaps the most cultivated man of his time. If there is a Christian culture, then here it is."[1]

In a vital sense, then, our first clue into Balthasar as a theologian is that his is a theology of *interdisciplinarity*. If theology expects to be relevant to the whole of life, to be cross-cultural, theology needs to holistic, needs to be "catholic" in the word's most denotative sense. Whereas being merely *disciplinary* implies a kind of underevolved and isolated monism, being interdisciplinary discloses something more gracious and relational and therefore something more theologically evolved. So then, if interdisciplinarity is about the dynamism of existence, of being, it should be about the dynamic engagement between various disciplines and modes of scholarship. In this sense, Hans Urs von Balthasar is the banner figure for interdisciplinary study. As a conscientious practitioner of this scholarly approach, Balthasar becomes a paragon of Catholic Studies: he is universal in his approach to theological inquiry, mining the resources of such disparate disciplines as Continental logic and Indian mysticism. As we shall see more clearly, his work is also the best optic through which to view the current academic movement of a "Catholic imagination" as an intellectual *and* cultural location, the imagination that negotiates logic and mystery, doctrine and revelation, ethics and aesthetics, attitude and beatitude, and, perhaps most important, "mentality" and sacramentality.

Born into a fairly aristocratic family on August 12, 1905, in Lucerne, "the most Catholic city of pre-secular Switzerland," Balthasar exhibited the signs of a scholar from a very early age.[2] Always one to read and play music, Balthasar combined these two powerful passions in his first book, *The Development of the Musical Idea: An Attempt at a Synthesis of Music*, published in Germany 1925 when he was just twenty years old. It is intriguing to observe that, even at this point, Balthasar's personality as a theologian is in full figure: he interrogates ideas that are communicated by the beautiful by uncovering the harmony of the disciplines as they work together to disclose both a narrative pattern and a logic that are native in an aesthetic idea. He constructs and reveals, in this case, a metaphysic of music. However, in the context of Balthasar's educational formation, his first book seems measurably dissonant, for his parents had removed him from what was the equivalent of a musical secondary school and transferred Balthasar to a Jesuit college in what would be the American equivalent of the middle of his senior year. Perhaps this first book was the reprisal of a mildly rebellious boy who would have preferred a life of music to anything else. In any case, his inclination toward theology did not manifest itself overtly in this early stint with the Jesuits. In fact, it can be surmised that Balthasar was originally unprepared to engage in the theological formation that he would later embrace when he left the Jesuit college soon after entering in order to pursue doctoral studies at the University of Zurich.

Balthasar's doctorate was in "Germanistics," (i.e., German literature, philosophy, and culture), his dissertation a study of some apocalyptic and eschatological problems in modern German literature. Again, Balthasar's topic illustrates his own native instinct for interdisciplinarity as well as the inclination to make fertile disciplinary connections between theology and literature, just as it presages the twentieth century's concern with endings—with the "last things" (*eschata*)—and with the idea of narrative "closure." Paul Fiddes astutely recognizes the turn to interdisciplinarity, particularly in the relationship between theology and literature:

> In fact there is a remarkable convergence going on between theologians and literary critics in their focus upon eschatology. Among the theologians, Jurgen Moltmann has been influential in claiming that eschatology is not just an appendix to Christian doctrine, to be abandoned to the enthusiasms of fanatical sects and revolutionary groups; since eschatology is the doctrine of Christian hope and witnesses to the God of hope, it is "the medium of the Christian faith as such, the key in which everything is set, the glow that suffuses everything here in the dawn of an expected new day." In the same tones, literary critics declare the basic nature of texts is eschatological, and that this dimension is too important to be left to the minority of interests of science fiction and disaster novels. Indeed, Jacques Derrida claims that the apocalyptic mood of the nuclear age "has been dealt with more 'seriously' in texts by Mallarme, or Kafka, or Joyce, for example, than in present-day novels that would offer direct and real descriptions of a 'real' nuclear catastrophe." All texts are eschatological, both in being open to the new meaning which is to come to them in the future, and also in being seriously open to the horizon which death gives to life, though the relation between this openness and the interior "eschaton" of the closure of narrative is debated as vigorously as theologians debate realized and future eschatology.[3]

Though Fiddes would do well to add Balthasar to his list of "theologians," his observations are no less compelling: theology and literature are not so much compementary disciplines as they access the one great discipline of being. In their own "styles" (a concept vital in Balthasar), they seek to describe the oneness and integrity of the human story that unfolds in God. Fiddes continues:

> Of course we must add, as does Mark Taylor, that this "emplotment" of history has not been understood by Christians as a mere *projection* of a concord fiction, but as the *discovery* of relations between events which have been plotted by the divine *Logos* into a scheme of promise and fulfillment, and which are sustained in their coherence by the presence of the Logos.[4]

Clearly, Fiddes is on to something and his approach to the theoliterary connection complements Balthasar fruitfully. Like Balthasar, Fiddes recognizes that narrative is a constituent element of existence, a theological provision—not merely a human construct grafted onto life by artists, a scheme that generally describes late modern and postmodern perceptions of narrative. In Balthasar's case, the result is not without humor. His literature doctorate turned out to be his only doctorate (besides multiple honorary theological doctorates); and he famously joked later that he found it hard to understand that people refer to him as a theologian when his expertise lay in literary studies. Again, the case is made for the fundamentally interdisciplinary nature of scholarship. In any event, Balthasar decided to put off the "last things" of literature until later—the eschatology of aesthetics, it is no surprise, is a main theme of his titanic trilogy—and he began to be irrevocably drawn to testing his theories more "practically," that is, from a decidedly religious base. So, in 1929, after submitting his doctoral thesis, he returned to the larger narrative of his own life, to the *via* of theology and vocation, and entered the Society of Jesus.

A Catholic Imagination (B): *Hallar Dios en Todas las Cosas*

In retrospect, Balthasar's transition from exercises in literary and cultural studies to Ignatian formation strikes us as entirely fluid. To a person who views image and narrative as central components of sound theological consideration, Ignatius of Loyola is a perfect spiritual icon on whom to fix. Ignatius's prayerful attention to diverse voices in his spiritual exercises (consolation, desolation, etc.) is analogous to the plurality of voices that exist in any good narrative and illuminate the dramatic structure inherent in being. Ignatius's emphasis on sacramentality, furthermore—that is, on the dynamic relationship among physical context, imagination, and faith—spoke persuasively to the young Balthasar and significantly influenced his theology. Also, the Ignatian emphasis on the centrality (and variety) of Christian *form*, on what Ignatius contemplated as "the mental representation of the place," the locale where we "see the great extent of the surface of the earth, inhabited by so many different peoples. . . . Here it will be to ask for intimate knowledge of our Lord, who has become man for me, that I may love Him more and follow him more closely,"[5] disposed Balthasar most favorably to the Ignatian brand of theological contemplation. Most important, perhaps, Balthasar was drawn in by Ignatius's exemplary approach to *freedom* and *mission*. Ignatius's romantic obedience to grace and revelation is itself an inchoate road map to a theological aesthetic: the fidelity of a hero or heroine to a noble goal in the face of mundane adversity. As such, Balthasar was ever and always prone to be a Jesuit.

It would also be legitimate to presume that the cosmopolitan reputation of the Society of Jesus would be appealing to "the most cultivated man in Europe," but, oddly, this fact did not did not really figure into Balthasar's experience as a Jesuit. In fact, aside from his academic formation at the theologate in Fourviére (just north of Lyon) and a short stint in Munich, Balthasar spent most of his days out of the Jesuit loop in Protestant Basel, a kind of Catholic hinterland in Switzerland. It was here where the great Lutheran theologian Karl Barth was constructing his indispensable *Church Dogmatics* while Catholics were flying under the radar. This situation seemed to fit Balthasar for a variety of reasons. First, as aristocratic and cultivated as Balthasar was, he was the kind of Jesuit who identified with Ignatius in the saint's more ascetic modulations. These "at once more missionary and more interior"[6] tendencies, it can be argued, ultimately prepared Balthasar for his traumatic break with the Jesuits in 1950. Second, Balthasar was able to teach young Catholics who lived in a more (theologically) pluralistic environment than Rome or Paris, which sharpened Balthasar's ecumenical sense. He was a renowned retreat master (leading over fifty of them in his years as student chaplain), and his sermons were broadcasted on the radio. Third, he served as a guardian of European tradition as an academic who was fortunate enough to be, quite literally, "above the fray" of World War II. His famous editing of *The European Series* (of anthologies) defended the multicultural heritage of Europe against the totalitarian specter of National Socialism and maintained the Catholic Social tradition of commenting forcefully on political issues, on prejudice, and on economic matters.

Important relationships in Basel sustained Balthasar. The first is the foundation of and participation in the secular institute of the Community of St. John (*Johannesgemeinschaft*)—an institute he founded with Adrienne von Speyr but without the endorsement of Balthasar's Jesuit superiors or the local bishop, an acutely important circumstance that helped shape the middle third of his life. The Community of St. John became important for many other reasons as well: it fulfilled Balthasar's need for community (especially after he dispensed his vows as a Jesuit); as a publishing house (*Johannes Verlag*), it gave Balthasar a venue in which to contribute intellectually at a critical point in the century for Catholic discourse; and it insightfully anticipated (and modeled) today's need for productive lay/clerical partnership. The next relationship is with his friendship with Karl Barth, a partnership that challenged and expanded his own theology and helped delineate its Catholic contours, particularly when it came to articulating the importance of the transcendentals that are so central to Balthasar's thought. It is fair to say that Barth's Christology, with its emphasis on the uniqueness of the historically revealed *Logos* (with all that this entails analogically), aided Balthasar's fledgling considerations about the nature of theological aesthetics, the analogy of being, and the Christological nature of time.[7] And, most important, his relationship with Adrienne von Speyr, whose role as Balthasar's mystical teacher deserves its own book-length space, was one of incredible depth and breadth and flourished until her death in 1967.

Truly, one cannot understand Balthasar without understanding Basel. It was there that the long reach of *ressourcement* trumped, even, the church culture of which Balthasar was so fond. In the true spirit of early church, it can be surmised, Balthasar recovered the true spirit of church. In obedience—to the Jesus of the gospel and the Christ of revelation—he chose to side with a more fully integrated community instead of one that was more narrow and officious.[8] Perhaps more important, Balthasar tacitly endorsed an ecclesial role for women. Notwithstanding the centrality of Balthasar's highly developed Marian theology, it is Adrienne von Speyr, most of all, with whom, as Aidan Nichols observes, "Catholic officialdom has only in the last few years begun to come to terms."[9] Ironically, it is Speyr—who had no formal training in theology—who served as Balthasar's most influential teacher, a flesh-and-blood tutor in matters of mystical theology, ecclesiology, and, most vitally, prayer. In this sense, Speyr can be seen as priestly; she takes up the mantle of Phoebe of Rome, and the two become further examples of de facto and bona fide priestesses who are denied their rightful place in history, it can be argued, by the curious machinery of sexual politics and hierarchical tradition.[10] In Basel, Balthasar was a perfect Jesuit, so perfect, perhaps, that he chose to disassociate himself from them. Yet, as Henri de Lubac tells us, he was an ever "fervent disciple"[11] of Ignatius, and his theology, as I suggested above, depends extensively on Ignatian thinking just as his spirituality depends on Ignatian action. In point of fact, just before Balthasar's death in 1988, there was even a move at a renewal of his Jesuit vows, as Balthasar and Jesuit Superior General Peter-Hans Kolvenbach were in discussion about such a possibility. It would be facile and ungenerous to speculate that this reconciliation was initiated because Jesuits are famously adept at capitalizing on a "commodity" and because the discussion about reunion occurred in light of the conventional recognition that Balthasar (along with Jesuit confrere, Karl Rahner) was one of the two most important Catholic theologians of the latter half of the century. The truth is something much more akin to trying to resolve a delicate and painful family argument. In a 1999 interview in the Jesuit periodical *America*, Balthasar scholar Werner Löser reports of a walking trip in 1973 during which the two discussed the matter:

> It was a long excursion. Along the way, Balthasar confided his personal thoughts and feelings about the Jesuits. He had left them in 1950. It was a very painful episode that he still felt more than 20 years later. I recall him saying, "I am still a Jesuit, but I live in exile. This situation is an ever-bloody wound in my heart." Now Balthasar was "a fervent disciple of St. Ignatius," as his friend Henri De Lubac once wrote. In fact, in his later years he tried to rejoin the Society of Jesus. Peter-Hans Kolvenbach, the superior general of the society, was ready to agree to his request in the 1980's. But Balthasar died in 1988 before it could happen.[12]

The relationship between Balthasar and the Jesuits is of fundamental importance. The Jesuit engagement with modernism, represented best in the person of Karl Rahner, provides a constructive backdrop against which to finish this short biography and move into an analysis of how Balthasar's work contributes to literary criticism and how it might fit with the postmodern "school." Rahner (1902–1984) was *the* archmodernist, theologically speaking. His "Supernatural Existentialism" and "Transcendental Thomism" were two of the important theological perspectives that underpinned the Second Vatican Council (1962–1965) and influenced theological inquiry for the following twenty-five years. Rahner, on the one hand, was a *peritus*, or theological expert, at Vatican II and influenced many conciliar texts. Balthasar, on the other hand, was not invited to the council. He spent Vatican II (as well as the years that followed) writing his great trilogy as well as many of his other shorter tomes. As Vatican correspondent John Allen observes: "While Rahner became an icon of the church's liberal wing, von Balthasar spoke for those who worried the dream of *ressourcement*, meaning a return to the sources, was being obscured by a post-1968 frenzy of rebellion. It should be stressed that despite their differences, the two remained friends."[13]

The enduring amity between the two men is refreshing to note. It underscores the amusing fact that the nature of the philosophical disagreement between Balthasar (or "Baltz," as Rahner like to call him) was simply (and ultimately) a matter of philosophy. Rahner was devoted to squaring Christian revelation within the philosophical scheme of Enlightenment rationalism, opting, in the final analysis, for the God of reason instead of the God of revelation. The "dream," as Allen describes it, is Balthasar's hope to return to a cosmologically more comprehensive metaphysic, one that relies noton what reason might "demonstrate," but on what revelation might teach reason, what grace might teach nature. Rahner, while not a complete Cartesian, had it the other way around: his theology, in the end, was eclipsed by the restrictions of Enlightenment rationalism, the eager arms of revelation amputated by the age of ideology. Löser describes the conflict well, and his own experience in grappling with Rahnerian thought illustrates a major problem in modern theology:

When I finished my philosophy studies in 1965, I searched for a theology closely linked with philosophy. I was aware that Rahner knew modern philosophy intimately—Kant, Hegel and Heidegger had all inspired his thinking. At the time, my philosophical interests were so strong that I did not think theology could be done differently. But in 1966 my view changed. One morning while reading one of his books, it suddenly struck me that Rahner's theology was limited by his philosophy. I also came to realize that he could not answer certain theological problems. It was a shock to realize this because for years I prepared myself to have Rahner as my theological guide. But I discovered that theology needs to recognize that its point of departure is the attentive listening to the word of God revealed in the concrete and contingent history of Israel and of Jesus Christ.[14]

Balthasar, too, was convinced of the primacy of revelation; and for all of its forays into the philosophy of aesthetic style, his theological aesthetics is a simple meditation on "the word of God revealed in the concrete and contingent history of Israel and of Jesus Christ."[15] In any case, the Roman Catholic magisterium began to see that both theological views were valid and that the theological character of the late modern age depended on negotiating the concerns of Balthasar and Rahner (and, of course, others). When Pope Paul VI formed the International Theological Commission as an advisory body to the newly renamed Congregation for the Doctrine of the Faith on May 1, 1969, both Rahner and Balthasar were named as members.

By the early seventies, Balthasar seemed to come in, as it were, from the cold. His great trilogy was in full swing (it would be finished in 1985, with epilogues to follow in 1987–1988), and he was finally serving the church more formally, more expansively, and more publicly. In 1972, Balthasar, along with a number of his colleagues and friends, founded the international cultural and theological review *Communio*, which now exists in the form of at least fifteen distinct and semiautonomous editions in different languages around the world. *Communio*, Balthasar wrote in its maiden issue, was meant to be an oasis of theological exploration, "a place of observation in which existing tensions and divisions are seen, to be sure, in all their seriousness and hardness, but in the certainty that they are already vanquished and embraced, in such a way that this certainty dictates a precise theological method and throws its characteristic light on problems," including the problem of divisions within the Church. In *Communio*, Balthasar and his companions envisioned something more than a journal and hoped that, as a kind of spiritual offspring of the Community of St. John, *Communio* would facilitate an intentional community in which "the value of communion and communication among the greatest possible number of reflective believers can be realized, as if all were simultaneously in the circle."

Throughout the rest of the seventies, Balthasar's constructive views on what the church can be, particularly as a universal culture par excellence, began to resonate more and more with church authority. Pope John Paul II was particularly charmed by Balthasarian thought and described Balthasar as his "favorite theologian."[16] This can come as no surprise as the two have very similar theological personalities. Fundamentally perceived as an academic theologian, John Paul II also recognized that Balthasar was, like himself, fiercely concerned with issues of justice and with the important intersections between aesthetics and ethics, between beauty and action, between love and responsibility, concerns that are not always obvious at first consideration. Because of this, perhaps, the two men, ironically, also share a common "image problem" and are constantly misinterpreted as right-wing icons of a domineering church. Balthasar, for example, was often perceived as an aloof, Euro-centric scholar whose work sustains bureaucratic hierarchy, an impeccably dressed aristocrat out of touch with the poor, out of touch with the church on the ground. Similarly, John Paul II, raised and formed in a totalitarian regime, is often critiqued on the grounds of perpetrating the ultimate mimetic foul: for being hypocritically authoritarian in his 1980s' rebuke of priests from Latin America who were trying to be Christ-like agents of liberation, just as he tried to do when he was a young priest in communist Poland. In addition, both have been accused of being insensitive to women, of being too "cerebral," and of being too backward looking.

Of course, many of these criticisms are valid and credible; but, like most criticisms, they are justified only against the most measured and considered qualification. Both men, in the end, defy such reductive labels as "conservative" or "liberal" or "reactionary." As honest intellectuals, they are best explained by the paradoxes and complexities that attend philosophical and theological speculation.[17] The identities of both men seem to be made manifest most clearly in curious nexus of a "coincidence of opposites," which points to another similarity among individuals who negotiate serious intellectual activity with serious faith commitments. For these two, the life of faith takes the day: for a gargantuan intellect takes a backseat in a theology that is done from the knees, especially when this theology comes to grips with the horizons of existence that challenge, tease, and confound us. This stipulation, of course, does not preclude the reality of suffering. On the contrary, it provides precisely for suffering, as Balthasar and Rahner found out in their own experience, as Pope John Paul II, one can imagine, found in his.

Which raises an interesting point, especially about one whose work was so fixated on the *eschaton*. There is some evidence that Balthasar, toward the end of his life, was ultimately as unimpressed with his devotion to intellectual investigations in theology as St. Thomas Aquinas was with his and that such activity really "amounted to a pile of straw" (so Aquinas was reported to have famously huffed from his deathbed), especially when compared to the gospel mandate of sowing love in a more "practical" venues. We know, however, that the work of the theologian, the purveyor of *doxa*, is always *praxis*—even if it seems impractical and politically irrelevant. Paradoxically, it is precisely in the formal variety of Christian *praxis* (a mandate that flows from the premise of God's historical Incarnation)—which includes the work of the scribe—that the unity of being is realized *doxologically*, a feature dismissed and neglected by post-Enlightenment disciplines. In the *doxa* of Christ, for example, we find the logic of Balthasar's (and John Paul's) Personalist philosophy, a logic that is radically practical. We find the mandate and model for the "I-Thou" encounter, brought to light so well by Martin Buber, by the example of the God who encountered us in real time and real place and who continues to invite us to encounter in the Spirit. Moreover, in the Christ of *praxis* we recover conceptual solutions to the ontological divisions that Balthasar critiques: the false dichotomies set up by Plato, reified by some strands of Scholastic Thomism, and then unmoored seriously by Enlightenment rationalists. The dyadic fracture of *doxa* and *praxis*, like other dyadic fractures, produces an array of negative social effects, many of which I'll discuss in the second half of this study in the form of narrative criticism. In Balthasar's estimation, the "dualistic mistake" is a primal mistake; but it remains with us, and it has very real consequences for present cultures, not least because it affects the fundamental ways we relate with one another. Balthasar is refreshingly candid, practical, and prophetic as he reflects on the issue in a later work, *Love Alone Is Credible*:

> But whenever the relationship between nature and grace is severed
> (as happens . . . where "faith" and "knowledge" are constructed as

opposites), then the whole of worldly being falls under the dominion of "knowledge," and the springs and forces of love immanent in the world are overpowered and finally suffocated by science, technology and cybernetics. The result is a world without women, without children, without reverence for love in poverty and humiliation—a world in which power and the profit-margin are the sole criteria, where the disinterested, the useless, the purposeless is despised, persecuted and in the end exterminated—a world in which art itself is forced to wear the mask and features of technique.[18]

As a trained philosopher, Balthasar recognizes the importance of duality, but he seeks to illuminate its structure more clearly. As Peter Casarella observes in a point that complements the above passage: "To understand the essence of being truly is to accept that a finite nature cannot be reduced to a metaphysical composition constructed out of different parts or elements, for irreducibility of form to expression is intrinsic to each being and manifests in being itself."[19] By cultivating the comprehensive nature of theological investigation, we may recover our "creatureliness," to use one of Rahner's terms. We may suggest ways to restore brokenness to wholeness both personally and collectively. Balthasar's final years seemed to be about this, about being socially active, about *animating* his theology in the light of unique faith claims. It is important to note that John Paul II collaborated on these causes.

Balthasar died on June 26, 1988, two days before he was to be vested as a cardinal. While he had refused the honor a couple of times prior, we can be sure he was going to accept on this occasion because of his Jesuit-ingrained habit of obedience, because of his friendship with John Paul II, and because he had already gone to Rome to be fitted for his cardinal's vestments.

It is clear, upon cool inspection, that Balthasar, in his negative appraisal of Enlightenment rationalism, shares an affinity with the philosophical position of most postmodern theory. His studious critique of Enlightenment structural hegemony reveals a strong aversion to the artificial certitude promoted by the rationalist tradition. Balthasar's experience provides an interesting thesis on which to dwell: postmodern perspectives can improve discourses in theology. If, indeed, there is a "crisis in meaning," as postmodernity does so well to show us, and theology, as mother of all disciplines, is the default site of meaning, then it stands to reason that theology must negotiate the claims that postmodern criticism posits. We must make sense of the "empty space" that rightly preoccupies the postmodern mind. We must make sense of the language, images, and activities we employ to describe this empty space.

As I noted in chapter 1, Balthasar observed that "when everything is blocked off, one must live in the interstices."[20] Clearly he was referring immediately to the challenges of modernity, but it is vital to note that his remark is a quintessential postmodern critique of modernism and a postmodern "solution" to the problem of modernism's overreaching cause-and-effect certitude. We dwell in the interstices; we attempt to derive meaning from hazy locales and dark junctions. So Balthasar's observation speaks volumes about where a scholar must reside as he sashays along the cusp of the twenty-first century. Balthasar himself lived and flourished in the "interstices"; he expertly met, rode, and then gloried in the storm surge caused by the grand cultural collision known as the twentieth century; and his own experiences illuminate the clarity of contradictions that only a healthy and just respect for interdisciplinarity yields.

Ressourcement, for Nothing Stands Alone

Balthasar was a force for change. He found the rote scholasticism that was de rigueur in his formation days at Fourviére overbaked and irrelevant and so railed against it. His emphasis on beauty, in fact, can be interpreted as a direct response to theological academies of the mid-twentieth century that fell into viewing theology as little more than a pedestrian systematization of codes and morals: "Was not Scholasticism itself already a false path, with its 'rationalization' of dogma, its dialectic hair-splitting and its all-too naïve use of secular logic?"[21] Whether romantically or otherwise, Balthasar wished to restore theology to its rightful place and rehabilitate the concept that theology, as mother of all disciplines, ought to be unapologetic about dwelling on its own magnificent beauty. Truly, it is no accident that Balthasar begins his most important work with a seven-volume meditation on Beauty, for Balthasar's organizing principle proclaims, "Philosophy ends with Beauty, theology begins with it." In this way, Balthasar (and of course his confreres in the *ressourcement* movement) replied to those theologians who, in their overemphasis on rationalism and linear investigation, would geld theology of its vital constituent parts. Balthasar, as we have seen, was particularly keen on this idea—that syllogistic logic simply cannot, in the end, explain the narrative and imagistic logic of salvation history and revelation. It cannot explain love. The dramatic structure of theology, for example, with its natural provisions for tension and release, conflict and reconciliation, error, and glory becomes a keystone for understanding this point.[22] Why did theologians deny this resource and exclude it from consideration? Why did theologians evacuate theological study of its very content? Balthasar was incredulous about this kind of foul play ("at Lyon, I quickly became disenchanted with my studies"),[23] and his reinstatement of the primary consideration of the beautiful serves as a righteous defense against the historical-critical movement, to name just one (ironically) myopic product of Enlightenment theology, as well as other incomplete approaches to theological investigation that preclude the beautiful essence of a theological existence.

But where does one turn for an intellectual escape hatch in such a complicated and hostile environment? What theological and philosophical resources exist for the disenchanted theologian? For Balthasar, the answer was clear: take an expeditionary survey of history and see where the train left the rails, and this maneuver would, in turn, provide the general constitution of his methodology. Balthasar possessed several postmodern instincts; but postmodernism, because of its general suspicion of history and its wariness about truth claims, is excluded as a fully integrated theological method. A turn to modernism was out, as we have established, in any of its abstracting and de-incarnating forms; the theology of Renaissance humanism was out because of its disproportionate emphasis on human efficacy; Thomism was out, ultimately, because the version of Thomism taught in the seminaries effectively compromised the mysteries of theological revelation by squaring it too narrowly with ancient Greek philosophy. Still, Balthasar was devoted to Aquinas—for his sophisticated approach to the transcendentals and for the fecundating, but narrow, intersection between *fides et ratio*—and did not want to jettison his influence altogether. There was the further issue of theological rhetoric. Which sources captured and conveyed the authentic beauty of Christian revelation? Which sources spoke profoundly and beautifully about the mysteries of prayer and the poetry of Eucharist?

To respond to these hosts of concerns, Balthasar had to fix his gaze on a period of some 3,500 years and then work his way back around to the present, a procedure that, as I mentioned above, became his theological methodology. He found intellectual and spiritual kinship in an "approach" now known as *ressourcement* and, in turn, became one of its most important figures. *Ressourcement*, not exactly a self-conscious movement (known often by its alternative appellation, *la nouvelle theologie*), announced itself first in France in the early twentieth century. Henri de Lubac's two great masterworks, *Catholicisme: Les Aspects Sociaux du Dogme* (1938) and *Surnaturel* (1946), mined the wisdom of the "old theology" so effectively that, after the long inebriation of modernism, the "old theology" appeared to be positively cutting edge and, ironically, *nouvelle*. Like many, Balthasar found Lubac's treatment and credible refraction of patristic and mediaeval sources refreshing and persuasive. Moreover, Balthasar's ardent regard for theological creativity and rhetorical warmth—the precise elements that he longed for in theological expression—were matched best, he decided, by the Church Fathers. He began to see a sturdy abode for the intersection between theology, philosophy, and the narrative arts, first in the writing of figures from early centuries CE and then branching out— *a-chronologically*—through different aesthetic moments in history: "That is why we must see in the Fathers great prototypes and models of intellectual power and Christian daring and interpret them with tact and tenderness and always take into account the hidden tension and symbolism between content of meaning and expressive form."[24] Clearly, Balthasar (and his colleagues of the new theology, specifically the Frenchmen Congar, Danielou, Bouyer, and, again, most important, Henri deLubac) was not after a utopian repetition of the golden age of Christianity (for "nothing would be more perilous than to demand from our completely different situation a pure return to patristic Platonism, heedless of the consequences").[25] The invocation of the Church Fathers is simply a perceptive engagement with history, one that presents an alternative road map that might enlighten, even, the Enlightenment Rationalists who, as practitioners of a strange brand of fundamentalism, were unprepared to entertain alternative epistemologies. Many artists and writers, of course, were imaginatively disposed to the new theology and could divine this map laid out by *ressourcement* theologians (which may explain the glut of activity in theology and the arts in the 1930s, 1940s, and 1950s, especially by Catholics); but it also provided direction for theologians and philosophers who were able to envisage the credibility of more nonlinear epistemologies.

Theology and Interdisciplinarity (C): Balthasar's Prolific Vision

For the map is, as Balthasar exemplifies, interdisciplinary. It does not rely upon or promulgate, merely, a rationalized cause-and-effect schema. It is, again, a *Kath-holon*, a vision of something open and universal. And the map gives cause to pause now and consider the ways in which Balthasar translated his ideas into prose, into a systematic theology. Therefore, it is judicious to map a relatively brief outline of some of the major topics in Balthasar's purview. I'll feature three important themes from three strands of Balthasar's work so as to offer both a modified bibliographic survey of representative Balthasarian texts as well as interpretive options for religious critics. The survey, in Balthasarian spirit, is in unequal length and by no means is meant to encapsulate the whole of his work. The first theme is the notion of *concentricity*, a central tenet of *ressourcement* theology and a theme that illuminates a central facet of Balthasar's theological imagination.

The early Christian commentators were deeply disposed to cyclic (i.e., circular, concentric) thinking. As theologian David Cunningham reports:

> We once marked the passage of time not by lines but by circles: the sweep of the watch hands, the close observation of the moon's phases, the repeating change of the seasons. In cultures much more in tune with nature than our own, one could never forget that the passage of time was cyclical. In our modern effort to domesticate time by forcing it into straight lines, we have eclipsed our own awareness of nature's cycles.... Christianity was born into a culture that recognized its place in the natural order. It has thus retained an awareness of the circular movement of time, even as our secular society has lost it. The regular cycles of Christian prayer, the repeating scripture readings and feast days, and even the circular nature of the worship service itself (with processions and recessions)—all these are small reflections of the Christian understanding of time in its cosmic scale.[26]

This tendency toward a concentric vision is a pillar in Balthasar's theological project, and he dwells on it specifically in his 1941 work *Cosmic Liturgy: The Universe According to Maximus the Confessor*, in which Balthasar illuminates Maximus's (580–662) circulating theology of procession and return (*proodos* and *epistrophe*), a fertile topic, clearly, for theological aesthetics and one that is central in my next chapter, albeit through the lens of Pseudo-Dionysius (Denys). Concentricity is also fundamental in Balthasar's 1943 monograph on St. Irenaus of Lyon (120–202), *The Scandal of the Incarnation: Irenaus Against the Heresies*, in which Balthasar shows how the Incarnation, according to Irenaus's vision, pushed out in all chronological directions and radically reoriented the nature of time, a "scandal," in one of the many ways Balthasar's employs the term (in this case he does so from its Greek form, *skandolon*, which means "impediment") to the Gnostic imagination. Most important, perhaps, concentricity discloses the very logic of God, that is, God's "Theologic," and Balthasar concludes the first volume of his *Theo-Logic* (1946) by offering a meditation that links love with the circular procession of God:

> God is love. This does not mean, of course, that his essence is substantial love, while his other infinite properties are dissolved into this love. There is an order here: love presupposes knowledge, while knowledge presupposes being. But the love that stands at the end of the sequence as the goal of its unfolding stands, in another perspective, at its beginning as the basic impulse underlying it. *Eternity is a circulation in which beginning and end join in unity.*[27]

Balthasar translator and commentator Erasmo Leiva-Merikakis qualifies this concentric theological imagination rather instructively, as one "that never treats a subject in isolation from all those other subjects which are naturally bound to it, but sees them as interacting concentric circles, distinct yet inseparable from a common center,"[28] an observation that enlightens us about the aims of both *ressourcement* and the deeper pathology of Balthasar's interdisciplinary vision, for "Christ is prior to all things and in him all things hang together."[29] In his introduction to Balthasar's *Threefold Garland* (1978), Leiva-Merikakis goes on to offer an excellent aesthetic example of this vision in his consideration of the icon known as *Our Lady of the Sign*, "('sign' here referring to the prophecy of Isaiah of Acaz)," which shows "Mary offering Christ to the world from a 'mandorla' on her breast, that is, from a 'window of heaven' consisting of concentric circles and out of which appears the Savior. The virgin herself, in turn, is surrounded by a greater mandorla."[30]

From a couple of disciplinary time zones away, Flannery O'Connor offers a complementary vision of concentricity in her 1957 short story "Greenleaf." Mrs. May, one of O'Connor's self-satisfied, by-your-bootstraps Pelagians (she believes in "looking busy"; she views heaven as the logical product of working long hours), gets hounded in the tale by a Christ-like figure. As the action rises, she, tired after her all her labors, struggles to make sense of it all:

> For some time she lay back against the hood, wondering drowsily why she was so tired. With her eyes closed, she didn't think of time as divided into days and nights but into past and future. She decided she was tired because she had been working continuously for fifteen years. She decided she had every right to be tired, and to rest for a few minutes before she began working again. Before any kind of judgment seat, she would be able to say: I've worked, I have not wallowed. At this very instant while she was recalling a lifetime of work, Mr. Greenleaf was loitering in the woods and Mrs. Greenleaf was probably

flat on the ground, asleep over her holeful of clippings. The woman had got worse over the years and Mrs. May believed that now she was actually demented. "I'm afraid your wife has let religion warp her," she said once tactfully to Mr. Greenleaf. "Everything in moderation, you know."[31]

The reader suspects by this point in the narrative that it is Mrs. May who has been warped by religion—in this case by the religion of modernism—and begins to sense that she is being enveloped by a conspiracy of "truing" elements. O'Connor methodically insinuates concentricity into her fiction—the circular nature of time and the circular unity of the cosmos—as a foil against Mrs. May's linear notion of salvation. O'Connor writes Mrs. May into a series of circular settings and situations (near a large milk urn, under a big red sun, in the middle of a pasture), and the action in the story itself escalates in a swirling manner. A bull, who has been circling her, wooing her most erotically (evoking the stag figure of *The Song of Songs*), finally gets his prey and pierces her with his horn through her heart:

> In a few minutes something emerged from the tree line, a black heavy shadow that tossed its head several times and then bounded forward. After a second she saw it was the bull. He was crossing the pasture toward her at a slow gallop, a gay almost rocking gait as if he were overjoyed to find her again. She looked beyond him to see if Mr. Greenleaf was coming out of the woods too but he was not. "Here he is, Mr. Greenleaf!" she called and looked on the other side of the pasture to see if he could be coming out there but he was not in sight. She looked back and saw that the bull, his head lowered, was racing toward her. She remained perfectly still, not in fright, but in a freezing unbelief. She stared at the violent black streak bounding toward her *as if she had no sense of distance*, as if she could not decide at once what his intention was, and the bull had buried his head in her lap, like a wild tormented lover, before her expression changed. One of his horns sank until it pierced her heart and the other curved around her side and held her in an unbreakable grip. She continued to stare straight ahead but the entire scene in front of her had changed—the tree line was a dark wound in a world that was nothing but sky—and she had the look of a person whose sight has been suddenly restored but who finds the light unbearable. Mr. Greenleaf was running toward her from the side with his gun raised and she saw him coming though she was not looking in his direction. She saw him *approaching on the outside of some invisible circle*, the tree line gaping behind him and nothing under his feet. He shot the bull four times through the eye. She did not hear the shots but she felt the quake in the huge body as it sank, pulling her forward on its head, so that she seemed, when Mr. Greenleaf reached her, to be bent over whispering some last discovery into the animal's ear.[32]

The clear allusion to the stag in *The Song of Songs* provides a biblical resonance for O'Connor's rendering of a cosmic space for divine union and redemption. The reference, archetypal in scope, serves her purposes in at least three ways: *anthropologically*, as a multivalent mythopoeaic theme that speaks to us in a pretheological way; *Christologically*, as a theologically credible representation of the idea that Christ passionately seeks union with us; and, of course, *aesthetically*, as O'Connor's unique artistic style and her own theological aesthetic present a startling depiction of a religious experience. Mrs. May is like many of us—a self-righteous protagonist who insists on living in a perfectible world that she can control. But such a world makes no provision for the gracious penetration of God; moreover, as O'Connor's depiction does deftly suggest, the assertion of this kind of a world, a world that forecloses upon the possibility and power of divine encounter, is, paradoxically, both a revelation of Mrs. May's fear and a tacit confession of her radical powerlessness. The sclerosis of her egoism is shattered by one violent action: an encircling piercing embrace, encircled in a field, encircled by the great "invisible" circle of the cosmos. This is a beatific vision for the ages: shocking in its marvelous symmetry and violent because violence is one of the only effects available to the late modern narrative artist who possesses a serious religious imagination.

Music, the second of the three mini-themes, reveals other interesting things about Balthasar as a prose stylist. One striking phenomenon confronts us when we consider his output carefully: the formal variety of his theological tomes conveys a deeply measured musical sense about them. His vast pieces, for instance, divulge scaled polyrhythms that crest and flow over the course of many pages at a quiet but measured (i.e., *andante*) pace. To some critics, these multivolume pieces (*Explorations in Theology*, four volumes; *The Glory of the Lord*, seven volumes; *Theo-Drama*, five volumes; and *Theo-Logic*, three volumes) are the precise spaces at which Balthasar's work seems dense and garrulous. However, if we interpret these works carefully (and in the spirit in which Balthasar constructed them), it becomes clear that Balthasar is garrulous only in the way that Mozart, Mahler, or Gorecki are garrulous. Each of Balthasar's "notes," to paraphrase Mozart in Peter Shaffer's *Amadeus* (1984), "belongs." Clearly, there is something daunting about these mammoth and dense volumes; but it is also clear that Balthasar ventilates his corpus with a series of shorter works, studies that convincingly illustrate his theological rhythm and compositional control. In fact, these shorter works, such as *A Theology of History* (1950), *The Christian and Anxiety* (1952), *Prayer* (1961), and *The Theology of Henri de Lubac* (1976), illustrate Balthasar's genius for dwelling on staccato theological "phrases," to sustain the music metaphor further, as well as his adeptness at concentrating some vibrant theological insight into shorter and more readable works. Leiva-Merikakis is again insightful on this matter. He assesses the variety of Balthasar's prose in his introduction to one of these shorter pieces, *The Three-Fold Garland*:

> The little book we here offer is a classical demonstration of the
> fact that the profoundest truths need not always be expressed in a

technical or esoteric terminology for them to retain their depth. Far from that: it is the simplicity of the well-chosen image, the directness of a sudden intuition, the whisper of a sentiment too delicate for words, that often best preserve and convey the whole range of meaning. A certain genius is needed to compress great richness into great simplicity, and in my opinion this book, without diluting it, contains the essence of von Balthasar's weightier tomes; and this is so, I may add, not in spite of the fact that the style here is non-technical, at times poetic and always full of prayer, but precisely *because* of these qualities. For this reason I would recommend these thoroughly accessible pages as perhaps the best introduction to the overwhelming and sometimes difficult work of Father von Balthasar. The long philosophical excursus and slow-motion expositions required elsewhere in his work are often the measure of his titanic effort in trying to bring to the mind of the world, the imbalances of a given cultural epoch and the exigencies of reason a bit closer to the warmth and the life emanating from the loving heart of God. But at the center, at the *point vierge*, this heart's mystery itself is utterly crystalline— invisible and unproblematic as the very air we breathe.[33]

The third of our featured themes will also, fittingly, serve as a hinge to the last portion of this chapter. The theme is stylistic pluralism, and it hinges on Balthasar's theological aesthetics. As Balthasar himself was a careful but rhapsodic prose stylist, he realized that theological writing could itself have an aesthetic quality about it and that numerous voices and styles resulted in at least one thing—a more interesting and descriptive theology. As a *ressource- ment* theologian, he was moved by the rhetorical power of patristic sources and was specifically fond of the theological visions articulated by Origen (185–254) and St. Gregory of Nyssa (d. 385) and wrote book-length studies of them. He wrote long monographs on St. Gregory Nazianzus (325–389) and Clement of Alexandria (d. 215) in *The Glory of the Lord*. Additionally, the contributions of major foundational thinkers such as St. Augustine (354–430) and Pseudo- Dionysius (AKA "Denys," fifth century CE) along with Maximus Confessor pervade Balthasar's work at every turn. As his forays into Patristics indicate, Balthasar's broad and variable intellectual interest, along with his copious output, provides the interested scholar with numerous topics for study.

The catalog alone at Johannes Verlag (the publishing house in Einsiedeln that Balthasar founded along with Speyr) lists over one hundred book-length tracts written by Balthasar. It is clear that he wrote much more than that, of course, but it is hard to generate an exact number since he wrote in many venues (sermons, occasional meditations, journal articles) and he collaborated with other authors. As Balthasar's cousin, Bishop Peter Henrici, former dean of the faculty of philosophy at Rome's Gregorian University, noted, "He wrote more books than an ordinary man succeeds in reading in a lifetime."[34] However, not all of this work is "digestible," as Nichols astutely observes, which, of

course is the case with any writer who produces so regularly and so volumi-
nously. For this reason, it is difficult to say just one thing about Balthasar as an
academic theologian, for it is clear his life's project concerns the whole of
theology, and that's no small affair.

Inchoate in Balthasar's preference for pre-Enlightenment sources is the
major stylistic observation about the relationship between theology and aesthetics. Balthasar devoted much of his writing to exploring the theological
properties proper to art and how an artistic imagination serves the mission of
the theologian; but he also dedicated himself to translating (and introducing)
original literary sources (i.e., poems, plays, and novels) from one language to
another. He entered the orbit of the French-Catholic literary revival of the early
to middle twentieth century and was captivated by what he found, especially in
the work of Charles Péguy (1873–1914), Paul Claudel (1868–1955), and Georges
Bernanos (1888–1948). More important, as we have mentioned, Balthasar
understood that theological discourse needed to have an aesthetic element
about it because of its uniquely important content. Theological writing is best
when it embodies the very mysteries it seeks to depict and when it is written by
those personally attuned with its content. And so Balthasar helps us navigate
the broad terrain of theological aesthetics and develop an appreciation for
theology as it appears in a plurality of settings, the literary setting being especially fruitful. Leiva-Merikakis astutely locates this double action of Balthasarian theological aesthetics and observes: "Balthasar seems to be saying, we
go to someone like Georges Bernanos not only for the highest kind of aesthetic
pleasure and illumination, but indeed for the deepest kind of concrete Christian reflection and guidance."[35] Balthasar's own appraisal of the literature-
theology connection speaks volumes: "It could just be that in the great Catholic
literary figures we find more originality and vibrancy of thought—an intellectual life thriving superbly in a free and open landscape—than we do in the
somewhat broken-winded theology of our time, which is satisfied with quite
slender fare."[36] Clearly, an integrated approach to aesthetic style serves as a
vehicle for exposing a symphony of doctrinal truth as well as the disclosure of
pluriform aesthetic transmission of meaning.

Balthasar also approaches aesthetics in the old Greek way, as "a sensible
manifestation of the spiritual."[37] In this schema, theological aesthetics can
tend toward pantheism and animism, to name two, just as it can tend toward
transcendental Trinitarianism, issues that Balthasar sorts through in his 1963
study, *A Theological Anthropology*. Balthasar, in the main, focuses on aesthetics
as they are mediated by and through humans vis à vis literary form. For this
reason, Balthasar is in a key position to contribute to the theological possibility that attends discourses in literary and narrative theory, for no other theologian of the twentieth century displays such a refined understanding about
the theological dimension of literary art. On this matter, of course, disagree-
ments flourish, especially around points that are precisely theological in
nature. For many have realized the theological quality of arts and literature
so profoundly that they have converted arts and literature themselves into

theologies. Balthasar, unlike many late modernists, never confused the two: the aesthetic mediates the divine and discloses a presence; but the aesthetic cannot, ultimately, be equivocated with the divine.

In his 1891 essay "The Soul of Man Under Socialism," Oscar Wilde wrote:

> A work of art is the unique result of a unique temperament. Its beauty comes from the fact that the author is what he is. It has nothing to do with the fact that other people want what they want. Indeed, the moment that an artist takes notice of what other people want, and tries to supply the demand, he ceases to be an artist, and becomes a dull or an amusing craftsman, an honest or dishonest tradesman. He has no further claim to be considered as an artist.[38]

Clearly, Wilde is correct in refusing to turn art into a commodity and subjugating it to the whims of the market or the ferocity of the state. However, Wilde's extreme aestheticism earned him and his dandified followers the lash of Chesterton's tongue: "The aesthete aims at harmony rather than beauty. If his hair does not match the mauve sunset against which he is standing, he hurriedly dyes his hair another shade of mauve. If his wife does not go with the wall-paper, he gets a divorce."[39] This aesthetic vision, pioneered by French poet Theophile Gautier (1811–1872), the first to declare "art for art's sake," later promulgated by French novelist Andre Malreaux (1901–1976) and, also, to an extent, by James Joyce, transmogrified art into religion. The aesthetes reckoned that the sheer variety of original aesthetic forms and artifacts, along with the potential for art to influence the world, was surely a sign that there were also a variety of original truths that were outside and independent of God. Balthasar, of course, denies this categorically. A multivalent aesthetic landscape does not challenge the existence of God or supplant our ideas about God; to the contrary, the plurality of aesthetic visions illuminates the explosion of expansive variations on a theme. Various aesthetics are not so much self-sufficient universes, but *styles*, according Balthasar, that dwell and pulsate in the one vast universe that is God. Stylistic variety is of such importance to Balthasar that, in addition to employing it as a regular component of his methodology, he devotes two large volumes of his meditation on Beauty, *The Glory of the Lord*, to surveying a representative variety of "clerical" and "lay" styles—musical riffs, really, to close the cello case—on what God is doing in the world and what the world is doing in God.

In order to better understand how Balthasar systematically negotiates the distinction between "truth" and "style," an amplification is in order, that of the dynamic play between *impression* and *expression*. On this matter, Balthasar owes a plain debt to Bonaventure, who was the first to employ the terminology in his doctrine of *expressio*.[40] This vigorous relationship (along with an almost inexhaustible array of other polarity structures) goes to the very heart of Balthasar's personalism, that is, his aesthetics of *encounter*. It also goes a long way in explaining Balthasar's approach to "truth claims." For Balthasar, the evidence of God's relation with us comes in two forms, "subjective" and "objective" evidence. The movement of God appears to us as in a "subjective" movement, mediated through some "sign," which impresses itself upon us, which radiates and adheres to the human person. The subject (i.e., the person) is then moved toward expression—the "objective evidence"—toward contemplation, creativity, or some other form of human action. The various forms of personal expression (in light of the Divine impression) become objective theological styles whose source is the same well or, as our ever-musical Balthasar has it, whose source is the same composer of music, "where they all play from the same score which both transcends and embraces them."[41] In a turn to early mediaeval theology of the Cappadocian sort, anything that is not so radiated by the Spirit is simply not of God, in a productive sense, and does not meet the criteria for evidence. To the extent the form is impressed and expressed, the splendor of God is revealed, as Nichols observes: "The living revelation is not only possessed of form; in Balthasar's view, it is also creative of form, able to call forth a vast array of great theologies whose inner form it inspires."[42]

Balthasar's democracy of sources and his apparent trading of "truth" for styles may not meet the muster of most theological skeptics. Be that as it may, Balthasar's theological aesthetics is premised on such maneuvers. It becomes clear that the "expression" of the "objective evidence" depends upon and proceeds from the theological imagination. As Balthasar scholar Peter Casarella elucidates in an essay that deals with a very similar topic (i.e., the aesthetics of eucharistic presence), discourses in theology, when juxtaposed against any other linguistic (or truth) claim, are at least *as* valid as purely rational proofs:

> Some will contend that employing concepts derived from the Christian view of Eucharistic presence to illuminate a theory of language constitutes a category error, for it results in an unnecessary and unwarranted mixture of philosophy and theology. To be sure, a sacramental theology of language can stand on its own only after being justified in the realm of philosophical hermeneutics and philosophy of language. Such justification goes beyond the bounds of this essay but would begin with a theory of what language makes present that neither instrumentalizes the function of the linguistic sign nor hypostasizes the active polarity between expression and form of the word.[43]

Casarella's point is well built. It is literature and poetics, precisely as aesthetics of presence, which have been concerned with grounding theological existence ever since there were plumes and parchment. Balthasar's project then is not so much to meditate on this fact, as it is to demonstrate how a literary aesthetic is both a constituent of a theological existence (as a formal artifact) and a host for the illumination and exposition of theological content (i.e., a text that is both a body and a site, a form, that hosts, for example, the beauty of eucharistic presence). Balthasar's treatment of various theological artists—those who wrote from their concrete experience and in their own vernacular—illustrates the many avenues of theological expression, the many varieties of form. Casarella continues:

> Thus, the key element received from a reflection on aesthetics, one we already encountered in the account of knowing, is that of manifestation (*Erscheinung*). This is the most explicit in the aesthetic experience of beauty where the heart of the issue lies in relation between expression and interior depth, between the manifestation and the non-manifested. In the *Divine Comedy*, when Dante meets Beatrice, she speaks not of herself but of an other. And yet, she is the Beauty that he encounters. This area of non-manifest depth belongs to the dimension of mystery in all beings, and particularly to infinite Being. It cannot be "bracketed-out" as some of the exact sciences want to do. Human knowing must include this dimension: "For it is only in this way that the figure which lies at the heart of the matter becomes legible as a figure of reality." (*GL I*, 446)[44]

Casarella does very well to shine light on the trajectory of Balthasar's theological program and to reveal the place of art and beauty in Balthasar's aesthetics. Balthasar is proposing a sacramental aesthetic: how arts and literatures, as "manifestations" of the beautiful, begin to reveal the mystery of the "non-manifest" dimension, the dimension that exists, paradoxically, beyond expression.

A Sacramental Aesthetics: The Analogy of Being as Compass for a Catholic Imagination

My short bibliographic expedition is meant to be a representative (if protracted) consideration of Balthasar's wide concern. The subjects he engages, the topics he explores, and especially his methods of transmission alert us to the advent of something unique in current discourses on theological expression: a fully refined *Catholic imagination*. To be sure, there is something at stake in making such a claim, yet Balthasar's work bears it out and provides a systematic endorsement of such a claim.

Unfortunately, some have built the notion of a Catholic imagination around the generation of cultish associations with Catholic cultural artifacts. Still, such an instinct is not entirely misguided, for the most fertile inroads into the topic do have to do with the possibilities for meaning that reside in cultural artifacts, albeit under a sacramental banner. In a vital way, Balthasar's Catholic imagination, articulated most fully in his theological aesthetics, can be seen as a category of sacramental theology, for his whole "system" is premised on a sacramental imagination as it has developed in the Roman Catholic tradition. His theological aesthetics outlines ways in which finite artifacts of the beautiful, when imagined, constructed, and described beautifully, can embody, demonstrate, and express the deeper realities of an authentic theological existence. I propose now to show that Balthasar's "system," which is premised on the transcendentals and which unfolds and "operates" sacramentally, is the best venue for proposing a legible aesthetics and the best compass for tracking the (re)emerging movement of a Catholic imagination in arts and literatures.

As I indicated in my introductory chapter, much work has been done of late on the idea of a Catholic imagination. Because Catholicism is often presented as a totalizing view, as a metanarrative to end all metanarratives, the concept of a Catholic imagination can be applied to various discourses and disciplines liberally and, perhaps, too carelessly. Andrew Greeley's book *The Catholic Imagination* (2000), for example, focuses on the Catholic imagination as largely a "tribal" phenomenon. Greeley is insightful in asserting that the Catholic imagination is primarily sacramental, that "Catholics live in an enchanted world, a world of statutes and holy water, stained glass and votive candles";[45] but his presentation, in the final analysis, is compromised by a fatigued apologia for Catholicism. The discussion unfolds through a series of vignettes that, at turns, vindicate and romanticize one reiterated version of catholicity. For example, Greeley spends the bulk of his space glossing over artifacts of Catholic culture in order to illustrate how the imagination manifests in everything from architecture to film. Clearly, his approach can be both interesting and productive, but his discussion becomes burdened by a stagnated ineffectuality that characterizes some methods of sociological study: he lays out the issues but offers little in the way of substantive theological commentary. Greeley's too cursory and incomplete study is typical of the laxity that often attends cultural studies. He perpetuates the kind of Catholicism-as-kitsch (again, "Catholics live in an enchanted world, a world of statutes and holy water, stained glass and votive candles") that distracts us from the more essential aspects of the theological/sacramental imagination, namely what God is mediating in, through, and with us and why this mediation is central to the various examples of cultural and artistic expression he offers. Certainly, Greeley can't be faulted too stridently, for his *Catholic Imagination* is a perfect example of what sociologists do, and Greeley is a competent one. But he also makes too many attempts in his book at hanging generally ephemeral cultural observations upon serious literary and theological principles that we are left wanting more sophisticated research and more expansive commentary.

Thomas Groome's *What Makes Us Catholic: Eight Gifts for Life* (2002) presents a similar limitation. Like Greeley's book, it serves the reader well as a mini-handbook of (American) cultural Catholicism. However, readers looking for deeper theological understanding will be dissatisfied. Like Greeley, Groome, who is a professor in religious education at Boston College, is interested more in the cultural and artistic manifestations of the Catholic imagination than he is in the theology that informs such an imagination ("But Catholic Christians should never think of the seven sacraments as apart from life. All must be appreciated as apex moments that heighten and celebrate the sacramentality of life in the world").[46] Groome's work is more catechesis than theological exploration, and he presumes only a minimal acquaintance with theology in his reader. It is fair to say that both Greeley and Groome fall into the camp of "bottom-up," *praxis*-oriented (as opposed to "top-down," *doxa*-oriented) Catholics and that their various visions of the Catholic imagination derive from this intellectual location. Moreover, this particular type of praxis tends to be less reflective or "intentional" than others. Because Groome's approach relies on a suspension of disbelief (i.e., most readers accept his premises without question), it ultimately skirts the essential components and the more demanding aspects claiming a Catholic imagination. This is not a critique, necessarily, because Groome knows his audience and his work serve an important function (and the same can be said for Greeley). But, as a stark contrast, it is precisely the inordinate theological rigor that Balthasar brings to the topic that makes him indispensable to any discussion of a Catholic imagination.[47] Balthasar's comprehensive treatment of the possibility that resides in any discussion of a Catholic imagination both sets him apart and provides a model for engaging the discussion.

As mentioned in chapter 1, a more interesting and scholarly approach to the idea of a Catholic imagination comes from cultural critic Paul Giles. In his seminal work, *American Catholic Arts and Fictions* (1994), Giles eschews transcendental claims in favor of an explicitly anthropological and cultural critique of (American) narrative art. Theology, in his view, is simply one among many other ideologies that influences and mitigates literary expression: "More illuminating is to conceive of a long tradition of Catholic arts and fictions, where texts analogically intersect and shed light upon each other, compositely forming a critique of some of the dominant modes and patterns within American literary consciousness."[48]

While Giles's work aids this study (in the sense that it is a watershed book in the study of a Catholic-aesthetic imagination), he, too, foregoes the opportunity to connect the dots to the deeper theology inherent in narrative art. In fact, he dismisses altogether the potency of the *analogia entis* as a transcendental rubric and relegates it to the status of a literary trope: "Unlike Foucault, I do not see the analogical impulse as having been simply overtaken by the march of human thought, but I would suggest that analogy be reworked not as a philosophical principle, but as a trope of fictional style."[49] For Giles, and so for many of his contemporaries, all phenomena is both mediated and insulated by culture, even by God. This approach, with its semiotic character, appears to resemble the sacramental dynamic of Balthasar's theological aesthetics, but it is riddled with problems from the start. Is mathematics, for example, also mediated by culture? Is love ultimately dependent on culture? In a way that seems Hegelian, there is, finally, reticence in Giles to stake a flag in the risky topography of transcendental belief, for belief, under his thesis, is simply a cultural exercise, not a central artifact of being. The Catholic imagination for Giles is rarely anything other than "the overlap of technique with ideology."[50] In this sense, his insights on the Catholic imagination are limited: his is an anthropological description of an essentially theological phenomenon.

For Balthasar, as we discussed in chapter 1, all hinges upon "form." The sacramentality that he proposes, of course, is grounded in such palpable "hinges" and so is nothing extraordinarily new, at least in the area of sacramental theology. What is new is the manner in which Balthasar visualizes his aesthetics: a composite schema built out of the palimpsest of the *analogia entis*, with a heavy emphasis on "analogy" as construed by Balthasar's other great mentor, the Jesuit theologian Erich Przywara. Balthasar combines his view of *analogia* with the enduring doctrine of *sacramentum et res*, which was developed first by Augustine, and then worked through significantly by both Aquinas and Bonaventure, among others, and shuttled into the modern age by Balthasar, Louis Dupre, and Gustavo Gutierrez, among others. For Balthasar, an informed contemplation of form is itself a sacramental act.[51] As a concrete expression of the divine, it bespeaks an opportunity for an expansive, loving encounter with all of creation and, of course, with God. This, of course, is a departure from form as Aristotle conceives it, for the form that Balthasar has in mind is revealed in history. Christ becomes the primordial form, the site from which we derive and proclaim a tangible relationship with God. Yet, this assertion of human power by no means domesticates the radical power of God for, as Balthasar states, "*analogia* implies a mysterious irreducible 'similarity in dissimilarity,'"[52] which reveals yet another aspect of sacramental aesthetics, to which we will return shortly: the idea of *revelation and concealment*. In any case, the sacramental nature of Christ is Balthasar's great meditation, and it informs the structure of his aesthetic program: all things are predicated on Christ; Christ is in everything we see that is beautiful, true, and good.

A propensity to imagine and visualize *sacramentum et res* is key, for it is the sacramental logic that underpins Balthasar's aesthetics. Historian Joseph Martos articulates the theology well:

> In the end the mediaeval theologians developed a threefold distinction in reference to the sacraments: the *sacramentum tantum* being the element which "was only a sign," *the sacramentum et res* being the element which was "both sign and reality," and the *res tantum* being the element which was "only a reality."[53]

Far from a one-to-one symbolic fundamentalism, the *sacramentum et res* proposes to endorse a diffuse intelligibility of signs. For Balthasar, the "both a sign and reality" aspect indicates a kind of certitude in mystery: certitude that we dwell in a meaning-bearing world, and mystery in that, to follow Maritain, meaning is ever-flowering and inexhaustible. In general, Balthasar's aesthetics appears as a rupture when juxtaposed against other twentieth-century philosophical opinions on the possibility of meaning, which was hitherto a concept either explained away as desire (by more mechanistic philosophers) or that was existentially untenable (by more nihilistic philosophers). The arts of the beautiful (because they are not merely thoughts) are in a very special position to respond to these claims. Art performs a sacramentality and so amplifies the connection between what is "worded" or "imaged" (i.e., the *kataphatic*) and what remains on the edge of expression (i.e., the *apophatic*). The content of the sacramental "performance" is revealed by analogy, grasped by the analogical imagination, and figured on a kind of grand concentric continuum.

The analogy of being, to offer another strategic reprise, is the fundamental component that lends light, life, and credibility to Balthasar's entire theological project. A creative reconsideration of the doctrine, furthermore, has inspired a new school of scholars to apply the "analogical imagination" to current problems in theology, philosophy, art, and literature, to name a few. However, there is a metaphysical question with which to reckon: this is the analogy of "being," not of "thought." Those philosophers who have followed Kant and dispensed with the ground of Being as a metaphysical first premise—philosophers such as Emmanuel Levinas, Jürgen Habermas, and Richard Rorty—have also denied the analogy of being any metaphysical veracity.[54] This intriguing debate will demand our immediate attention in very short order.

A simple description of the *analogia entis*, therefore, comes with ambivalence: on one hand, the concept is simple—a child can explain it in a sentence. We understand one thing in terms of something else. On the other hand, the analogy of being has a complexity about it that no language can access (because language for some, as I discussed above, is ultimately incapable of accessing anything). The tension suggested in this ambivalence is perhaps where the heart of the question about analogy lies; and many postmodern scholars, whatever their religious or philosophical commitments, have ended up fixated on this tension, on this gap. The implications of this tension for theology, philosophy, and literary studies are positive. Analogy, we will observe, resists polarities and gains clarity and light in negotiating opposites. Analogy doesn't claim to say anything conclusive about anything else, which protects ambiguity, if that's a value, as well as mystery, if that's another value, and doctrine, if that's yet another. Most important for Balthasar, analogy discloses a relational pattern that comes from the heart of the universe, a pattern premised on the dynamic and constructive love of the *imago Trinitatis*. Analogy's double action that reveals a third reality prizes both the finite and infinite reaches of our imagination. Analogy reveals as it conceals; it discloses similarity in the very same motion that it discloses difference. Analogy safeguards what postmodern theorist Michel de Certeau (following Nicholas of Cusa) calls the *"complexio oppositorum."*[55] Since negotiating opposites such as these is perhaps what moves up most forcefully toward theological speculation and contemplation, analogy can also serve as a good topic on which to conclude a chapter. And to begin a new one.

3

Sacred Arrangements

Balthasar, Flannery O'Connor,
and the Glory of the Lord

To appreciate a beautiful form, you have to see it as a whole and
from every angle, or, in the case of musical beauty, you have to hear
it with all its harmonies. There is always something new to see or
hear, and yet it is still the same thing, beauty ever ancient, ever new.
—John Saward, 1990

I have seen
not behind but within, within the
dull grief, blown grit, hideous
concrete façades, another grief, a gleam
as of dew, an abode of mercy....
—Denise Levertov, from *City Psalm*, 1964

Nothing is profane for those who know how to see.
—Flannery O'Connor, c. 1962

Seeing the Form: A Christological Aesthetics

the verb took over all the power
and blended existence with essence
in the electricity of its beauty
—Pablo Neruda, "The Word"

The above epigraph locates a key contention in the debate between
those who assert that our experience as humans is represented best
by a performance of unstable and socially constructed "texts" (or
"discourses") and those who believe that our experience is better described as a sacred drama of persons who respond freely in a dynamic

hierarchy.[1] The excerpt comes from Pablo Neruda's famous poem *La Palabra* ("The Word") and is a celebration of the constructive potential of words and language. In the poem, Neruda reconfigures the traditional (in this case, biblical/Christian) trajectory of "the word" and avers that the word was not eternal but "born in blood." In his quest for a poetics of word-as-agent, Neruda then appropriates (and beautifully so) a decidedly eucharistic language. The poet writes, in a classic resignification of Christian signs, that he "drinks the pure wine of language ... the blood which expresses its substance." The locus of contention in the particular epigraph that I cited lays in the idea that "the verb took over" power and is misguided, paradoxically, because it seeks to limit the very power of the word that Neruda seeks to proclaim. For the (Christian) theist, the Word—the *Logos*—is eternal, revelatory, and normative. *Logos* combines God's dynamic, creative word (as in Genesis or in John's Gospel, in speaking or singing the world to being) with personified preexistent wisdom (as in Proverbs or Sirach, the wisdom packaged in language) as both the instrument of God's creative activity (as in the Christian scriptures and in the other "theological aesthetics" we are presently exploring) and the ultimate intelligibility of reality (as in traditional Western philosophy and theology). In the Christic imagination, the word does not "take over," construct, or merely represent (even though it can do these things): the word *is*. In the end, Neruda's poetic resignification gelds (or spays) the word and excavates it of its eternal power.

Siphoning off the power of language is not Neruda's intention. As a poet, he reveres the word and seeks to unite with it. He imagines that "language extends even to the hair" and that, in a poetic parody of Cartesian abstraction, it is the self-generated word, not thought, that creates: "(the word's) arrangements awe me and I find my way through each variation in the spoken word—I utter and I am." Without being too fussy about it, what puzzles the reader is the concession that the word can only extend to the hair but not to any further outpost (or inpost) of being and the realization that, in this case, Neruda's idea of transcendence is so imaginatively and spatially limited. For Neruda and the philosophy *La Palabra* represents, while it may indicate a certain kind of transformative power in language, the poem does not make available the final fullness on which such a poetic philosophy fundamentally relies. In other words, the poet has faith in the word and its ability as constructive agent, but the faith proposed is both self-generated and limited. Neruda's poem, in an ironic twist, lacks faith's essence: it lacks the faculty of intuition. It is intuition that spiritually senses both the word and all that is veiled by the aesthetic of the *word*; intuition that is primordial in poetry because it links the material to the spiritual, the present to the eternal, the signifiers to the signified; intuition that is the poet's third eye, the eye that gazes quietly through, even "the myth of presence," so that it might see what else is actually there.

The point cannot be emphasized enough. In his 1953 study *Creative Intuition in Art and Poetry*, Jacques Maritain assesses the poverty of Neruda's approach (i.e., the purely secular turn in poetics) as essentially one grounded in a misunderstanding of theological and philosophical liberty, an axial point, it is worth mentioning, in Balthasar's theological program as well. Maritain reflects:

> And because poetry is born in this root life where the powers of the soul are active and common, poetry implies an essential require- ment of totality or integrity. Poetry is the fruit neither of the intellect alone, nor the imagination alone. Nay more, it proceeds from the to- tality of man, sense, imagination, intellect, love, desire, instinct, blood, and spirit together. And the first obligation imposed on the poet is to consent to be brought back to the hidden place, near the center of the soul, where this totality exists in the state of a creative source.[2]

La Palabra resonates in this passage, especially in the imagery of "desire" and "blood"; but the architecture of poetic making, Maritain asserts, also requires nonmaterial components. In short, Neruda's poem seems a celebration of mere materialism and mere positivism and all those Promethean perspectives that would disallow the mysteries of the unseen.

My brief consideration of Neruda's philosophy of poetry is vital because it discloses a precise and subtle point of contention in the ongoing clash over hermeneutical approaches. It also provides a good transition from our discus- sion of the analogy of being that concluded the last chapter. For many devo- tees of strict modernist structuralism, for example, there is nothing signified outside the text. In the same spirit, their postmodernist/post-structuralist off- spring place an equal emphasis on the power of the text(s), but exactly in con- tradistinction: the postmodern "text" (or "meaning," but this term is com- pletely problematic in postmodernism to the ironical point of being taboo) is "located" in the area that is to be or has been "transgressed" or ruptured. The text (or "discourse," more likely), in turn, either actively subsumes this "trans- gression" and recalibrates itself, thus assimilating the transgression into a newer, shinier text (à la Foucault), or *it* (i.e., what is *signified*, what *it* might mean) remains deferred outside the text in the playful nether regions of *sur- plus* and *excess* (à la Derrida).[3] Obviously, both trends, in addition to making ample use of quotation marks and italics, indicate a myopic "bottom-up" ap- proach to reading the world (reality, texts, memory, history, mystery, phenom- ena, and so on), and both are trends that deny the challenge to see something else at work in the world of the word besides human fabrication. This chapter, among other things, seeks to engage this critical tension and to discuss the fascinating differences that exist in some current approaches to reading texts and, therefore, "reading" the world. Principally, though, the chapter aims to illustrate how the analogical imagination—vis à vis Balthasar's *Glory of the Lord*—continues to be a valuable resource for critics today. I hope to show how a careful consideration of some select narrative art can endorse the *word* in all its fullness: in its potency to have a plurality of dynamic meaning and its freedom to exist in its incarnate quality of finitude.

While I'll include important supplementary examples—from the hands of Walker Percy and William Everson—the central "artifact of Beauty" in this case is from Flannery O'Connor's short story "Revelation," published in 1964. It has been well established that O'Connor's work is generally excellent as an aesthetic aid or literary interlocutor to any conversation about art and representation. Moreover, her's was a prophetic voice that helped square a sense of theistic presence with some of the sclerotic tendencies of the modern world. A notion entertained less in O'Connor studies is how she, like Balthasar, anticipated some of the specific problems that modernism would bequeath to its next generation; and her prophetic voice rises yet again to help us make sense of postmodernism of art and representation as we've grown to interpret them since 1945. As Paul Giles has pointed out, O'Connor's work "negotiates the postmodernist fragmentation and discontinuity"[4] in an exemplary fashion and provides her readers with much more than the subtle literary catechesis with which most of us associate her name:

> But in O'Connor this modernist strain finds itself crossed with absences and discontinuities of postmodernism, predicated as it is on a world of philosophical fragmentation and difference. It is this paradoxical sense of incompleteness and displacement in O'Connor's writing that ensures her fiction comes to carry a larger aesthetic complexity and significance than the rigidity of the neo-scholastic dogma professed in her letters and essays might imply.[5]

This is not to say that O'Connor's entrenched neo-scholasticism is unimportant, for it quite clearly and quite thoroughly informs her work. And since it does, we will certainly respect its presence here. Additionally, Jacques Maritain, whose *Art and Scholasticism*, O'Connor wrote in a 1957 letter, was "the book I cut my aesthetic teeth on,"[6] is central to this discussion, particularly in Maritain's tripartite conception of beauty's "first stage." I have apportioned the heart of my chapter, in turn, along Maritain's conceptual guideline for beauty—in *integrity*, in *proportion*, and in *radiance*—in order to contemplate more acutely how the opposing critical camps compete under these various criteria of beauty. Balthasar, of course, is likewise attuned to such categories, so there will be another level of concord—namely that of a coherent theological aesthetic that ascends from these various sources to reveal a uniquely Catholic imagination. In the fourth section of the chapter, I attempt to take what was learned about the *word* in the first three sections and apply the lessons in a very close reading of O'Connor's "Revelation," particularly as a literary embodiment of a Catholic imagination. I hope, in this manner, that the chapter may achieve at least a semblance of the harmony that Maritain's categories seek to illuminate, just as I hope also to demonstrate how O'Connor's story, because it depicts these categories as they appear in a world that is fallen, can speak instructively to the reader who has divorced his or her critical gaze from traditional modes of inquiry in preference for the prism of postmodernism. Like Balthasar, O'Connor shakes, shuffles, and stirs ancient categories of beauty precisely so the categories may be revealed more clearly, more profoundly, and, finally, more meaningfully.

Since the theological aesthetics I explore in this chapter are specifically focused on language, much of my text will be devoted to unpacking language or, to be more specific, to unpacking a word. The word in this case is *hierarchy*. *Hierarchy* denotes, connotes, and implies a powerfully sacred concept that gains its fullest meaning when attached to the transcendental referent that much postmodernist theory, in its wholesale critique of theism as a critical category, denies or dismisses. The radical misunderstanding of *hierarchy*, as it turns out, is also the central theme in O'Connor's "Revelation."[7] *Hierarchy*, then, provides entrée into a wealth of issues that surrounds Balthasar's aesthetic; and it is my position, along with O'Connor and the rest of the *ressourcément* school of theological aestheticians, that our misreading of *hierarchy* and the powerful mystery that the term represents is precisely what thwarts our ability to conceive of a world that, while fallen and free, is also sacredly arranged. *Hierarchy* has become "one of those old words of grace," as Walker Percy mused, "that are worn smooth as poker chips."[8] What may rescue this fragmentation, as Percy's literature so often explores, is the disposition to see the beauty of the hierarchical drama and to see and assent to the dynamism of the form of the One who calls us by name. For these reasons, along with O'Connor and the other mediators of the "poetics of Incarnation,"[9] my conclusion tends toward a Christology as an incarnational ground for relationship, community, and transcendental beauty. Let us then begin, but, first, some basics.

Integrity: Rethinking *Hierarchy*

... to another mighty deeds; to another prophecy; to another discernment of spirits; to another varieties of tongues; to another interpretation of tongues. But one in the same spirit produces all of these, distributing them individually to each person as He wishes.
                                    —1 Corinthians 12:9–11 (New American Bible)

The passage from St. Paul underscores the giftedness of creation and illuminates the symphonic nature of absolute being. Each component of being receives from the Spirit an invitation to mission and a call to community. While Paul's vision indicates a traditional sense of an intentional orderliness to the world, it also emphasizes "difference," a key in critical and cultural theory. The passage conjoins the palpable location of absolute being (i.e., God's generous self-communication in Christ) to a temporal community (e.g., Corinth). By the same token, it also locates, in both a literal and metaphorical sense, the nexus of our participation with absolute being in a "body," which is "not a single part but many." These two tropes rhetorically accomplish and illuminate Paul's hope for unity;[10] but they also indicate how Paul, both here and in other Pauline writings, is meditating just as much on the notion of difference as he is on the hope for unity in Christ. After all, he has just said in his letter (cf. 1 Cor. 7) that while he "wishes that everyone be as I am," he realizes that each person has "a particular gift from God, one of one kind, one of another." All things, all gifts, it becomes exceedingly clear, are essential to being—Paul's foot, Priscilla's ear, even Silas's (as legend has it) weak eyes. We grasp the ordained potential and the ultimate harmony of our "parts," our gifts, when we assent to their ordination and, paradoxically, assent to their freedom to move within the body of being. The unity that Paul illustrates, furthermore, is strengthened by variety and by the innate potential of different elements to tend to the unity that created them. It is particularly important that Paul "works out" this new theology to the Greco-Roman audience of Corinth, for the letter can be interpreted as, among other things, a reply to the ontologically incomplete effects of Platonic dualism and other dyadic Hellenistic philosophies that influenced the region.[11] Paul is essentially introducing a bold new cosmology: a Christianized sense of the Greek concept of *hierarchy*, in which unbridled duality and plurality are subsumed in the mysterious logic of the Incarnation, the triune economy of God, and against the grand mystical symphony, the *ekklesia*, of "Him in whom we live and move and have our being."[12]

St. Paul's concern with the cosmological character of Christian *integrity* is well known.[13] The first few centuries after the circulation of his letters provided both the chronological spaces for Pauline theology to grow as well as the theologians with whom Paul's work could enter into dialog. In time, crystallization of seminal theological, ontological, and ecclesiological concepts such as *hierarchy* began to emerge. However, just as terrestrial luminosity can be swallowed up by the same dust that produces it, the same can happen to the razor sharp gems born of metaphysical inquiry. When language, for example, becomes dislocated from its source, from the community and tradition that sired it, it indeed becomes a free agent—so free that it begins to divest itself of its original location and sense of meaning and ultimately ends up in the dustbin of unintelligibility. It is for this reason, perhaps, that our understanding of *hierarchy* has simply eroded into the solipsism of a merely contextual understanding.

The greatest impediment to understanding *hierarchy* seems to be the vivisecting mechanism that illuminated its beauty and richness in the first place.[14] It is no secret that the Church Fathers devoted a healthy amount of time to repudiating the polarizing effects of philosophical dualism and theological bifurcation that were afoot in (and, of course, before) the early centuries of Christianity, whether in their Pharisaic, Gnostic, Pelagian, or Manichean forms, just as some today are devoted to debunking their Jansenistic, Cartesian, and deconstructionist ancestors. Augustine, for example, resisted ultimately the dualistic imagination that had played a major part in his own early ontological formation. He hunted for a "third way" to approach reality, a way that both denied the (ultimately) static character of dialecticism and mirrored the fecundating trinitarian reality that he saw behind all of creation. Certainly, Augustine knew the rhythms of the dialectic: he was pretty sure there was *being* and quite certain there was *living*. The third part of the triad became *understanding,* an intellectual structure, according to Balthasar, that becomes the precise point of clarity in Augustine's primary intuitions about being:

> The point is not to establish an empty identity between being and thinking, nor an original "tension" between subject and object; it is an attempt to find a place for the most fundamental order of being in the world within the original act of consciousness. This not only radically invalidates every dialectic between concept and existence, but also the unfruitful dialectic between thought and life whose divisiveness fills the history of modern thought. Rather, Augustine lays the foundation for a major thesis of Thomas Aquinas' when he says, "I know that I can only know if I am alive, and I know this all the more certainly in that I become more alive by knowing." "To be in order to be alive, to be alive in order to understand."[15]

Balthasar asserts that this realization contains the whole of Augustinianism, in that it is both a repudiation of dualism and a refutation of the character of Plotinus's hierarchy and other forms of Neoplatonism that would certainly "see hierarchical principle" but ultimately relegate it into a kind of pantheism.[16] O'Connor, as a distinctly Catholic artist, is equally wary of dualistic bifurcations and categorically rejected, for example, the Manicheans' heretical separation of sprit from matter and critiqued other contemporary (and often Catholic) artists' separation of grace from nature in their art. For Augustine, and for Denys who follows him, being is not *dialectical* but *analogical.* The analogical, as discussed last chapter, introduces the third term or option, which in turn provides relief to the heaviness and insularity of dialectical coupling. Thus, a "third way" is made available—not by envisioning a "this or that" world, but by employing the analogical imagination that sees the mystery of the world, linked in Christ, with a conciliatory sense of a "both/and," a sacramental wingspan that reaches out from that which is concrete to that which is universal.[17] As Balthasar astutely points out, in the Christian era, dialectical Greek philosophy came to represent "the misuses of genuine religious thought for purposes of Promethean speculation." Neither Augustine nor Denys, with whom we shall deal more explicitly in short order, wants to borrow from systems that assert dualism as primordial "but to return what has been borrowed to its rightful owners."[18] Such a desire speaks to the very heart of *hierarchy.*

Hierarchy is normally employed as pejorative term. It carries with it a haversack of negative connotations, among them, ironically, well-established linguistic and grammatological associations that suggest generation-wide hegemony at the hands of terms like *hierarchy* (like *authority,* like *economy,* perhaps, even, like *hegemony*). Certainly, in human experience, there have been (and continue to be) systematic abuses of hierarchical power and categorical examples of despotism—whether in language, in political and spiritual life, or elsewhere. Most every page of history carries with it the just imputation of guilt upon powerful political "hierarchies" who have imposed their will upon the masses and have often perpetrated evil schemes. Sanctioned structures of seduction and injustice, manifold incidents of the inured "power" of the colonizer wielded upon the colonized, innumerable instances of dubious authority asserted by armed thugs over the dispossessed and disenfranchised, chronic abuses of insidious forms of hierarchy (usually patriarchal in nature) systemically inserted into human communities. These corruptions of hierarchy have bled out into a broad swath of suffering that hangs over the generations. This we have seen; and more is the pity when terms such as *hierarchy* have come to be associated exclusively with history's anthology of ill will especially when such negative associations are based on a fractured understanding of what *hierarchy* actually connotes. The subversion of language, in this regard, is itself a transcendental dispossession and therefore strikes one as a double injustice. *Hierarchy*, then, is an exemplary linguistic scapegoat; and a literary inspection of the term exposes an interesting array of critical tension.

Excursus (A) Lost in the Cosmos: Walker Percy
and a Theology of Language

Broken bottles, broken plates,
Broken switches, broken gates,
Broken dishes, broken parts,
Streets are filled with broken hearts.
Broken words, never meant to be spoken,
Everything is broken.
—Bob Dylan, "Every Thing's Broken"

In one section of the introduction to his recent book, *Love's Sacred Order*, theologian and philologist Erasmo Leiva-Merikakis attempts to clarify ways in which some postmodern scholarship has misappropriated and misunderstood language. Viewed from the sphere of the popular academy, Leiva-Merikakis's efforts can be seen to share a kinship both with the *ressourcement* theologians of the early and mid-twentieth centuries, and with the present "radical orthodoxy" movement of Anglican scholars Graham Ward, John Milbank, Catherine Pickstock, and others; but such an association (i.e., association to movements at all, especially those with charged monikers such as "radical orthodoxy") would fail to do the topic or Leiva-Merikakis's work ultimate justice. Like Pickstock in particular, Leiva-Merikakis attempts to rescue language from its post-structural fragmentation, from its divorce of sign from signified.[19] In this way, Leiva-Merikakis's project is to out-Herod the Herods of current cultural and critical theory by lining up the "floating signifiers" and "decontextualized contexts" in his own critical crosshairs:

> "Sacred order" is an attempt to render in more comprehensible English the Greek word hierarchy. In our secular understanding of the term, we do not often remember that the term arose in an exclusively

religious context as an attempt to see all creatures in the whole created order, from cherubim and seraphim to the humblest pebble on the ocean's floor, in their relationship to their uncreated Source and to one another.[20]

"Relationship" is precisely the point, for the pesky problem of what words (as signs) signify is fundamentally an issue of relationality. A fair amount of current scholarship in hermeneutics, however, would have us believe that language is both ontologically and culturally inorganic; that it possesses no meaningful relationship within itself or with preceding historical "contexts"; that language gives us "no place to start," is nonreferential, and has nothing at all to do with "meaning," let alone transcendence. I disagree. Clearly, questions about relationships among language and history and culture are by their very nature metaphysical, have everything to do with the imagination and with seeing, and therefore have everything to do with meaning. But to take the approach, whether out of playfulness, narcissism, or nihilism, that words, narrative moments, and linguistic structures do not aid in the conveyance of metaphysical meaning or to deny the valuable connections between language and life is to divorce oneself arbitrarily from history, from community, and ultimately from any meaning whatever.

If we don't think language can aid intelligibility, consistency, and meaning, consider several recent instances in which the absence of a credibly articulated linguistic aesthetic has affected political economy. After the events of September 11, 2001, a politically divided congress sang "God Bless America" together with one voice. Even though the song beggars interesting questions about "which God?" and "which America?" to which each individual was referring as he or she crooned the tune, a sense of community was somehow created in the simple utterance of the song. In this case, Balthasar's symphony of meaning is achieved in spite of probable differences in intention. Let us turn the wrench tighter and consider another charged issue in which language is central: the issue of marriage. Who can be "married?" Is marriage simply a matter of historical precedent? What about anthropology? What of sacramentality? What about common law or parenthood? Is marriage a civil or religious state? What power ought churches have in this regard? Grammar, clearly, is everything in these debates. Consider something even more basic and practical: the issuing of an apology. In both the case of the USS *Greeneville*'s accidental sinking of the Japanese Trawler *Ehime Maru* in 2001 and the infringement of United States' spy plane into Chinese airspace later that year, the shrewd formulation of apology, even more than material reparations, meant everything. To the chagrin of some academics, these apologies, even across the horizon of language, were neither constructed nor received as random free play of signs but as important activities in human reconciliation. But the diminishment of language as practical agent has been evolving in a major strand of literary scholarship and has reached its apotheosis in the "secular understanding" of which Leiva-Merikakis speaks. Many adherents of the deconstructionist project have determined that language is not an instrument of metaphysics but rather another artifact of human insularity, another piece in a detached cultural game. O'Connor, for her part, anticipated the darker implications for aesthetics and metaphysics that this cavalier approach to language and signs entails. Her fiction, letters, and essays serve as a literary counterfriction to a world in which the relational, linguistic, and, finally, theological value of language has atrophied. She wrote in 1963:

> Unless the novelist has gone entirely out of his mind, his aim is still communication, and communication suggests, at least to some of us, talking inside a community of which one is a part. One of the reasons Southern fiction thrives is that today a significant number of our best writers are able to do this. They are not alienated from their society. They are not lonely, suffering artists gasping for purer air. Although there are a few who always run from the South as from a plague, in general the Southern writer feels the need for expatriation less than other writers in this country. Moreover, when he does leave and stay gone out of choice and continues to write about the South, he does so at great peril to that violence between principle and fact, between judgment and observation which is necessary to maintain if fiction is to be true. The isolated imagination is easily corrupted by theory. Alienation was once a diagnosis, but in much fiction of our time it has become an ideal. The modern hero is an outsider. His experience is rootless. He can go anywhere. He belongs nowhere. Being alien to nothing, he ends up being alienated from any kind of community based on common tastes and interests. The borders of his country are the sides of his skull.[21]

O'Connor's congenital (and highly nuanced) anti-intellectualism aside, her message applies today: for those who subscribe to post-structural "meaning," for example, insularity and detachment reveal a kind of liberty. Since we can ourselves construct language (and relative meaning), there must not be anything that conclusively qualifies as "true." Since we ourselves, by our own shaping activities, can construct reality, there must not be any order or form in the universe for the prudent, imaginative, or aspiring person to discern, nothing that transcends.

From this perspective, anything beyond the ken of language becomes an ontological and grammatological anomaly, a demystified "excess of meaning" that contravenes, for better or worse, the idea of metanarrative. Such hermeneutical preferences, even though they are binary and dialectical in nature, cannot even be categorized among traditional misconceptions about dualism, because there is, in the end, no semiotic dance partner implied on the other side of the veil of the deconstructionist "system," nothing to link what is "excessive" to what is ordinary, nothing to which a symbol or a word corresponds. On the contrary: the relationship, because it is egocentric in character, forecloses, oddly enough, upon any possibility of authentic relationship with the "other" that it claims to seek—dialectical, grammatological, aesthetic, analogical, mystical, and so on. True relationship demands this risk of open-ness, which Walker Percy, among others I have mentioned, holds up as a structurally triadological (and therefore analogical) act. Following C. S. Peirce (1839–1914), the founder of philosophical pragmatism, Percy wants "to offer a new and more coherent anthropology," which is logically based on Peirce's notion of *thirdness* and theologically based on the communal relationship of the Trinity.[22] Against the deconstructionist program, Percy, with Peirce (who, ac-cording to Peirce scholar Donald Gelpi, was clearly the best logician of his era), stressed the same conclusion that is at the heart of Balthasar's aesthetic program: "the one great way to get at it, the great modern rift between mind and matter, was the only place they intersect, language."[23]

Percy holds that a recovered sense of the unitive power in language shines light on the idea that the intelligibility of experience finds its model in the mysterious procession of God. This "intelligibility," for Balthasar, is likewise linguistic (at least in one way) because it finds its prime analogical example in the *Logos* as John the evangelist perceives *Logos*, that is, as "cosmic reason" formed in flesh and propelled by love.[24] It's high theology, to be sure, but the analogical applications simply validate the transcendental intelligibility of human encounter and human community. Conversely, the final form of com-munity that deconstructionism allows, because the system precludes the "transcendental turn," is the tendency toward the atomization of communities. Adherents of postmodernism/post-structuralism will claim that hegemonic hierarchies (and that the human habit of viewing reality as a constructive and dynamic hierarchy) are precisely to blame for such atomization, that they wield and have wielded, as I mentioned above, oppressive power. *Hierarchy*, from this perspective, creates not a circuit of harmony but rather a proliferation of destabilized selves. I reiterate that it is the perversion of *hierarchy*, in our view both of the self and of being, which has instigated this dangerous decon-structivist reduction.[25] To explain this rupture away as, for example, a mythic novelty or philosophical construct is to engage in both an unimaginative metaphysics and a misreading of history. The fallaciousness of the position reaches its ironic climax when one realizes that the whole of postmodernity is itself premised precisely on history, on collective wisdom, and on relationship. George Steiner gets to the core of the matter:

> The deconstructive discourse is *itself* rhetorical, referential and alto-gether generated and governed by normal modes of causality, of logic, and of sequence. The deconstructive denial of "logocentrism" is ex-pounded in wholly logocentric terms. "Metacriticism" is criticism still, often of the most evidently discursive and persuasive kind. . . . They have invented no new speech, no immaculate conceptionaliza-tions. The central dogma, according to which all readings are mis-readings and the sign has no underwritten intelligibility, has precisely the same paradoxical, self-denying status as the celebrated *aporia* whereby a Cretan declares all Cretans to be liars. Immured within natural language, deconstructive propositions are self-falsifying.[26]

As one such "metacritic," Walker Percy sympathizes with Steiner. Percy, of course, is better known as a writer of highly reflexive metafiction, but his work uniquely serves both ends of the literary spectrum. Moreover, Percy is vital to any discussion about a theology of language, especially in the uneasy tension that surfaces between the areas of deconstructionism and theological aesthetics. As a novelist—one who began to write only after he converted to Catholicism, a fact that raises interesting issues—Percy's work is characterized by a scrupulous attention to language, sometimes, some critics will argue, at the expense of narrative clarity. Still, it is widely agreed that Percy integrated the concerns of theology, philosophy, and semiotics creatively and insightfully and that his work, along with that of O'Connor, serves as good example of what an accomplished theological aesthetics looks like in late-modern literary settings. It is also fascinating to note that Percy's intellectual and spiritual mentors—namely Aquinas, Maritain, Marcel, and, most important, Kierkegaard—were also favored by Balthasar, especially in the way that these figures articulated relationships among philosophical and theological aesthetics, among anthropology, Christology, and narrative art.

As a bona fide semiotician (Percy has written extensively on language, sign, and transmission of meaning), Percy is intrigued by codes—codes in consciousness, behavior, and language—and, of course, by the transmission of codes. His 1977 novel *Lancelot* examines the possibility for the existence of the mediaeval code of chivalry under the decayed moral umbrella of the late twentieth century. Lancelot (Lance) Lamar, attorney at law, though, is a defeated man. The Arthurian allusion of the title is obvious: Lancelot is a fallen knight. The narrative is Lancelot's first-person "confession" from an "aberrant behavior ward" where Lance recounts a series of recent episodes to his childhood friend, Percival (the pure knight in Arthurian legend), now a Catholic priest. Lance attempts to explain his motivation for torching his home and killing his wife (along with a couple of others) amidst the storm-surge chaos of a violent hurricane. Yet, in one perspective, Lance can be viewed as a character more closely aligned with Kierkegaard's "knight of faith." Beaten down by his own hopeful idealism (in this case, the liberalism that met the failed project of Johnson's "Great Society") and besotted by booze because of it, Lance "awakens" in midlife to find that a few other things are out of kilter as well—chief among them is the revelation that his daughter, Siobhan, has been fathered by another man. On the heels of this discovery, Lance suddenly finds himself in some brand of Kierkegaardian-aesthetic-phase disaster in which his genteel Southern landmark of a home is transformed by Hollywood moguls (through the agency of his libertine wife) into what amounts to a "location" (both cinematic and actual) for the performance of soft-porn manners that typified popular culture of the mid-1970s. Lance initially "rolls" with the scene; but he also begins systematically to observe his guests and, in time, decides that, among other things, all men are rapists, all women like to be raped, and society approves these behaviors by rapaciously consuming the entertainment culture that performs and presents these transgressions as behavioral norms. Lance's findings are aided, of course, by other psychohistorical factors, not least of which is Lance's memory of catching his mother *in flagrante delectio* with his uncle when he was a child. In short, Lance's variable experiences lead him to believe that modern culture is decadent and dissolute and that humanity has lost the "knightly" code of meaning. As a Southern gentleman, the last guard of chivalric virtue, he decides to reject the dominant culture from which he is alienated and become a knight of faith: "So overnight I became sober, clear-eyed, clean, fit, alert, watchful as a tiger at a water hole. Something was stirring. So Sir Lancelot set out, looking for something rarer than the Grail. A sin."[27]

Since the code of meaning has been subverted by modern culture, Lance's quest manifests itself as a kind of anti-quest. Lance, as a modern knight facing a crisis, decides to reorient his quest toward sin and "evil" since " 'Evil' is surely the clue to this age, the only quest appropriate to the age. For everything and everyone's either wonderful or sick and nothing is evil."[28] There is logic in this quest, clearly, and it is found in a kind of theological inversion, one of the only modes of interpretation that makes constructive sense of violence. Because the world is turned upside, his faith is put not in goodness, which has been carefully interviewed by culture and then cast aside, but in evil. Following the famous formula O'Connor describes in her essay "The Fiction Writer and His Country" (1957) regarding the Catholic novelist and distortion ("To the hard of hearing, [Christian writers] shout, and for the . . . almost-blind [they] draw large and startling figures."[29]), Lance bears a familial resemblance to O'Connor's alienated anti-pilgrim Hazel Motes, who acts out of similar convictions in *Wise Blood* (1955). By blending grotesquerie with a measured sense of comedy, Percy manages to distance himself from Lance's peculiar odyssey but also to offer the reader a credible ethical exposé in prose. The code of love, according to Lancelot, has been reduced to the petty trafficking in serial orgasms, the "only earthly infinity"; the knightly quest for the Grail is now "the little Volkswagen with the make love not war sticker pulling in this very moment with the same mousy little coed at the wheel, the same two homosexuals holding hands next door, a quiet decent couple actually, much like any other couple, raper and rapee, with needs like yours and mine plus an occasional tube of K-Y jelly."[30]

Chivalry is a paradoxical concept in that it blends militarism with Christianity, but it does endorse enduring virtues such as grace, civility, loyalty, and honor. This tension is central to Percy's presentation in *Lancelot*. The amplification of Lance's chivalric vision triggers us to wonder at knights of other ages. We are struck with the fact that these are not moderate characters after all—Kierkegaard himself was anything but moderate, and his insistence of the structure of "either/or" reveals the Gnostic and Manichean flavor of his imagination. But how often is moderation associated with the radical experience of prophetic encounter? Prophets, as we have seen, are rarely known in their own time or place, and moderation diminishes the volume of the knight's prophetic voice to a whisper, if even that. In this sense, deconstruction, which is the diminishment of the relationship between values and words, aids in eroding valuable codes and inspires a kind of revolt. Lance, as distorted as his code appears, at least acts with passionate intensity. And have we ever heard, before now, *passion* and *postmodernity* in the same sentence?

To pull on the thread of Kierkegaard "either/or" option for the knight of faith is also to engage in a deeper reading of *Lancelot*. The "dialog" between Lance and Percival illuminates distinctions within the theological imagination, between the Gnostic and the "incarnational" imaginations. For the majority of the novel Percival does not respond to Lance: he simply stands gazing and listening: "You gaze at me with such—what? Sadness? Love? What about love? Do you think I can ever love anyone?"[31] Percival only responds at the end of the novel when Lance hurls a series of Gnostic ultimatums at him: "You are silent. Very well. But you know this! One of us is wrong. It will be your way or it will be my way...there is no other way but yours and mine, true? *Yes.*"[32] While Percival responds in the affirmative, perhaps as a conclusive theological and existential rebuttal to Lance's various negations, it is also clear that Percival's *yes* psychologically pacifies the unstable Lance. Percy then equivocates Lance's Gnostic dualism with mental illness, a psychospiritual split that, in its rupture, underscores the inseparability of psychological reality from theological reality. Albert Gelpi comments:

> Lance's sense of the dualism between body and spirit is so radical and extreme that body equates to sin—specifically sin as sex. The bodily existence is living sin without the redemptive Incarnation. Spirit becomes a hopeless, unrealizable ideal (like chivalry). Percival as a Catholic should be able to affirm the Incarnation as the redemption of fallen, sinful body, not Gnostic redemption *from* body, but Incarnational redemption *of* body.... Do Percival's few responses offer a counter to Lancelot's tirade of Gnostic/Manichean despair? Is Lancelot's Chivalry a true code, or a falsely Gnostic one? Is the novel, in the end, Incarnational?[33]

To respond to Gelpi's last question, the answer is yes—the novel is ultimately an endorsement of the incarnational imagination precisely because it discloses the heavy price paid for our estrangement from such an imagination. Its absence discloses the postmodern "gap" left behind by an incarnational presence. Yet, Percy does not hang Lance out to dry, for the humanity of Percival's *yes* somehow protects Lance from total annihilation. Percival's *yes* is itself a linguistic invocation of chivalry, an invitation to mercy in a fallen world. As Percy writes in *Lost in the Cosmos* (1983): "My own conviction is that semiotics provides an escape from the solipsist prison by its stress on the social origins of language."[34] Percival's *yes*, then, is an incarnational emblem par excellence; in a most critical moment of significant theological drama, Percy's response becomes a pastoral obligation. Analogically speaking, just as the Incarnation of God validates an array of transcendental and theological relationships, human language provides the link that signifies the value of our interpersonal relationships. Deconstructing the novel thus reveals one important gap that exists within the theological imagination: the relationship among signs, what the signs might signify, and the persons who stand so tenuously in between.

But deconstruction is precisely concerned with annihilating the false dichotomies that fire the Gnostic/rationalist mind-set; and, it is exceedingly clear that much of the deconstructive project, in its makeover of the word, is premised on the value of casting aside oppressive and restrictive modes of epistemology. I believe that the spirit in which the movement arose was one grounded in historical necessity, in philosophical justice, and in intellectual creativity and that the project has been a good challenge to traditional modes of theory and metaphysics.[35] However, while not all post-structuralists propose a limited and godless metaphysic,[36] the movement of deconstruction tends, if not toward atheism, then at least toward a tight-lipped cynicism about God; and I believe both to be fallacious positions. In his 1968 study *The Death of the Author*, literary critic Roland Barthes described the approaches to textuality characteristic of post-structuralism "as an anti-theological activity ... since to refuse to fix meaning is, in the end, to refuse God and his hypostases—reason, science, law."[37] Because of perspectives like these, there is the growing tendency to state that, ultimately, to follow Derrida, nothing can be signified. The next step in this process, as Milbank (and others before him) has pointed out is nihilism, and this is where we are presently: the point at which deconstruction becomes *destruction*, which in my opinion is a devolution into a basic, primal fury that will destroy the world, resulting not only in the demise of language, but also in the demise of art, of aesthetics, and ultimately in the demise of both the receiver and the sender of signs, that is, in the demise of the human person.

Percy is likewise concerned about the postmodern shape of nihilism and delves deeper into the topic in his 1987 *The Thanatos Syndrome*, a novel with similar atmospherics to *Lancelot* (indeed, atmosphere is everything in Percy). This time the setting is Feliciana, a Southern world in a bubble, a kind of never-ending, pre-apocalyptic cocktail hour on a shabby veranda. Somebody, quite literally, has put something in the drinking water of Feliciana parish, and the natives are behaving peculiarly, which of course is Percy's way of suggesting that the community has lost its wits, that its sense of *hierarchy* and order has been scuttled. In an extended dialog between two of the novel's main (if marginalized) characters, Dr. Thomas More (a name with historical significance of course, and More appears in other fiction by Percy) and Father Smith, Percy expostulates on the postmodern assassination of language, which Smith sees as the heart of what is afoul in Feliciana. Their conversation takes place in the marginalia of one of Balthasar's *interstices*, in this case, the six-by-six fire tower that Father Smith calls home. Thomas More, a psychiatrist, is marginal because he's just returned from a two-year prison term for malpractice and his license is in limbo; Father Smith is marginal because, as More observes, "he's gone batty, but batty in a way I recognize." Father Smith has retreated to his tower "to watch for signs." Father Smith engages Dr. More in a latter-day Socratic dialog:

> "The signs out there"—he nods to the shaggy forest—"they refer to
>   something, don't they?"
> "Right."

"The smoke was a sign of fire."

"That is correct."

"There is no doubt about the existence of fire."

"True."

"Words are signs, aren't they?"

"You could say so."

"But unlike signs out there, words have been evacuated, haven't they?"

"Evacuated?"

"They don't signify anymore."

The conversation unfolds in this fashion but concludes, strikingly, with Smith's asking More to help "assist" with mass, a turn in the discussion that quietly reveals that the reconciliation of "mind and matter," as Percy stated it above (and the reconciliation of our *thanatos syndrome*, our anger, our death instinct), does in fact reside in language, the language of liturgy. In the Real Presence of the Eucharist, and all that the Eucharist entails theologically (as in cosmic *Logos*, as in real communion with the eternal Word, as in relationship with the form of forms, as in a faith in history), language achieves its decisive enfleshment. "Goodbye, Tom," Father Smith says, smiling cheerfully, "There are dangers down there, Tom, you might not be aware of. Be careful." " 'I will,' I say, stepping down, wanting to be on my way."[38]

The demise of the signifier has negative implications for those who view reality *sacramentally* and analogically. One realizes that many aspects of post-modern thought conjugate to beget a fickle child who, as he hides from his parents in the Disneyland of postmodernity, rides *It's a Small World* over and over again, mistaking the different languages of the songs he encounters for totally different songs. But all is not lost: perhaps as the kid shuts the lamp at bed, the signal tower of his own day, he will be touched by an intuition or an insight that clarifies and recovers the day's experience. He may retrieve a renewed understanding of analogy and discern it, as Lynch counsels, "as that habit of perception which sees that different levels of being are also somehow one and can therefore be *associated in the same image,* in the same and single act of perception." What is not of the large and variegated fabric, Lynch continues, "we may lump together under the word 'Manichean:' all those habits of per-ception which instinctively dissociate."[39] Ultimately, the child may under-stand, as Derrida did before he died, that some things *are not* deconstructible, that, as Balthasar asserts, truth is symphonic. There are many glorious vistas and splendid horizons, but it really is a small world after all.

Proportion: The Analogical Imagination

But grace was given to each of us according to the measure of Christ's gift. Therefore, it says: "He ascended on high and took prisoners captive; he gave gifts to men." What does "he ascended" mean except that he also descended into the lower (regions) of the earth? The one who descended is also the one who ascended far above all the heavens, that he might fill all things.

—Ephesians 4:7–10

Before I get too far afield, let us return to our examination of *hierarchy* and how this specific word is exemplary when it comes to disclosing problems with several current conceptions of order, relationship, and community and suggest how O'Connor will make use of such distorted conceptions in "Revelation." In his text, Leiva-Merikakis's remarks about the abrogation of the contract between word and world are occasioned by a reference to Denys (who is more often referred to "clumsily" as "Pseudo-Dionysius,")[40] the Areopagite, the anonymous Greek writer who wrote in about the year AD 500 and with whom we, in the Christian tradition, chiefly associate the concept of *hierarchy* with "the arrangement of all sacred realities": "with procession and return and many essential adagios, but also the fundamental structure of the doctrine of God, of the angels, of the 'sacred' cosmos (with structures based both on function and rank), of the ecclesiastical hierarchy...."[41] Although not much is known about Denys himself, other than the fact that he was a contemplative Syrian monk, he has had monumental influence on theology: biblical, mystical, and systematic. Denys is a central stylist of the theological aesthetic that Balthasar proposes, and his vast insights on the arc of existence can inform the vocabulary of the religious critic. Consider, for instance, how all three theological venues (biblical, mystical, and systematic) resonate in the following excerpt from his *Celestial Hierarchy*:

> For each of those who is allotted a place in the Divine Order finds
> his perfection in being uplifted [*mystical*], according to his capacity,
> towards the Divine Likeness; and, what is still more divine, he
> shows forth the Divine Activity revealed as far as possible in him-
> self. For the holy constitution of the Hierarchy [*systematic*] ordains that
> some are purified, others purify; some are enlightened, others en-
> lighten; some are perfected, others make perfect [*biblical, as in 1 Cor.*
> *12*]; for in this way the divine imitation will fit each one.[42]

O'Connor was also very familiar with Denys. She writes to the famous "A" (AKA Betty Hester) in 1955, responding to Hester's questions about mediaeval mysticism: "he wrote treatises on the Angelic Hierarchies and on the Names of God which were very influential for mediaeval mysticism. You would enjoy this book (*Mysticism*, by Evelyn Underhill).... I read it last spring is how come I know all this. It's a mine of information."[43]

Hierarchy in the Denysian schema is a beautifully structured distribution of light, in which the highest choirs transmit the light received from the "Divine Source" to the heavenly intelligences, to the intermediate orders, and so on. This primordial taxis originates in the absolute unity of God and affirms cosmic variety; but from our (human/terrestrial) perspective, "order" and taxis seem to imply a foreclosure upon the possibility of will and personal agency, especially to those of the "lower orders." This possibility can be viewed, with good reason, as a threat to freedom by most of us, whether we are secular critics or not. However, when one meditates upon the mystery of Denys's hierarchy, one begins to see the sacred order of which Leiva-Merikakis speaks. The diminution of being that we find glancing down the ladder in Denys's hierarchies is not a defect in creation or a curtailment of our freedom, as some modern scholarship would have us believe. In fact, as Leiva-Merikakis makes clear, it is just the opposite:

> Nothing could be farther from the hierarchical vision of Denys, which, despite the Neo-Platonist terminology used, is at its core thoroughly biblical and Christian. For him the descending hierarchies signify the *difference* from God and from each other proper to each kind of being, but not *distance* or *estrangement* from God, since the whole order of hierarchies came about, not as a result of a defect, emanation or degradation of the Divine Being, but indeed as a result of the wise and good act whereby God freely chose to create a world, *this particular world*. Thus, an order results that is sacred both because it has God as absolute Source and because it is *the* order willed by God. Such a world and such an order, in turn, are an incessant source of glory for God, because all beings within abide at their posts fulfilling the tasks assigned to them by the Creator.[44]

It is fitting that a stone should be a stone and a tree should be a tree and that these things are ordered just so—for all things proceed through and participate essentially and proportionately in the Divine Hierarchy, or, as historical theologian Mark Delp has it: "Every being is what it is in respect of its capacity to receive the gifts of God. A rock only has the capacity to receive being, an animal receives being and life, but a soul receives being life and intelligence."[45] In *De Musica*, Augustine weighs in a bit more pragmatically on the matter: "We must not hate what is below us, but rather with God's help put it in its rightful place, setting in right order what is below us, ourselves, and what is above us, and not being offended by the lower, but delighting only in the higher.... Delight or enjoyment sets the soul in her ordered place."[46] All of creation is a procession of "gifts," freely given and (meant to be) freely received, for this procession from Divine Light is gratuitous and lush. It only appears cumbersome or lethargic when viewed as, say, a detached ego (as in the post-Enlightenment scheme) or as a substrate of Platonic or Neoplatonic cosmology, which, in the end is supercilious in its consideration of matter and creation.[47]

The metaphysical notion of the "analogical," a concept held in the collective gaze of much current discourse, clearly owes a precious debt to the "hierarchical imagination" Denys envisions. His cosmology is derived from a composite consideration of the mantle of being—biblical sources, observations of nature, and prayerful intuition, which he then (and Aquinas after him) fashioned into a hierarchy of causes. This hierarchy is motored, if you will, by the doctrine of the analogy of being, which has been reconstituted in present scholarship as the *analogical imagination*. In whatever form it is drawn, metaphysical properties inherent in analogy are striking in that analogy is able to describe, according to Jesuit scholar William Lynch, the structure of all existence by avoiding the dualistic extremes of viewing the world *univocally* (everywhere the same) or *equivocally* (everywhere different). In this way analogy is able to negotiate the opposites. Consider the Denysian resonance of the following passage from Lynch's *Christ and Apollo*:

> The act of existence descends analogously, *ana-logon*, "according to a proportion." The degree of existence is always measured by a degree of possibility, by the degree of fullness of being any possibility may receive. The form of a mouse can receive only so much. No one yet knows how much the form of a man can hold. But the proportion is always one and the same and altogether unvarying. It is always a proportion of "existence according to possibility." That has been and always shall be. It is an absolute invariant. All being therefore is one and the same, completely predictable, and with a decision that never changes as it advances in its processes. . . . Existence, as it descends, is analogous. It is never the same act of existence. It is a completely new fact; it must be new; for it must itself adapt to the new materials which it confronts, adapting itself in its bone and heart to the bone and heart of each new subject of being, each new part of the total organism. So too with the analogical idea, with our inward thinking about being. . . . We can never come up with one logical core and say it will satisfy the requirements of all the subjects. Only the proportion is the same; but the two parts of the proportion are always changing. The act of existence is always different; so too is the possibility, the material into which it enters.
>
> In other words, in an analogical organism of unity and its epistemological counterpart, an analogical idea, everything in the subjects is always the same, and everything is altogether different.[48]

Such a conception of the analogical makes the politically delicate notion of *hierarchy* more heterogeneous and therefore more credible (not to mention more palatable) to the postmodern consciousness.[49] It negotiates the opposites of similarity and difference and invites some sense of unitive meaning and mystery in a world that has come to be characterized by (a decidedly unanalogical) relativism, indeterminacy, and ambiguity.

In recent discourses, the concept of analogy has been criticized as structurally delusional. Literary critic Denis Donoghue observes in "Christ and Apollo" (an essay on the contribution of William Lynch) that the main complaint from such critics is that analogy "is complicit with the Aristotelian-Thomist rhetoric of identity presence and substance" and that to follow such entrenched conventions of analogy privileges "substance" and relegates the "accidental" to second-class status. In this way, according to Gilles Deleuze, the "same" is primary and "difference" is secondary, a deconstruction that is hegemonic and unfair. Donoghue sees the argument but ultimately rejects it: "I don't see why, to make the point that analogy implies identity and difference at once, you have to jettison Aristotle and Aquinas: analogy, in the scholastic tradition, acknowledges identity-and-difference at once, just as metaphor does."[50]

Donoghue's insight reveals the deeper implications of the analogical for aesthetics and poetics; and Lynch, for his part: "The matter, therefore, of fixity of dogma has no relevance whatsoever for the poet; but whether dogma fixes or frees the imagination has every conceivable relevance for him."[51] Fairly considered, then, the analogical imagination can stanch the wound of deconstructionism and can provide space, finally, for the reunion of the *sign* with the *signified*. How revitalizing to say, with confidence, something meaningful about something else.[52]

Radiance: Procession and Return

For once you were in darkness, but now you are the light of the Lord. Live as children of light, for light produces every kind of goodness and righteousness and truth. Try to learn what is pleasing to the Lord . . . everything exposed by the light becomes visible, for everything that becomes visible is light.

—Ephesians 5:8–10, 13–14

As I stated above, a central figure in Denysian cosmology is the analogical character of Divine Light. Certainly "light," as a trope, is a common Greek conceit; but for Denys, light has a transcendental quality in a specifically religious sense: it is a primordial autograph of the Christian Trinity, a "Divine Name." Denys speaks of God in this way as suprasensible Light, a shaft that "gushes over" and enlightens the hierarchy of being—Celestial, Ecclesiastical, Natural. In this way, God is the ray of "Divine Bliss . . . Eternal Light, perfect, in need of no perfection, purifying, illuminating, perfecting . . . Himself the Origin of perfection and the Cause of every hierarchy, He transcends in excellence and holiness."[53] Light imbues all of creation; and each different thing—from highest to lowest—is expressing the light that has been impressed upon its nature, the light that "pre-exists in the undifferentiated Super Essence."[54] As Balthasar observes well, light informs Denys's hierarchy to such an extent that it constitutes the very trajectory of Divine Being—which, for Denys is based on the classic mediaeval concept of *exitus et reditus*, the inexorable procession of all things from God, away from (but remaining within) His Light, and their ineluctable return to Him. Balthasar observes: "So finally, according to Denys, all is in accordance with the great flowing movement of being itself as *procession and return, proodos* and *epistrophe,* so that what is ultimately important is to trust oneself to the direction of this flow, recognizing in the procession the source, and in the return the goal."[55] The challenge to see God lies in the "trust" to see the world that God creates, orders, and reveals.

Such a conception of trust has far-reaching implications—individually, onto-logically, corporately, to name a few, and of course ecclesiologically, or, as Chesterton puts it:

> I meant that in one sense we see things fairly when we see them first. That, I may remark in passing, is why children have very little diffi-culty about the dogmas of the Church. But the Church, being a highly practical thing for working and fighting, is necessarily a thing for men and not merely for children. There must be in it for working purposes a great deal of tradition, of familiarity, and even of rou-tine. So long as the fundamentals are sincerely felt, this may even be the saner condition. But when its fundamentals are doubted, as at present, we must try to recover the candour and wonder of the child; the unspoilt realism and objectivity of innocence.... *We must invoke the most wild and soaring sort of imagination, the imagination that can see what is there.*[56]

And herein lies one modern response to the many just inquiries about agency and freedom: the full appreciation of Dionysian hierarchy, like all sys-tems that are moored in mystery, requires the creative imagination, the will to trust, the desire to see, and, perhaps most important, the gift of faith. In short, the vision requires conversion, an interior turning that "is the converse of a psychological act. It is the turning of the self to the otherness of being."[57] Those who are not disposed to the mystery will not see it. Thus, while all of Dionysian hierarchy—from mystical to celestial to terrestrial—transmits the providential life to all that is "below," they constitute for the *aspiring* soul that unites itself to them "a spiritual ladder from Earth to Heaven which is seen to correspond with the threefold Way traversed by all great mystics—the Active life through the way of Purification, whereby men become true servants of God; the Inner Life, the Way of Illumination and of real sonship with God; and the Contemplative Life, which is the Unitive Way whereby men may attain to true friendship with God."[58] Speaking in terms of literary analysis, one can interpret the randomness of floating signifiers as the nebula of meaning, or one can contemplate his or her experiences as something mysterious, as something that participates in the largeness and lightness of being revealing the form of the Beautiful.[59] *Ressourcement* theologian Henri de Lubac situates the choice well:

> If God had willed to save us without our own cooperation, Christ's sacrifice by itself would have sufficed. But does not the very existence of our Saviour presuppose a lengthy period of collaboration on man's part?... God did not desire to save mankind as a wreck is salvaged; he meant to raise up within it a life, his own life. The law of redemp-tion is here a reproduction of the law of creation: man's cooperation was always necessary if his exalted destiny was to be reached, and his cooperation is necessary now for his redemption. Christ did not come to take our place—or rather this aspect of substitution refers

only to the first stage of his work—but to enable us to raise ourselves through him to God.[60]

As Balthasar demonstrated in his own theological approach, to yearn for God and to desire God is to dispose ourselves toward God; and when we seek to see God's face, we then become complicit in our own "return." In this way we see that the Christian approach to life is as much a "doing" as a "saying," it is our action in the "divine-human drama."[61] The dramatic mandate reunites the estranged bedfellows of *orthopraxy* and *orthodoxy* and rightly places emphasis on the acting person. "Character is not a fact, but an act," writes the Personalist philosopher Emmanuel Mounier, an action that, because it is personally dynamic, orients us toward a view of existence that fits, among others, the theological tradition of *exitus* and *reditus*, the challenge of human freedom, and the theological aesthetic at work in O'Connor's fiction.[62] As O'Connor said, "All good stories are about conversion,"[63] instigating, perhaps, an *aesthetics of volition*: if we don't make the turn, if we do not seek and pray for *metanoia*, we will simply remain in partial sight, gazing, as St. Paul muses, "indistinctly, as in a mirror" right back at ourselves and at ourselves only. In essence, we will never have any clarity about *hierarchy* in the true sense of the word until we, as persons created to move in being, join with God, with Absolute Being, in the mystical return to himself, or as Delp puts it: "Once there is return, there can be hierarchy, and once there is hierarchy, things have a divine orientation."[64] Clearly this statement implies freedom—and Balthasar, as we shall see in chapter 5, is wise to focus on it—freedom for the individual to turn either toward divine radiance so as "to see the form," to see the arc of light enfleshed in a theodramatic and "meaning-bearing" world, or toward the freedom to remain under the lamp of our own, more dim illuminations: "The theological aesthetic is no philosophical conceptualism. The beautiful form is not a "static" idea: it is a dramatic "doing," its radiance pulsating with the hidden energies of being. The meanings that shape its form tend upward, toward the absolute meaningfulness in which it participates, and outward, toward its audience. In the degree that the form can contain the radiance, or surplus, of being, it obtains a relation to reality. The meaning that has been tightly bound in artistic form captures the radiance of reality itself. The beautiful object presents existingness, not essences."[65] The concept of *hierarchy* asserts an order, to be sure, but one that is qualified. Cleary, the concept has been eroded by history and therefore is too often dismissed by the bulk of critics today, critics who have jettisoned most of their ontological and theoretical links to God whether in "good faith," Barthesian whimsy, or, as Balthasar reckons, "through the fateful loss of sight which befalls whole generations."[66] But even for scholars with faith commitments, *hierarchy* can impose itself as a presumptive intimacy with God, a warm and fuzzy domestication of God because of the belief that language, through analogy, can access the divine. Such a conception can seduce one into thinking that God is ultimately knowable and, in the end, absolutely similar. Denys's system ultimately denies this turn; Augustine himself struggled with this question and Balthasar writes about it with characteristic clarity:

The doctrine of hierarchical number, the highest level of which rests in God and forms the ideal world of the Logos, is the clear expression of this conviction. This hierarchy cannot be translated into quantitative terms of a mathematical picture of the world (in which identity, and no longer analogy, would have to predominate) without first banishing the soul of Augustinianism. On the other hand, neither can it be portrayed as a mystical monism, because Augustine was constantly aware of the always greater dissimilarity between God and his creatures, and indeed right to the end (in the struggle against the Pelagians) continued to become increasingly aware of it. Once these dangers are excluded, his hierarchical world-picture becomes a secure and open framework within which a whole Christian millennium was able to develop the rhythms of its thought and life in all directions.[67]

The "framework" and "rhythms" of which Balthasar speaks point to the sacramental character of being, where the Creator "made all creatures *symbolon* or symbols in relation to the divine and allowed human beings to know and love God."[68] This delicate negotiation of the mystery is well explicated by the systematic theologian Alejandro Garcia-Rivera:

The analogy of being brings the human being into the incomprehensibility of God through the sensuality and presence of the natural objects of the world. All finite things in one way or another reveal something about God even while, as St. Augustine described, they give witness that 'I am not He who made me.' Indeed, it is because of the analogy of being that there could even exist a language about God. At the same time, however, the very act of conceptualizing God, of attempting to speak about God reveals God's utter otherness.[69]

Garcia-Rivera offers a most refreshing interpretation about the ways that "the other" can and does aid in our own "construction." The encounter with the other (through God, with God, in God) results in a dynamic relational bloom that reaches inward, then outward, in full relational flower of self and community. In this way the encounter is ontologically and sacramentally full: transcendent, transubstantive, and transformative.

Excursus (B) *God Is a Word, an Unspoken Word*: Revelation, Concealment, and William Everson

We Catholics are much given to the instant answer. Fiction doesn't have any. Saint Gregory wrote that every time the sacred text describes a fact, it reveals a mystery. And this is what a fiction writer, on his lower level, attempts to do also.

—Flannery O'Connor, *Collected Works*

For Denys, though, God is "over,"[70] that is, "transcendent."[71] Derrida, as a bona fide commentator on Denys, was critical of him precisely on this score and rejected his negative theology as a self-canceling proposition because it attached a positive value upon God from the nebulous regions of language, which, as Derrida saw it, is never definite. Derrida wants to respect the apophatic integrity of "the Wholly Other" that language purports to speak of, and of whom nothing, finally, can be said (as *apophasis* is, literally, "unsaying"). Literary critic Luke Ferretter has considered this point carefully and exposed Derrida's misperception, which in turn exposes a critical point at which postmodern theory falls short: while we know rationally that God is ultimately "unsayable," we also know God is God by what is written on our hearts, by what is formed in us, of us, and by us. The point that Derrida neglects, according to Ferretter, is *the process*, what Denys describes as something "beyond words, something unknown and wholly unrevealed. . . . What I wish to do is sing a hymn of praise for the being-making procession, the absolute divine source of Being."[72] Ferretter qualifies the misconception further, noting that Denys's "account of theological language makes clear that, although the term 'Being' is to be attributed to God in an analogical sense, its referent is a procession of the divinity, and not the divinity itself, about which nothing can be known or said, including the proposition that it is the fullness of Being."[73] In God's transcendence, to the delight of Derrida, "symbols are only 'legible as pointers to that God Who remains totally different no matter the analogies.'"[74] This representational geometry touches the very heart of God's bottomless radiance and takes on meaning when we contemplate the power of aesthetics (or postmodern "texts," which Ferretter discloses as artifacts of "the process")—particularly, the power of the cross and in its intersection with human history. It is another way of describing how sacred symbology tends to be "both/and"—both *analogical* (and thus relational, expansive, and "horizontal") and *over*, that is, *anagogical*, to introduce a key term, "lifted up" (and thus metaphysical, sacramental, and "vertical,")—a relational dynamic that actively influences our conception of an all-encompassing theological aesthetics. As Garcia-Rivera observes:

> The contemplator of these sacred formations will not thereby climb upward but will be lifted up by another force. This uplifting takes place by means of the formation: the movement is not away from the images as undesirable, but precisely through them as the means to the higher realm. The Scriptural symbols are not disparaged but are rather valued in their temporary but indispensable role in the uplifting process. Yet the movement here described is not just vaguely or metaphorically up: it is to their divine simplicity.[75]

The anagogical sense, then, is an indispensable critical option for literary critics. While strict postmodernists will deny that anything is "over," they will recognize the integrity of the immediate aesthetic artifact in its own unique presentation. Religious postmodernists will appreciate anagogical sense in that it interprets the finite object in connaturality with the creator and is thus uniquely intimate with the limitless transcendent. Clearly, the tensions categorized under the postmodern banner of *différance* expose, oddly enough, the one area in which premodern and postmodern theology become profoundly intelligible to each other. Indisputably, the central issue is that of language (or grammar, more likely), that is, how things are "put" and communicated. Derrida's most recent analyses bear this out; and in the years before his death, he began to reconcile theological language on this score. But others have not. For them, the classic dynamic between *revelation and concealment* may offer an additional texture on which to demonstrate how this reconciliation might take place. As such, Balthasar found the concept valid and profoundly attractive. He ultimately figured it as a normative (if theologically mysterious) component of his aesthetic program:

> But not for a moment is the singularity of this analogy, its irreversibility, forgotten: things are *both* like God *and* unlike him, but God is not like all things. Already there is a pointer to this expressed in the fact that God is in all things in his immanence and yet in himself independent, transcendent over them, and therefore even his immanence is comparable with none other.[76]

Clearly, the disclosure/concealment relationship can also be seen as a complementary component to the analogical imagination and therefore as fundamental import to aesthetics and representation. *Revelation and concealment* illuminate God's paradoxical nature. The dynamic proposes that God is both immanent and transcendent, for instance, and that God is present as much in negative *apophasis* (again the *unsaying*) as God is in positive *kataphasis*, in the *speaking with*. In both scenarios, there is a moment, however fleeting, of liminality, of incarnated existence, that initiates (and validates) the analogical process. The media employed in representing the arts of the beautiful, under this logic, say something about God (or being or truth) and point to a presence; but these "symbols" simultaneously indicate a poverty of speech about God and point to the postmodern *aporia*, a kind of absence or "trace." It is at this point also that we realize our prosaic descriptions about this "process" are suddenly out of their depth and that we must turn again to aesthetic order to gain any real clarity about it. A judicious turn to poetry seems appropriate here, for poetry is unique in that, as a logocentric aesthetic, it can mysteriously embody and mitigate the infinite confines of language as sign.

William Everson (1912–1994) was himself a practitioner of a holistic theological aesthetic. Everson was a poet, printer, and literary critic. Everson became a Catholic in 1949; soon after, he entered the Dominican order, first as a lay brother (under the name Brother Antoninus), then as a novice. He left the Dominicans in 1969 to live out his days holistically, a poet, a printer, a publisher, a naturalist, a husband, a father, and a teacher. Characterized by a generosity of spirit, Everson realized one potential of a Catholic Californian: to be a monk of the canyon he called Kingfisher Flat; to be a scout for the poetics of the Incarnation; to be, himself, a dusty, sanguine, beauty-in-God sacrament, he left us "A token of the poet's inimitable/ Credential—his consecrated blood."[77]

Everson's "You, God," from his collection *Hazards of Holiness* (1962), is an excellent illustration of the theology of *revelation and concealment*. The poem is generated by an excerpt from the book of Job ("A land of darkness, and of the shadow of death, / without any order, where the light is as darkness.") "You, God" is also tonally similar to Job in that it is no faithless complaint against God. Rather, Everson explores a poetics of relationship, his poem an impassioned incantation that intones upon the awesome mystery of existence: the things that God shows us, the things we are left to wonder at, and the mystery (and animosity) of living on the horizon of death:

> If I beg death, God, it is of you.
> If I seize life, God, it is out of you.
> If I lose, if I lose,
> It is unto you.[78]

The repetition of the third line of the strophe emphasizes the poet's acceptance of his own radical dependence on God, positioning the contemplation of the drama of his existence against the precipice of death. The poet conveys awareness that submission to God's power also means acceptance in participating in the ambivalent, indeterminate grammar of God's self-communication:

> Existence is mine,
> But you
> Broach a nothingness
> Breached out of nowhere
> Always you are not.[79]

Compositionally, the line "Always you are not yet" is a peerless poetic inscription of *revelation and concealment*. The line holds together both positive and negative attributes of God, the immanent and transcendent, the sayable and unsayable, the created and uncreated. Moreover, juxtaposing "always" flush against "you are," which is then negated by "not," exposes the precise tension we run into as pilgrims of the absolute. We see and feel divine presence at the very moment the presence escapes so that we are left feeling arid and alone. This kind of structure reveals the "double helix" of Eversonian poetics, the ebb and flow of *revelation and concealment*, which for Everson constitutes, simply, the "integral" vision of being and living.[80]

As any reader of Everson will testify, Everson's "integral vision" is powered by a profound sense of eroticism. Likewise, there is something intrinsically fecundating about the theo-poetic dynamic of *revelation and concealment*. As a process of divine outpouring, it describes the erotic and carnal quality of creation and of life. Emotionally, even (perhaps especially), we can grasp this element intimately. We can track the fleeting-ness of *revelation and concealment* in the ecstatic moment of human lovemaking: the feeling of utter fulfillment that advances on the spirit thrown against the reality of this self-same beauty receding to who-knows-where? Everson's poetry dwells on the *hierarchy* of sexual intimacy again and again and contemplates the ways that truths in human passion correspond with divine reality. Albert Gelpi, writing about Everson's 1957 "watershed" poem "River-Root" ("the most sustained orgasmic celebration in English, perhaps in all literature"), pursues these connections. Gelpi observes how Everson draws out such analogies in "River-Root," which in the poem materialize in the erotic intimacy of a married Catholic couple and the relational dynamism of the triune God: "The graphic physical details of intercourse are innocent in their directness, and their cumulative physicality serves both to ground and be sublimated by the sudden illumination as sexual union yields the Beatific vision and the procession of the Trinity becomes the kinetic drive in the sexual act."[81]

Everson's steady gaze upon the intimacy of human relationship restores the rightful place of *eros* as primary in an aesthetically comprehensive vision. It also demonstrates the importance of gender and sexuality in the rendering of a careful aesthetics of the Incarnation, not to mention a recovered understanding of *hierarchy*. This vision applies equally to his concept of the individual person who possesses the attributes of the feminine and masculine (and the divine) in his or her own being, attributes whose distinctions become opaque and borderless, particularly in the peak experience of divine encounter.[82] Everson's poem "The Raging of the Rose," from his 1967 collection *The Rose of Solitude*, engages this dynamism, specifically in the format of *revelation and concealment*. The rose, as a twice-potent image, is another of Everson's double helixes. In the poem, the "Rose" is both Christ and his Father, both Christ and his Mother. And it is more: the Rose is "the multifoliate particularities of the whole. / In the presence of person / The Rose, invincible, rages and affirms . . . The ecstasy of presence."[83] The Rose is the "point of mystical intuition" at which the double-natured God "immolates Himself, / Makes himself new Form / Constellates being." The Rose is the human person[84]—the tensions of the self, even, of *anima* and *animus*—"Two egos, / Selfed in unison, modeled on the subsistence of Christ." The Rose is revealed and completed in Christ, but so, too, is it concealed and "indwelt":

> Flesh and Spirit,
> Spirit and Flesh,
> Transmuted together,
> Sealed in Christ,
> The indwelling.

In the revelation of the Rose, the value of human personhood is revealed and endorsed by the primordial and eternal "Rose" (and "She exults" at this), but it is also concealed to a trace by the spending of its own self ("Burns, the coal of itself"). In the dynamic drama of creation and destruction, penetration and reception, and "the *act* of existence," our *esse* is proclaimed:

> The crest of release
> That liberates freedom
> In the primacy of response,

The *act* of existence.
As act, being: His *esse*: to be.
So she: I
In us: He is.
We Three:
Free.

Everson exposes an explicitly trinitarian poetic: "she" and "he" in relationship beget the poem. A trinity, then is revealed by the poem; but because it participates in the holy *perichoresis* of the Trinity (that is, the *divine dance*), the poem mirrors the swirling trinitarian logic that it simultaneously creates.

"The Rage of the Rose" concludes with a call to action ("Beat it up to synthesis!" "Pound it to perfection! / Make it be!" "Confer beatitude upon it!"), so that what is concealed might remain in a constant state of formal revelation. The poet prays for the unity of being (within the multiple textures of being) that the proclamation of the image of the Rose, as "Reality unfolded," promises. We will revisit Everson later, but let us conclude here with the last lines of the poem so as to illuminate another conclusive instance of the rotating, paradoxical quality of *revelation and concealment*.

On the four wings of the Cross,
In the ecstasy of the crucifixion,
In the blood of being,
In the single burn of beauty
BE!
So that
In you,
The consummate
Vision of the Other:
In you,
I Am![85]

In Everson, we can acutely observe how poetry and literature can uniquely reveal the most ineffable mysteries. Moreover we can move outward from the poem and begin to see why Divine Manifestation can be construed (but not limited by) hierarchical, analogical, and aesthetic categories. Historically, it can be read as a transfiguring of Greek style: "an aesthetical expression for communication and word"[86] that keeps the divine word rooted in palpable reality and keeps it from becoming pure illusion or merely representative. The whole aesthetic phenomenon has always been rooted in mystery because such manifestations perpetuate the mystery of God who in His revelation is ultimately "ever greater and ever more hidden."[87] The aesthetic quality of the word, then, is nimble and creative: it maneuvers confidently between the Scylla of Cartesian abstraction and the Charybdis of Derrida's *logophobia*. The aesthetic imagination is figuratively cruciform and endorses, ultimately, the axial miracle of all time—the embodiment of Light, the Absolute made Image, the Word made flesh and made beautiful—"The Glory of the Lord": the Incarnation.

Just as good postmodernists do, in these pages, we have sought to hold so many complementary, if variable, strands together. We have referred to the "eternal word" and spoken about "divine light"; we have seen how both word and light can exist in the same space; we have seen, first hand, how the mediaeval theological concept of *revelation and concealment*—a swirling eddy of a dynamic that asserts both similarity and difference in one image—can enlighten postmodern discourse. Our task now is to concretize forcefully by a sustained consideration of one literary "form," a negotiation that will lend vital insight to the metaphysics of language, to our experience with the divine, and to the larger aims of this discussion.

Form, Inversion, and O'Connor's "Revelation": Order Is Nothing without Love

Yet how is this? For I am no disbeliever in spiritual purpose and no vague believer. I see from the standpoint of Christian orthodoxy. This means that for me the meaning of life is centered in our Redemption by Christ and that what I see in the world I see in relation to that. I don't think that this is a position that can be taken halfway or one that is particularly easy in these times to make transparent in fiction.

—Flannery O'Connor, Collected Works

Through the 1980s in particular, much scholarly work was devoted to considering Flannery O'Connor (1925–1964) and her theological vision. While much of it was penetrating and credible, in the end (and with a few exceptions), the theological commentary on O'Connor's work left much to be desired. Generally, the interpretive work was being done by critics who were either theologically disoriented or by critics who viewed O'Connor's theological concerns as something akin to a psychological tick. After a relatively lengthy critical hiatus in the 1990s, more monographs and studies on O'Connor have recently appeared, and these with more decidedly theological trajectories.

In this chapter, I have devoted space to the consideration of Percy and Everson as theological aestheticians. Both of these writers were of the Balthasarian sort—literary theologians endowed with interdisciplinary sensibilities who survey the variegated forms and settings of God's Incarnation. O'Connor can be numbered among this group as well. Her Christology, of course, bears its own stamp and finds full expression in the way that O'Connor depicts human freedom in her fiction, whether it's the simple and finite human freedom in the form of exercising the quotidian choices in our daily lives or the freedom that participates in the infinite, that comes from seeing in the quotidian the presence of God.[88] As I mentioned in the introduction of this chapter, it is ultimately this developed sense of Christology that fully illuminates all of being (not just thought) and provides the incarnational and historical ground for relationship and community. Moreover, the whole notion of a theological aesthetics, specifically as Balthasar has meditated upon in multiple volumes, depends fundamentally on *seeing* Christological form at work both narratively and actively or, in other words, *theodramatically*.

The incarnational imagination ponders God's desire to be with us. It is a disposition to see God in all things—sacramentally, passionately, paradoxically— even if this vision is inchoate or opaque. The self-donation of both the Father and the Son and, in a special way, the assent of Mary reveal that we are (more or less) free or, as Karl Rahner has it:

> Because in the Incarnation the Logos creates the human reality by
> assuming it, and assumes it by emptying *himself*, for this reason there
> also applies here, and indeed in the most radical and specific and
> unique way, the axiom for understanding every relationship between
> God and creatures, namely the closeness and distance, or being at
> God's disposal and being autonomous . . . Christ is therefore man in
> the most radical sense, and his humanity is the most autonomous
> and most free not in spite of, but because it has been assumed, be-
> cause it has been created as God's self-expression.[89]

The Incarnation achieves many things for us; but the essential mystery in it resides in the fact that it ever illuminates the trinitarian reality of God's love and God's preferential passion for relationship. Even though we remain quite free to refuse it, the Incarnation invites us to "hear" God's love and to have "it" done according to God's will.

Like many of us, however, O'Connor's Ruby Turpin is prone to have *it* done according to *her own will*. A self-satisfied character head-scratchingly aware of her own goodness and contemptuous of anyone who is not quite like her, Ruby presents herself to us as a latter-day Pharisee. Her routine visit to the doctor's office with her husband, Claud, initiates the beginning of a powerful discovery in Ruby and gives O'Connor both the occasion and the narrative space to present some applied theology. In this section, I will discuss how the theological aspects I discussed above embody and pulse in O'Connor's short story "Re-velation." In this way, I hope to illuminate more vividly the possibilities that abound when we read the literature of the Catholic imagination through the eyes of Balthasar's theological aesthetics.

At the critical moment of her sustained and nuanced revelation, when all from Ruby's perspective is decidedly *out of order*, she calls out—to the setting sun, to the huddled pigs in retreat, "panting with secret life" in the pen's corner, to the silence, and so to God: " 'Go on,' she yelled, 'call me a hog! Call me a hog again. From hell. Call me a wart hog from hell. Put that bottom rail on top. There'll still be a top and a bottom.' "[90] Throughout the pages that lead up to this angry ejaculation, O'Connor has rendered a character fixated on arrangements, on "tops and bottoms," on social pecking orders, and on dis-positions.[91] So crucial is the idea of arrangement, of reified *hierarchy*, that the story opens up in a doctor's office with Ruby musing precisely on her place in the crowd in which she presently finds herself: "Next to her was a fat girl of eighteen or nineteen, scowling into a thick blue book which Mrs. Turpin saw was entitled *Human Development*. . . . Next to the ugly girl was the child, still in exactly the same position, and next to him was a thin leathery old woman in a cotton print dress. . . . She could tell by the way they sat—kind of vacant and white-trashy. . . . Worse than niggers any day, Mrs. Turpin thought."[92] The purgatorial implications of a waiting room of a doctor's office in the eschatological hierarchy is really our first clue that, in "Revelation," O'Connor is in the land of *hierarchy*, as I have charted it in this chapter; and Ruby's obliviousness about her own flawed understanding of order only adds to the darker psychological humor of her situation as her utterances begin to reveal the smudged map of her own human development. In fact, our acknowledgment of the purgatorial character and trajectory of the narrative as a whole is crucial in order for us to realize the dramatic deeper textures of Ruby's revelation, an encounter that promises to "burn (Ruby's) virtues clean."[93] Her hierarchical imagination, furthermore, resonates so audibly (structurally anyway) with mediaeval (and scholastic) theology, that one begins to hear the distorted voice of Denys in all of this:

> Sometimes Mrs. Turpin occupied herself at night naming the classes of people. On the bottom of the heap were most colored people, not the kind she would have been if she had been one, but most of them; then next to them—not above, just away from—were the white trash; and above them were the home-owners, and above them, the home-and-land owners, to which she and Claud had belonged. Above she and Claud were people with a lot of money and much bigger houses and much more land. But here the complexity of it would begin to bear in on her, for some of the people with a lot of money were common and ought to be below she and Claud and some of the people who had good blood had lost their money and had to rent and then there were the colored people who owned their homes and land as well. . . . Usually by the time she had fallen asleep all the classes of people were moiling and roiling around in her head.[94]

Ruby roils and moils because she has it all backward, and her vantage point is distorted, "as if she were looking at it through the wrong end of a telescope."[95] The point O'Connor is making in this narrative is a deeply Christological one and is also the revelation that lights this chapter: without love, there can be no order. Without the desire to and practice of love in the way Jesus shows us, our perceptions about the world and our place in it are severely skewed. As the French Catholic revivalist poet Charles Péguy writes in "Hope," trying to make Christological sense of God's kenotic gift of the cross:

> That hard, rough bark and those limbs which are like a confusion
> of huge arms,
> (A confusion which is an order)
> And those roots which thrust into the soil and lay hold of it
> like a confusion of huge legs
> (A confusion that is an order)[96]

The order we perceive is really not order at all. Like our vision of beauty, standards of "order" are inverted; what we perceive, because we are fallen and can only trust our instincts in conditional ways, is often the obverse of order. The God revealed in Jesus proclaims these paradoxes. Jesus clarifies that sacred arrangements are not based on, for example, sanctimony, pride, and acquisitiveness, but rather on humility, respect, and mutuality, to name a few. In her unsparing, but ultimately loving critique of Ruby (and the Ruby Turpins of the world and the Ruby who resides in each of us), O'Connor is stating these facts strongly; and in "Revelation," she enlists the tactical aid of Denysian cosmology to illustrate the precise fissures in our understanding. For Denys's meditations about *hierarchy* come out of the heart of mystical moments, where all is charged with hierophantic energy of God and all is seasoned with God's breath. In these moments of true encounter, God's spirit of understanding dwells within us in a special way. To couch the phenomenon in Greek terms, *hierarchy* is to be construed as *kairos*, as infused radiance of understanding in the never-ending eternity of God's moment; O'Connor, in order to demonstrate radical difference, is showing us how *hierarchy* appears to most of us most of the time. We, who dwell in quotidian *chronos*, who struggle in the mundane, have a botched sense of *hierarchy*. Our native ability to see such relationships at all has become complicated: too often and too typically obverted, awkward, and clumsy.

The element that O'Connor employs to suggest a Denysian base, fittingly, is light. O'Connor lights her narrative with cinematic skill, and the degree of radiance fluctuates in direct proportion to the credibility of the language a character speaks or the action he takes. When we first meet Ruby, we at once know we are in the presence of a contradiction, "Her little bright black eyes took in all the patients as she sized up the seating arrangement."[97] Later, when Ruby is in the heyday of pontificating about the finer points of social arrangements and caste, "a grotesque revolving shadow passed across the curtain behind her and was thrown palely on the opposite wall," suggesting that Ruby's insights, like the shadow, are precisely devoid of light, are, in fact, parodies of light. And later still, Ruby's face is "very dark and heavy" when she hollowly rationalizes the events of her afternoon to her obsequious farmhands who toady her with promises of revenge ("Lemme see her. I'll Kill her").[98] In contrast, Mary Grace, Ruby's antagonist and the story's unwitting vessel of grace, is accompanied by intense varieties of light, all of which are present in and mediated by her eyes. When she first encounters Ruby, "her eyes smolder and blaze"; in reaction to one of Ruby's dubious nuggets of waiting-room truth, Mary Grace slams her book shut, and her "eyes seemed lit all of a sudden with a peculiar light, an unnatural light like road signs give"; at the moment of the violence in the narrative, at which Mary Grace tosses a book (thus ostensibly tossing the *word*) at Ruby in the form of a textbook entitled *Human Development*, Mary Grace's eyes "seemed a much lighter blue than before, as if a door that had been tightly closed behind them was now open to admit light and air"; and Ruby looks back "into the fierce brilliant eyes" as Mary Grace confronts her with a most mysterious communiqué: "The girl raised her head. Her gaze locked with Mrs. Turpin's. 'Go back to hell where you came from, you old wart hog,' she whispered. Her voice was low but clear. Her eyes burned for a moment as if she saw with pleasure that her message had stuck its target."[99]

Because of this encounter, Ruby's own vision is touched and contravened. She is graciously destabilized so as to be prepared for the turn: "Her vision narrowed and she saw everything as it were happening in a small room far away . . . and she saw everything large instead of small,"[100] her world turned upside down. Ruby may have a genteel disposition, but, again, gentility is nothing without love. O'Connor illustrates this defect rather subtlety in "Revelation"; but its Christological implications resound. After their visit to the doctor, she and Claud nap away the afternoon to recuperate from the commotion:

> Claud slept. She scowled at the ceiling. Occasionally she raised her fist and made a small stabbing motion over her chest as if she was defending her innocence to invisible guests who were like the comforters of Job, reasonable-seeming, but wrong.
>
> About five-thirty, Claud stirred. "Got to go after those niggers," he sighed, not moving.
>
> She was looking straight up as if there were unintelligible handwriting on the ceiling. The protuberance over her eye had turned greenish-blue. "Listen here," she said.
>
> "What?"
>
> "Kiss me."
>
> Claud leaned over and kissed her loudly on the mouth. He pinched her on the side and their hands interlocked. Her expression of ferocious concentration did not change. Claud got up, groaning and growling, and limped off. She continued to study the ceiling.[101]

As if to test a hypothesis, as if to test her own warthoggedness, Ruby solicits her core being for love but finds that her need for love has deepened. Her sterile response to her husband does not annihilate their particular love, but it reveals her new sense of displacement. She needs God's gracious love; and her arid response to more quotidian expressions of love, for the mystically inclined, serves as harbinger for the long haul of a bona fide conversion.

O'Connor's frequent use of sun imagery has called forth much critical commentary on the sun as God or eye of God. Arthur Kinney writes that "we get a further extension of meaning from a passage she [O'Connor] marked in a study of St Bonaventure that reads, 'From the theological tradition St. Bonaventure received the Augustinian principle that the Word is the Sun of the mind, the light thanks to which created spirits are able to see intellectually.'"[102] In "Revelation," O'Connor represents this theological principle most systematically as the narrative resolves and the day begins to gloam. Ruby's errant thinking about *hierarchy* crystallizes against the backdrop of a sun "that was a deep yellow and now like a harvest moon," and the gaze of a sun sacralizes her epiphany from "behind a wood, very red, looking over the paling of trees like a farmer inspecting his own hogs." The warm glow of our creator nudges his child toward vision ("What do you send me a message like that for? How am I a hog and me both? How am I saved and from hell too?"[103]) so that light transfers sacramentally through the finite ("The color of everything, field, and crimson sky, burned for a moment with a transparent intensity"), through the orders, through the pigs, even, who "had settled all in one corner around an old sow who was grunting softly. A red glow suffused them," until the "visionary light settled in her eyes."[104]

Light informs the *exitus et reditus* unfolding in the narrative, and all of creation is joined together, almost conspiratorially, by a Denysian gushing of light as Ruby receives her mystical vision. The strength of O'Connor's prose and the seriousness of the phenomenon depicted (i.e., the restoration of the dynamic integrity between sign and signified, the retrieval of the meaning of *hierarchy*) reveal the refinement of O'Connor's theological aesthetics:

> She saw the streak as a vast swinging bridge extending upward from the earth through a field of living fire. Upon it a vast horde of souls were rumbling towards heaven. There were whole companies of white-trash, clean for the first time in their lives, and bands of black niggers in white robes, and battalions of freaks and lunatics shouting and clapping and leaping like frogs. And bringing up the end of the procession was a tribe of people whom she recognized at once as those, who, like herself and Claud, had always had a little of everything and the God-given wit to use it right. She leaned forward to observe them closer. They were marching behind the others with great dignity, accountable as they had always been for good order and common sense and respectable behavior. They alone were on key. Yet she could see by their shocked and altered faces that even their virtues were being burned away. She lowered her hands and gripped the wall of the hog-pen, her eyes small but fixed unblinkingly on what lay ahead. In a moment the vision faded but she remained where she was, immobile.[105]

"Revelation" climaxes in this passage as O'Connor expresses her narrative's fundamental mystery. By paradoxically casting an unexpected shape of hierarchical light and transfiguring the warm communal rays of Denys into the trope of a violent fire that burns us clean, that burns away what we think are virtues, Ruby truly sees how we are made to be, how we are fundamentally "arranged." The topsy-turviness of this vision takes Ruby's legs from her (and ours as well, if we are attentive); and we observe how O'Connor's theological aesthetic credibly describes a most complex theological event by dexterously negotiating the mystical integrity of the Denysian schema with the rigid mandate of Balthasar's *Form of Forms*: the incarnational Glory of the Lord. In the narrative, Ruby begins to see the dramatic reality of her own return. She stands against God's revelation of the grace that is unmeritable. God does not want us for our piety or our various artifices; God wants us simply for ourselves. God desires to see our faces, desires our turning to Him, so that we might love fully and authentically, so that we might love like Jesus.

For one who knew the difficulties of writing about conversion, O'Connor does so convincingly. In an authentic conversion, there are so many theological and relational dynamics at work that it becomes dizzying to distill the particulars. Literary critic Northrop Frye's conception of the "U-shaped narrative" demonstrates the ways that a sophisticated literary imagination can uncover deeper realities. O'Connor retrieves the notion of *hierarchy* through *procession and return* and *revelation and concealment*. Borrowing theologically from Augustine (as well as from early archetypal myth patterns both in biblical narratives and elsewhere), Frye's theory hinges on the idea that apocalyptic events, actions, or images signal both narrative "ends" as well as, ironically, eschatological beginnings. Paul Fiddes comments on the implications of Frye's vision: "Thus the cataclysmic end to the order of nature symbolizes a destruction of the way of seeing that order which keeps us confined to the world of time and history as we know them. This destruction of our conventional structures of understanding is what all art is intended to achieve, and what all scriptures aim to do. 'Apocalypse' means 'unveiling,' and as the final phase of a sequence of phases of revelation within the total biblical story, this narrative unveils the true meaning of all previous scriptures."[106]

While the eschatological finality of Frye's vision implies that, supernaturally speaking, the end organizes the beginning, the insight also contains a more analogically immediate relevance for the dynamic structures of the natural world and the mysterious quality of narrative art. Obviously, this must be the case because of the character of the analogy of being as well as the objectivity of the Christology that this chapter, with its compass firmly fixed on Balthasar, proposes.[107] Fiddes's observation also aids us in understanding how the totality of that which is veiled (i.e., a glimpse into the mystery God's order) is made clear by the unveiling of the particular piece of the puzzle (for example, the call to actually practice the love that is at the heart of God's incarnating of Godself), which, in turn, adumbrates the mystery of the totality to begin with. In effect, then, Ruby's revelation about her habit of practicing disordered love, her practical neglect of bona fide Christian love, shows her that ultimately *she must love*. The "hieratic" unveiling, furthermore, trumps all prior understanding of her own ontological orientation and signals the critical turn toward God.[108] The nadir of the "U" in Ruby's narrative of conversion signals both her advancement in understanding as well as the initiation of her slow-going return to God, or, as Frye has it: "As we follow the U-shaped curve . . . from alienation to resurrection, we encounter these images on the upper slope of the curve, suggesting 'a nature transformed into an environment of human meaning.'"[109] Because of the postmodern suspicion of absolute claims, the turn to eschatology is precluded. Still, it is clear that eschatology as Frye and Fiddes conceive of it may make some space for dialogue.

The Gracious Catastrophe: Removing Splinters from Our Eyes

An eclipse of the sun is something that occurs between the sun and our
eyes, not in the sun itself.

—Martin Buber, *Eclipse of God*

Let us contemplate Ruby's return further, as a horse making for the post. In
her Job-like moment of creaturely disgust, Ruby, fittingly, yells her various
complaints to the heavens from the center of "all that she owns," only to be
answered by her own "garbled echo." She then asks (or rather "roars"), shak-
ing her fist, "in a final surge of fury," her penultimate question: "Who do you
think you are?"[110] The answer she receives is one for all the ages: strikingly
pliant, conclusively multivalent. For the natural theologian, the form of her
question reveals its own sacramental unity and mediates a divine revelation.
Likewise, for the mystically inclined, the answer comes in the form of her
hieratic epiphany, her interior vision of order revealed. For the postmodernist,
the answer comes to Ruby reflexively and self-referentially, that is, performa-
tively, in the very utterance of her own question. And for the evangelist, similarly, the answer is found in the question and is its own prophetic voice. Ruby
mouths the very question of God that God asks of her: "Who do you think *you*
are?" How fitting that, in a chapter that seeks to navigate words and silences,
forms and absences of form, meanings and indeterminacy of meanings, Ruby's revelation comes both in language, which, because language and interpretation are fundamentally relational acts, bestows rich variety in truth, as
well as in the Grand Silence ("In a moment the vision faded but she remained
where she was, immobile"), a concealment that reveals a still greater "language" and promises a still greater variety in truth. To me, this is as sound a
representation of the reunion of the sign with the signified as one can render.
In the unifying space where day meets night, Ruby asks how she can be a hog
and her at the same time, how she can be from hell and saved, too? These
opposites, like all opposites, are negotiated in and through Christ. The form is
reconciled with the formless, the act with the essence, and so on, all orders of
creation turning toward the Grace that builds on nature and opens its arms to
gratefully embrace God's gift of *hierarchy*. Gawronski observes:

> So theology itself is the correct ordering of Heaven and earth, of
> angels and men, singing praises at the throne of the Unseen: the
> Word surrounds the middle of Silence. Words proliferate the further
> one goes from the centre. Once again, the silence is not an *empty*
> silence, but rather the divine silence which summons a correspond-
> ing hymn of silence as it were with which to be honoured in its
> hiddeness: "theology will be careful . . . to honour with silence the
> hiddeness of God which towers above."[111]

Ruby's experience coincides with this mysterious unity as she makes her
turn toward home, "her slow way on the darkening path to the house," her

movement toward the heart of God. Out the darkness of her decentered center comes the light, and Ruby begins to realize that she does not walk alone: "In the woods around her the invisible choruses had struck up, but what she heard were the voices of the souls climbing upward into the starry field and shouting hallelujah."[112] It's not likely that she will forget this encounter; and I close this section with one of Gabriel Marcel's meditations that speaks to this very mystery:

> Each one of us becomes the center of a sort of mental space arranged in concentric zones of decreasing interest and participation. It is as though each one of us secreted a kind of shell which gradually hardened and imprisoned him; and this sclerosis is bound up with the hardening of the categories in accordance with which we conceive and evaluate the world. Fortunately, it can happen to anyone to make an encounter which breaks down the framework of this egocentric topography; I know by my own experience how, from a stranger met by chance, there may come an irresistible appeal which overturns habitual perspectives just as a gust of wind might tumble down the panels of a stage set. . . . But it is an experience which leaves us with a bitter taste, an impression of sadness and almost anguish; yet I think it is beneficial, for it shows us in a flash all that is contingent and—yes—artificial in the crystallized pattern of our personal system.
>
> But it is, above all, the sanctity realized in certain beings which reveals to us that what we call the normal order is, from the higher point of view, from the standpoint of a soul rooted in the ontological mystery, merely the subversion of an order which is its opposite.[113]

Too Late Have I Loved Thee: Word, Incarnation, and Beauty

> If even creatures so convoluted and imperfect can accomplish something, how much more might creatures greater than they in the strength of their faith and love accomplish? And what about those who are even higher than they are? Divine humanity, the Incarnation, presents itself as the highest rung on the hierarchical ladder. To move mountains with a word is not for us, but this does not mean it is impossible. Were not Matthew, Mark, Luke, and John miracle workers by virtue of their having written the gospels?
> —Czeslaw Milosz, "If Only This Could Be Said"

And so we find ourselves back where our chapter began: with the *word*. Amidst all of the cacophony that swirls in our arguments about whether words can and cannot mean, what words do and do not say, we rightly wonder how it is we can find any meaning at all in language, image, and act, how we find any significance at all in the realm of aesthetics. But somehow we do find meaning. There remains in us the certitude of the still small voice that endorses, faithfully and reasonably, the pluriform connection between sign and signified, between existence and essence, between act and idea, and between heaven and earth. We could not make such important claims, as the Polish-Catholic poet Czeslaw Milosz comments in the above epigraph, were it not for the historical reality of the Incarnation, were it not for the existence of a prime analogate that originates in love and links all that is seen with that which is unseen—the eternal Word without which all other words are "without meaning," *meaning-less*, and meaning/less. In this chapter, we have recovered this fact; and as a by-product of this recovery, we have witnessed the surprisingly symmetrical relationship that exists between the postulates of classic mediaeval theology and the fundamental issues at work in postmodern critical concern: both traditions are deeply invested in the notions of absence, otherness, and difference. But of course, there remains the penultimate difference, and this difference is not simply a matter of idealism or of language: it is location, a home for the heart and the mind.[114]

Our examination of *hierarchy* has been an exemplary case study in interrogating our assumptions about what words can mean. We find that our assumptions about whether to construe sacred order as top-down or bottom-up or vertical or horizontal are ultimately misguided and wrongheaded, much to the delight of both mediaevalists and postmodernists alike, both of whom are made uneasy by straight lines. In many ways, the circular taxonomy of *procession and return* and the "double helix" of *revelation and concealment* provide more valid clues about sacred order more than any other metaphysical geometry we might consider. Clearly O'Connor demonstrates this more than once in her fiction, as concentricity is of prime value in her imagination. In "Revelation," it is no less the case. Circularity regulates the tale, from its narrative arc, through its indictment of disordered social circles, right down to the shell of the narcissism that encases Ruby's heart. Clearly, O'Connor's "Revelation" is an exemplary theological text, but it is also an exemplary aesthetic instance of a Catholic imagination. The narrative demonstrates that the Christological condition of God stimulates the analogical imagination in order to reveal what we are (and what we are not) specifically because it seeks to balance and negotiate polarity structures such as Rahner's "closeness and distance," lightness and darkness, *word* and *referent*, and *sign* and *signified*, to name a few.

> the verb took over all the power
> and blended existence with essence
> in the electricity of its beauty

4

Breaking the Waves

The Cry That Finds the Ear of the Heart

Thus play I in one play many people
And none contented.

—William Shakespeare, c. 1597

What is sown is perishable, what is raised is imperishable.
It is sown in dishonor. It is raised in glory.
It is sown in weakness, it is raised in power.
It is sown in a physical body, it is raised in a spiritual body.

—St. Paul, c. 56

A dramatist is one who believes that the pure event, an action involving human beings, is more arresting than any comment that can be made upon it.

—Thornton Wilder, 1958

This is to smell the infinite fragrance, and taste the infinite sweetness of divinity . . . by embracing and kissing the place where the persons stand or are seated, always taking care to draw some fruit from this.

—St. Ignatius of Loyola, c. 1541

The *Pathos* of God: A Trajectory for Dramatic Art

As essential as the divine *Word* is to Balthasar's theological program, the word, as an aesthetic icon, lacks any potential for transforming persons in the world without an intelligible and constructive theory of dramatic action to complement it. More to the point, Balthasar's aesthetic program is unique in that when we speak of his aesthetics, we are always also implicitly referring to his Theo-Drama and his Theo-Logic as well, for, like the transcendentals on which these theologies are premised, Balthasar's aesthetics, dramatics, and logic are interdependent upon one another. The transition from aesthetics to dramatics, though, is unique in its own right, and, as such, it merits distillation and recognition both in its role in the history of theology and in the shaping of literary theory. Aesthetic form reveals the beautiful, to be sure, but the beautiful lacks any ultimate power or efficacy if it does not include a sustained sense of ethics (and ethics are always tied to "action"), a sense of the active performance of the "good" that Christ, to take the penultimate example, demonstrates in the Gospels. On this point, Balthasar scholar Aidan Nichols provides a good observation: "The criticism that the Christ of aesthetics is reduced to an icon, that Balthasar has de-potentiated the power of Christ's words and deeds which are meant precisely to challenge human self-understanding and to elicit the self-commitment of human freedom to the cause of the Kingdom of the world is also off target. The art of God in Jesus Christ, in *Herrlichkeit*, is explicitly *narrative* art."[1] As we saw in the last chapter, theological truth can find harbor in unique aesthetic moments (moments encased in words, for example), but these moments, while stable and meaningful, are not inert and static. Christianity is essentially a living *praxis*; it is not a museum piece, merely, of word concepts that confess doctrine and tell us what we should believe. As Balthasar notes, Christianity is the religion of the "Go and do Likewise," the exhortation that concludes the parable of the good Samaritan and challenges Christians of every stripe in every age. Christ's mandate toward action shows the New Testament to be "not a textbook but Spirit, a collection of occasional writings referring to Christ's exemplary conduct and indicating how Christians ought to act."[2]

That "action" is at the heart of Christianity, of course, and has vast implications for theories of dramatic art. And while literary theorists of all sorts have sensed the fertility of the connection and have devoted vast spaces to locating and discussing the "God question" (whether decoding Christianity, for example, out of Fitzgerald or Updike or encoding it into Hemingway or Carver), few have articulated the debt that theology owes to narrative and drama—particularly theology seen through the prism of Christianity—as creatively and systematically as Balthasar has:

> No theological textbook has found it worthwhile to refer to the names of *Shakespeare* or *Calderon*. We have shown, however, that all of today's influential theological trends—aware of the inadequacies of systematics as practiced so far—converge towards a theological dramatic theory yet without being able to reach it.... It is time, therefore to attempt a synthesis: theology is pressing for it from within, and from outside—from Drama—we have so much material at our disposal.[3]

The current trend toward some theologies of art and beauty notwithstanding, the flaw perpetrated by modern theology lies in its general indifference to literary and poetic sources. As I noted in chapter 1, the literal ignorance of theologians on matters literary and artistic, coupled with a general unwillingness to delve into the literary character implicit in both (scriptural) revelation and other theological discourses, has resulted, arguably, in a kind of crisis: hosts of exegetes looking for a theological beauty that is not available to them because of the constraints set up by the very methods of inquiry either foisted upon them or in which they willingly engage. Often, the result is an assortment of bland interpretations and incomplete theological considerations. Balthasar presses on this issue in the *Prolegomena* of his *Theo-Drama*:

> But when exegesis begins to go its own way and becomes scientific, dogmatics increasingly becomes a 'textbook,' and only apologetics, placed before the other two retains the appearance of dialogue. Now, however, the latter, no longer nourished by the drama of revelation, looks more like an instruction manual for fencing or wrestling. The answers are ready-prepared, the question is not allowed to present a real challenge nor is the person of the questioner.[4]

Again, we are struck by Balthasar's refreshing propensity toward the interdisciplinary approach to theology, for theology, simply, demands the facility for conceiving existence in large scope, for painting in both wide and narrow strokes, and then singing about what is painted in multiple octaves. But it's more than that, as Wilde's famous epigram reports: "The stage is not merely the meeting place of all the arts, but is also the return of art to life." Theater itself, as, perhaps, the most democratic and "human" of the arts, has been a most fertile site for exposing aesthetic interdisciplinarity especially in regards to the nexus between art and meaning. To view the theater phenomenologically, moreover, is to see the mechanisms in which dramatic art becomes liturgical: the theater, like liturgy, navigates, negotiates, and recapitulates the deep sense of mystery that good drama exposes. Theater binds us all together; our participation with dramatic art—at any level—reveals our need for participation simply because, as Nichols concludes by virtue of Balthasar's great teaching, drama is intrinsic to divine salvation.[5] Balthasar comments broadly but incisively on this aspect:

> But for as long as theatre has existed, in all its high periods—which were clearly characterized by something over and above the business side of things—people have asked more of drama than this. People have sought insight into the nature and meaning of existence, things that cannot simply be read off from its immanent course but radiate from a background that explodes the beautiful and gripping play on stage—which suddenly becomes inwardly relevant to the spectator—and that relates it to something that transcends it.[6]

Even Plato, who was not easily given to sympathizing with mundane aesthetic or dramatic forms (what Nichols in this sense revives as the "theatre of the world idea"),[7] also concluded that drama was not merely an exercise in human immanence and figured existence into a transcendental drama in which "each of us living beings is a puppet of the gods. Whether we have been constructed to serve as their plaything or for some serious reason is something beyond our ken."[8] Balthasar cites this instructive passage from Plato's late work, *The Laws*, and comments:

> Life is a play in the presence of God insofar as it is an education according to the Muses and enters into the divine-life-rhythm; but at the same time this rhythm is a gift from God: God is the real mover. Thus man moves in the proper order when he allows himself to be moved as a divine marionette by God.[9]

Plato's insight exudes a special credibility, of course, and Balthasar salutes it as an early artifact of Theo-Drama; but, according to Balthasar, Plato's shackled view of "the actor" bespeaks a stunted conception of the human liberty that Balthasar sees at the heart of his theodramatic vision: there must be authentic liberty before there can be authentic relationship, let alone before there can be collaboration in mission. Balthasar clearly will depart from Plato on the person-as-marionette aspect of the passage: in Plato, we are constructed as a toy for the gods; in Theo-Drama, we are made to relate dialogically; we "allow" ourselves, as Balthasar holds, to be moved by God. Again, to return to the vision gained in theological aesthetics, to be agents of our own growth and fulfillment, we assent to participate in the great dialog of hierarchy, the great gift of God.

Balthasar indicts the myopia of theological discourses that preclude the opportunity for such a "dialogue," for "dialoguing," even beyond its role as indicator of salubrious psychological and sociological health, is God's original olive branch, God's original invitation to relationship with humankind. Moreover, without the sense of encounter that a posture toward dramatics and dialogue include, theological activity can only be depicted as a series of sterile propositions. Balthasar reminds us that theology can learn much from both literary/dramatic art and literary/dramatic criticism precisely as an antidote to such facile leanings. Literature, film, and drama are dialogic by their nature and so illustrate a key aspect of our very being: that, because God is relational (depicted most conclusively in the subsistent and fecundating dynamism of the Trinity), so, too, are we. Indeed, as Ian Watt so persuasively argued half a century ago, narrative form is constituted by the very possibility for many voices to participate and encounter one another in active engagement.[10] Such a conception, moreover, is also scripturally rooted: our plots and narratives—like the multitextured nature of salvation history of which "theology will have to reflect without ever coming to a finished conclusion"[11]— unfolds on the "world stage." If theology is, as Balthasar concludes, "full of dramatic tension, both in form and content, it is appropriate to turn our attention to this aspect and *establish a kind of system of dramatic categories*. Ultimately the Catholic *'dialectic' between nature and grace* presupposes that such a system can be of use to theology: a natural dramatic dimension is presupposed by, and prefaced to, the supernatural drama, which adopts it after having first clarified and transformed it and brought it to its true proportions."[12] These kinds of concerns constitute and classify the broad scope of Balthasar's theodramatic program.

The "dialectic" that Balthasar proposes appears in *Theo-drama* as intersubjective dialog, the "I-Thou" encounter that is at the heart of every authentic relationship. Balthasar meditates upon this central structural dynamic and outlines a theory of intersubjectivity in his dramatic program. The hierarchy he lays out is so obvious as to be shocking. As Edward Oakes observes, Balthasar "foregrounds" his dramatics by utilizing "all of the theatrical and dramatic metaphors embedded in theology."[13] In this spirit, Balthasar illuminates the intersubjective character of his Theodramatics by offering another recovered sense of *hierarchy*, this time in the dynamic of the sacred relationship between "role" and "mission."[14] Specifically in *Theo-Drama*, this *hierarchy* takes the form in the dynamic interplay among author, director, actor, and audience. Balthasar carefully meditates on each "role" in his *Prolegomena* and proposes a kind of cosmology of theatrical duties. He also realizes, though, as starting point, the fluidity of each role, that "these roles interact as a result of the energizing of the players' esprit de corps," which is a "'happening,'" during which "there are great authors who have acted in their own plays, and even produced them," and "there is no reason why the boundary between auditorium and stage should not be obliterated; the spectator may join in the action throughout or part of the time, sharing in the 'authoring' and introducing things he would like to see."[15] Intersubjectivity, as a phenomenon that is uniquely "active" and uniquely human, is then quite indispensable to theodramatic theory. As such, I'll offer some remarks about it in this chapter; however, because Balthasar, as a theological personalist, discerns that intersubjectivity is the crux of all philosophy, it becomes an even more central concern in his *Theo-Logic*. The transcendental dynamism of intersubjective relations may best show us the immanent logic of God as an interpersonal Trinity and our economical association within the Trinity. Therefore, I've reserved the bulk of my meditations on *intersubjectivity* (as a kind of postmodern code word for "persons in relationship") for chapter 5.[16]

But theorists in postmodernism will also find much about Balthasar's theodramatic theory that they like. The "world stage," as I cited above, cannot presume conclusions to our drama; by the same token, world authors, directors, actors, and audiences cannot presume *final* judgment on other world authors, directors, actors, and audiences (again, roles each of us play, according to Balthasar's schema, at various turns). This kind of "undecidability" is decidedly *un*-Enlightenment and illuminates yet another intersection at which dialogue opens between postmodernism and Balthasar's perennial (or at least epoch neutral) approach. Consider Balthasar's passing comment on the "texting" of the Jesus of the Gospels:

> In the Gospels, we cannot guess from the question what Christ's
> answer will be; almost every time the answer is so unexpected
> that it sounds like no answer at all. Or perhaps the questioner was

asking the wrong question? All answering comes from the creative Holy Spirit. Of course, theology cannot think of competing with the word of revelation; but unless it too is inspired—in this here-in-now situation—it cannot interpret the word. The Spirit is empowered to utter a fresh and central answer to every situation: this not only produces a genuine pluriformity of theologies but at the same time their genuine unity—albeit not the kind found it textbooks. Christ's church is always from the very outset the integration of these apparently irreconcilable elements.[17]

If we interpret the above passage carefully, we can see the heavy thread of postmodernity running through it. Clearly, Balthasar is holding up Christ as the locus of ultimate unity (and, as he footnotes, it takes Henri de Lubac's methodology of *paradox* to get there),[18] a claim that runs contrary to postmodern hermeneutics because it is absolutizing. But a more careful reading reveals the way Balthasar uncovers and honors the indeterminate (but no less "true") mode of the Jesus we encounter in the Gospels. Jesus speaks the truth under His own logic (not the logic of the Enlightenment rationalism). The truth, while cosmologically unifying, is culturally pluriform and open; this truth, moreover, is practical and relevant to "the here-and-now situation," a vital aspect of Christianity that asserts it as an essentially political and pragmatic theology, even though the manner in which it is to be political is largely misunderstood by many of Christianity's adherents today. In this light, we are again struck by the creativity of Jesus who chose to teach chiefly through the method of parable. Since the parable is a distinctly narrative (and thus dramatic) format, Jesus' use of the form reveals both the profound importance of story and the need for keen interpretative senses. The dialogic quality inherent in the "telling," furthermore, coupled with the multivalent options in the "hearing"—both of which are "foundational" values in postmodernism—not only endorse the general validity of theodramatic criticism, but also offer *Theo-drama* as a fresh categorical option for religious criticism in general. This is a notable development chiefly because religious criticism, as an interpretive lens, has been marginalized for some time now by the atheistic wing of the postmodern school.

So Balthasar, working from the historical and geographical context of postmodernity, remains an excellent interlocutor for postmodernism. Moreover, careful consideration of his work addresses and assuages postmodernism's more tail-chasing tendencies. The first goal of postmodernism is to critique the excesses of Enlightenment; the second is to dismantle modernity's edifices of homogeneity and its ramparts of certainty. Balthasar, along with the theologians artists of *ressourcement*, identifies intimately with such goals. Consider the following passage, in which Balthasar, in a rare moment of shared inquiry, begins to sound like some type of postmodern conference-hopper, concluding his keynote address in a panel for *arts therapy*:

How can theatre, as a public institution, bring people together who hold different world-views? What is it (for surely it cannot be simple

amusement) that unites these people who come with active expectation and readiness to "enter into" the action? Under what denomi-
nator does it bring them through the performance? It is a very long
time since the theatre had a homogenous audience, such as the ba-
roque theatre had on which it could exercise a deliberately didactic
influence (compare the "ruthless formative power" of French classi-
cism). Yet it still has the power to place man in acute, inescapable
situations that strip him naked and confront him with the unavoidable
question: Who is he, this being who exists in a terrible finitude?[19]

There are other similarities between Balthasar and postmodernism—the apophatic attention to lacunae, gaps, and *aporia*; the creative consideration of horizon of meaning; the idea of an *inscription* (of being "inscripted" by power
structures, by the *Other*, etc.) upon individuals—with which this chapter will
deal shortly; but it is Balthasar's theodramatic theory that is prepared to serve
as the brightest stage on which the dramatic tension among premodernity,
modernity, and postmodernity might be played out.[20]

Clearly, it is no accident that Balthasar places Theo-Drama precisely between his aesthetics and his logic in order to emphasize the spatial centrality
of God's dramatic action in, with, and through the world. In the last chapter,
we saw how the problem (i.e., locating intelligible meaning between theology
and literary art) was oriented around conceptions (and misconceptions) in
grammar: whereas Enlightenment-vein modernism produced a theology of
language that became too abstract and idealistic, mainline postmodernism, in
reaction, vivisects the potential of language so that it loses the ability to mean
anything at all. Balthasar's theological aesthetics, following the insight of
Maurice Merleau Ponty (1908–1961) is "being's witness," and Balthasar mitigates this conflict creatively by providing a kind of recovery that reconciles,
to the extent that it is possible, both sides. Clearly, a similar enterprise is afoot
in Balthasar's five-volume *Theodramatik*; and this chapter will present corre-
lations among God's *word*, our re/action to the word, and our subsequent
turns to dramatic performance—to Theo-drama—as a response. In this way,
we move to recover a more valid hermeneutic, one that unflinchingly sees the
anthropology of love and receptivity—mysteries founded in creation and in
the kenotic action of God's incarnation, executed decisively in the events of the
Easter triduum, remaining present in the outpouring of the Spirit—through
an optic that commissions and demands the engagement of all of our faculties. In every case we need to turn to narrative and dramatic art for both content
and demonstration.

Theo-Drama and the Cinema of Transformation

Unfortunately, any comprehensive treatment of Balthasar's dramatics is beyond the scope of this discussion. My goal here is to isolate several essential
aspects of Balthasar's theodramatic theory and demonstrate how they "play" in

and through a select example of recent dramatic art. In this chapter, Lars von Trier's film *Breaking the Waves* (1996), the first installment of his *Golden Heart* trilogy, will serve as the main canvas on which to illustrate and test our claims.

Breaking the Waves is set in a repressed, deeply religious community in the north of Scotland, where a naïve church cleaning woman, Bess McNeil (Emily Watson), meets, falls in love with, and marries an outsider, Jan (Stellan Skarsgaard), a Danish oil rig worker as randy and virile as he is carefree and devoted to Bess. Their relationship, with the polar extremes of Jan's presence and absence, alludes to the kind of pining romanticism more prone to appear in nineteenth-century seafaring tales. Indeed, romanticism itself, with all of its multivalent qualities, is a vital subtext of the film. Trier conveys well the desperate profundity of Bess and Jan's love, and the early days of their marriage are full with the exploration of a broad range of human intimacies, not least of which is the comprehensive foray into erotic love. But the intermittent and prolonged separations that come with Jan's work steadily asserts the painful reality that erotic love is transitory, a fact that Bess denies until the day Jan is to return to his rig. On her own, Bess prays to God that Jan comes back to her for good. Jan does return, but his neck has been broken in an accident that would have been avoided had Jan not come to the gallant aid of a colleague. Because of his paralysis, Jan and Bess are no longer able to be sexually intimate; and because erotic expression is a very condition of Jan's being, the absence of it slowly erodes his spirit and diminishes his will to live. Drugged up on painkillers and imprisoned by a desire that can't be met, he reaches out to Bess from the wilderness of his existence, urging her to take other lovers ("It's for me, not you"), and then to return to him with a detailed account of her encounters. After some resistance (she faints), Bess resigns herself to Jan's requests and begins a unique sexual mission. The more deviant Bess becomes in her sexual behavior, the more she dialogues and prays to God about it; the more rank the nature of her sexual encounters, the more resolved she becomes in continuing them. She is certain that her actions are now intimately guided by God and have become material aides in Jan's recovery. Annihilating even the most liberal boundaries of social protocol, Bess stands by her man: she descends into the debauched world of offshore prostitution, has calumny spoken about her around the town, is beaten, raped, and finally murdered. Jan, however, makes a miraculous recovery. His health restored, he goes to work on "rescuing" Bess. With the help of his friends, Jan creates a ruse in order to save Bess's body from a traditional burial among the other "outcasts" of her community. In a scene that conveys both the beauty and the hyperbole of traditional hagiography, Bess lay in uncorrupted state in a makeshift coffin on a warehouse floor. Jan venerates Bess and makes his prayerful farewell; his mates then abscond with the body and leave the coffin. Two funerals follow: in town, Bess is being "consigned" [21] to hell by her pastor and buried in the earth of a Scottish Boot Hill. Meanwhile, quietly at sea—so quietly, in fact, that the burial is inferred to and not seen (a detail not lost on the Christic imagination)—Bess's body is given to the sea. In the days that follow, Jan retreats into a kind of depression but is roused from it by another miracle: the inexplicable ringing of church bells from high in the North Sea sky. The film ends thus—in a cinematic triptych, in an exposition of life in three dimensions. Trier begins the shot on the oil derrick but "rolls up" in ascent, rising to the sky, pulling back through actual church bells ringing—an unmoored belfry in the clouds—the perspective expanding so that we view the derrick from on high. The camera eye, the ringing bells, and the stunned men on the derrick: inexplicable trinitarian theophany.

Similarly jolting plotlines characterize the final two episodes of the *Golden Heart* trilogy, *The Idiots* (1998), and *Dancer in the Dark* (2000), as well as the first of the *America* trilogy, *Dogville* (2004), and it becomes clear that Trier is making creative use of the trilogy format as an aesthetic framework that might disclose his theologically trinitarian point of view. Indeed, the trilogy seems tailor-made for such an excursion, not least of all given the fact that Trier (the "von" part, unlike Balthasar's, was added in both tribute to and imitation of the great director Eric von Stroheim) wrote and directed these films just after he converted to Catholicism.[22] Trier's technique of working in "threes" is in itself an important artistic methodology. It reveals a kinship of approach not only with Balthasar, but also with literary artists such as Dante, J. R. R. Tolkien, or Sigrid Undset. It also aligns him with filmmaker Krysztof Kieslowski (who, as another Catholic filmmaker, approached his material—particularly his 1993–1994 *Trois Couleurs* trilogy—with a trinitarian imagination), not to mention both Ingmar Bergman and Carl Theodor Dreyer. All were visionary artists who saw the value of exploring religious concepts through the narrative medium of the trilogy.

The mode of trilogy is instructive of course, but the aesthetic connection between Balthasar and Trier's *Breaking the Waves* is our main focus here. The formal structure of *Breaking the Waves* relies heavily on additional components of literary and liturgical architecture. Each segment of the narrative is separated and framed by chapter titles, and a montage of seventies rock plays over the highly stylized, almost iconic, paintings of various points in and around Scotland's Outer Hebrides. As in liturgy, Trier employs music to suggest thematic transition and to "cover" the empty structural spaces. Such elements contribute significantly to the film's literary and dramaturgical heart. Cinema, especially the way Trier and the other members of avant-garde group "Dogme95" approach it, has become a direct offspring and guardian of the aesthetic purity that theater has always promoted and protected. In addition, cinema, like liturgy, makes ample space for music to be a formally essential part of the picture. This aspect is extremely intriguing, in regards both to Balthasar (for reasons I adduced in chapter 2 of this study) and to Trier (because music is central to his cinematic vision and is integrated in such a retroactive way as to make it truly pioneering.) My concluding remarks in this chapter will seek to illustrate how this aspect is profoundly theological—in scope, meaning, and possibility for meaning. Like music, the dynamism of Theo-Drama markedly opens further liturgical possibilities that may be conveyed in a piece—the companionship of so many aesthetic and dramatic constituents moving us toward the innards of deep theological meaning. In this way, sensitivity to both the substantive and structural mysteries of music quite literally restores drama to its "senses." Let us now turn to Balthasar and take a brief look to see how his dramatic program facilitates this reunion.

Like a classic five-act play, Balthasar's *Theo-Drama* is organized on a five-volume trajectory. It is composed as follows:

  I. Prolegomena
  II. The Dramatis Personae: Man in God
  III. The Dramatis Personae: The Person in Christ
  IV. The Action
  V. The Last Act

Clearly, Balthasar's sensibilities as a literary scholar shine through in this construction. Balthasar sets up the plot (the *Prolegomena*), introduces the various players and their roles (*The Dramatis Personae*), orchestrates and depicts the rising action (*The Action*), and then offers a careful, qualified, but ultimately open "resolution" (*The Last Act*), a resolution which gains substantive credibility when viewed teleologically and eschatologically. The central premise of *Theo-Drama* (beyond its encouragement toward a contemplation about the variety God's incessant action on the world stage) is to provide an analogical foothold and a discerning rationale of why we, as persons, continue to create, participate, and spectate our own various kinds of stage plays. As Balthasar observes: "Life manifests a fundamental urge to observe itself as an action exhibiting both meaning and mystery,"[23] and the reason that this is the case lies in the very order of the universe and the human person's role within it. Aidan Nichols is incisive on this point:

> Every personal mission—and it is the happening of such missions which makes the life of the Church drama-filled and provides the materials for Christian theater—contains something of the universally relevant mission of Christ. Just as in the Old Testament there were pre-figurations of Christ, so in the plays of Shakespeare, for example, characters can post-figure Him.[24]

Trier's protagonists, as characters "in their own independent drama" meet, especially by virtue of their unique context, the criteria for the "post-figures" of Christ that Balthasar's theology proposes. For all independent dramas, in Balthasar's schema, are yoked together in a single, total drama that encompasses all the individual actions "because all encounters between God and man are included in the drama of Christ (*Theo-Drama* III, 33–40). The latter not only supplies the play's content but actually opens up the acting area in the first place (*Theo-Drama* III, 41–56)."[25] The poetic spirit of Hopkins resonates here. We again see a way to play among Hopkins's kingfishers in ten thousand places and how, as such, they authentically incarnate and achieve key aspects of theological recapitulation.

A Catholic Imagination (C): Moving through the Finite

Because it meditates upon and qualifies the relationship between faith and action, Balthasar's turn to dramatics also reveals the uniquely Catholic contours of Balthasar's theological vision. Moreover, it provides credible justification for the idea of a Catholic imagination as both an artistic location and as a category for the theoretical critique of all art, but dramatic art in particular. It can be argued, in fact, that theological distinctions between Protestant and Catholic conceptions are what also propel Trier's vision in the *Golden Heart* trilogy, and the manner in which he studies these differences becomes itself another defining aesthetic moment in our understanding of what kind of content it is that makes an imagination Catholic.

Like Balthasar, Trier establishes a polarity between Protestant and Catholic sensibilities from the very outset of his trilogy. Balthasar qualifies the Catholicity inherent in Theodrama, drawing historical distinctions of important sectarian differences within the Christic imagination. He dwells on these in the early pages of *Seeing the Form* and the *Prolegomena* to his *Theo-Drama*: "In Germany, after the initially positive attitude to the theatre, it was primarily Calvinism and North German Lutheranism which took a campaign of annihilation against the stage. In the Protestant towns of Switzerland they were successful, whereas in the Catholic areas the Jesuit drama (the continuation of the learned, middle-class drama) was able to celebrate its triumph."[26] Trier is also seeking to interrogate differences within the Christic imagination as he sets *Breaking the Waves* in the cultural location of extreme Protestantism, that of the Presbyterian Free Church, a very rigid wing of Scottish-Calvinism. This world, while Protestant, is decidedly "Old Europe" and in no way is inhabited by the traditional aesthetic figures who dwell in American Protestantism, such as Cheeverian WASPS, who languorously wade through soft middle age, staving off daily some unnameable *ennui* as they tour the circuit of lapsed Presbyterian cocktail hours. What we have in *Breaking the Waves*, though, is a community dwelling in a long tradition of dedicated (if imperial) asceticism, the shadow of the sober Scottish Reformer John Knox lurking behind every unadorned corner of church and township. And Trier is intent on mining the differences between the aesthetics of Catholicism[27] and the staid quietness of serious Knoxian Calvinism, itself a version of Christianity that is chartered upon an anti-aesthetic theology: "O Papists! Where shall you hide from the presence of the Lord? You have perverted his law; you have taken away his ordinances; you have placed up your own statutes instead of his. Woe and damnation abide you!"[28]

But Trier is careful not to make sweeping indictments against particular religious practices, no matter how retrograde or eccentric they might appear. He is more concerned with the human psychological structures that exist underneath and around religious expression. For example, he is intrigued by the fact that fundamentalism exists not only in practitioners of Scottish Calvinism but also in devotees of Catholicism, Islam, and Judaism (not to mention many agnostics and atheists who themselves operate on the same fundamentalist machinery they often lampoon and reject). In an interview with Danish film historian Stig Bjorkman, Trier expands on this point. The following remarks are a response to the question, "What role does religion play in your approach?" and Trier's account lends more insight into the malleable shape of the theological imagination without compromising the complicated dynamism of his own Catholic identity:

> Probably because I'm religious myself. I'm a Catholic, but I don't worship Catholicism for Catholicism's own sake. I have felt the need to experience a sense of belonging with a religious community, because my parents were convinced atheists. I flirted with religion quite a bit as a youngster. You perhaps search for a more extreme religion as a youngster. You either go to Tibet or seek out the most rigorous of all faiths. With total abstinence and such like. I think I have a more Dreyer-like view of the whole thing. Because Dreyer's religious view is in essence humanistic. He also accuses religion in all his films. Religion is accursed, but not God. It's like that as well in *Breaking the Waves*.
>
> My intention has not been to criticise a particular religious community, such as the one that exists in this Scottish environment. That doesn't interest me. That is far too simplistic. And it's nothing I want to concern myself with. To adopt a viewpoint that is easily accessible and universally applicable. That's like fishing in shallow water. In many ways I also have an understanding for—or rather, *that* people are engaged by spiritual questions and that they are so in an extreme manner. It is just that, if you want to create a melodrama, you have to furnish it with certain obstacles. And religion provided me with a suitable obstacle.[29]

As a convert and an artist, it is fair to surmise that Trier responds favorably to the version of "drama" proposed by Catholicism. Still, in *Breaking the Waves,* Trier is careful to offer a vision that seeks to recover the "universal spiritual" that the human religious spirit seeks but that is impeded by all too common psychosocial patterns and practices that are often sired and endorsed by religious communities. This position is further supported by Trier's choice of setting. Initially the film was to be shot in Jutland (the Danish hinterland and the scene of another famous 1987 cinematic gloss on the Catholic imagination, *Babette's Feast*), and then in Ireland. The cultural idiosyncrasies of Trier's final choice of Northern Scotland become, then, of secondary importance. In order to offer a credible context for dramatizing and post-figuring Jesus, Trier needed something of a *universale concretum et personale*, a particular setting renowned for its religious austerity; but his focus was equally fixed upon the sacramental/ transcendental realm, on the universal and eternal. This, of course, is not to diminish the importance of setting in any way, for all of the action must work through a finite locale, or, as William Lynch has noted, "Faith is the ability of the finite to lead somewhere"; but, while setting mediates, Trier's first and ultimate concern is with universal perspective.[30]

However, it is clear that Trier also has a specific theological point in *Breaking the Waves*; and though he does not designate the socioreligious force that propels or explains Bess's actions—so as to fall into the trap of cinematic dogmatism—it is clear that Bess's theological personality is explicitly Catholic. A bold assertion, to be sure, but it becomes clear upon close inspection. The logic, imagery, and trajectory that are encoded in the responses to her prayer reveal a "theology of the body" that is articulated and negotiated most consistently by Catholic aesthetic tradition. Trier, then, lays out a kind of Catholic-map work in his presentation of Bess's journey, particularly in his emphasis on Bess's body as the flashpoint of theological transformation. Emily Watson's astonishing performance, moreover, adds indispensably to the making of such meaning in that the spiritual data of her character is so expertly rendered.

The first clue comes in an early scene with the couple making ardent love. Bess gazes directly into the camera—to the viewer-as-community, to the panopticon eye of God—and sweetly says, as if in response to a great discovery, "Thank you." Jan replies, "What did you say?" Bess then quickly fixes on Jan's eyes: "Thank you," their lovemaking joining heaven and earth, an erotic site of sacramental love. Soon after, Bess experiences other sensory awakenings. Jan is the first to awaken Bess aesthetically and to liberate her from her life-without-art. He delights in *watching* Bess *watch* her first movie and celebrates the joy that good aesthetic mediation can provide. However, we are mindful of the world that Jan invades by acknowledging Calvinism's antipathy toward the employment of "graven images" as a means to both theological expression and understanding. Cultural critic Ann Kibby recounts Calvin's hostility to aesthetics as "the incomparable boon of images, for which there is no substitute, if we are to believe the papists. Whatever men learn of God from images is futile, indeed false." Kibby suggests also that "Calvin conceived of Catholic visual art as existing in opposition to those living icons, Protestants themselves who constituted the proper visual art of Christianity."[31] The irony of the Calvinist position is brought to full flower in *Breaking the Waves* in that Bess offers herself as a perfect Christian, a Protestant who is both living and speaking the gospel; yet she is rejected sharply by the very community that purports to value Calvin's anti-aesthetic approach. It is both striking and ironic that this particular truth is disclosed and realized through the "graven image" of film.

The Prophetic Moment: A Liturgy That Joins Word and Deed

Another clue that the Catholic imagination is at work in *Breaking the Waves* is rendered to us in a fashion that is at once more ingenious and more heartbreaking. As viewers, our main information about Bess's theological encounters is revealed in a series of her "conversations" with God. These monologues, which take place in the empty church that she daily cleans, add depth and dimensionality to her character and help move the plot. But they also divulge an essential character complexity by suggesting the presence of mental illness: Bess's split personality. One part of Bess's psyche plays the God role (when Bess/God speaks in a severe, chastising, and paternalistic voice), and the other plays the passive and willing child, hanging on every directive from on high, an analysis that gains psychological credibility when we consider her personal formation and history. Bess was raised fatherless, and her main male influence is her grandfather, a dispassionate elder in the church community, devoted much more to it than he is to Bess. In presenting Bess as a schizophrenic, Trier is emphasizing the polarity of the *dialectical imagination*. The schizophrenia becomes a metaphor for the religious world that Bess inhabits. Her "unorthodox" spirituality serves as a kind of parody of a religious (or ideological) tradition that presents a view that all of creation is radically polarized. Bess's schizophrenia reflects a dualistic Christianity; and her prophetic moment leads her to resist the limits of this vision and to "protest" to it by will, word, and action. In this way, Bess sounds out a bell of protestation against the great Protestant dominion of the "either/or." It is precisely in this sense that *Breaking the Waves* is a powerful and disturbing dramatization of the incarnational vision emerging from the dualisms of an extreme Calvinism. Trier depicts this aspect most subtly, and it is a quiet clue to the terrain of a most ingenious analysis of differences that exist within the wide scope of the Christic imagination.

In his *The Analogical Imagination* (1981), Catholic theologian David Tracy is similarly bent on locating such distinctions. Tracy approaches the issue of a polarized religious imagination by using the different strokes of systematic theology. As Tracy posits, if we discuss the Catholic imagination, then at the very least there must be something like the Protestant imagination. Tracy concludes that Protestants tend to engage in what he calls a *dialectic imagination* and Catholics in one he terms an *analogical imagination*. He relegates the distinction between the two to the realm of family quarrel, which, of course, read properly, is Tracy's attempt at saluting each side of the problem, making the space for both conceptions of the imagination to exist. Thus, while the analogical/dialectical poles represent antithetical while complementary inclinations in any imagination (whether Protestant or Catholic), these poles also describe prevailing and defining differences between the Catholic/Protestant mind and imagination. Generally, the analogical imagination stresses the presence or immanence of God in Creation, while the dialectical imagination stresses the absence or transcendence of God. Tracy finds that classic Catholic texts exhibit the analogical imagination more prominently, while classic Protestant texts bear greater witness to the dialectical. Tracy stresses that for the believer, the different tendencies are actually complementary.

The Analogical Imagination, as we have suggested before in these pages, is no groundbreaking work. Rather, it is a late modern version of examining and articulating the ancient duel between dualistic and triadic modes of perception. While Tracy clearly favors the analogical mode, "which is a language of ordered relationships articulating similarity-in-difference . . . constituting the whole of reality . . . focused, interpreted, related through newly formed propositions to the other analogues as similarities-in-difference by the primary analogue, the Christ event,"[32] and sees the turn to the analogical as a more productive means of fostering religious pluralism than the more divisive "this-or-that" dialectical mode, he concludes, as I mentioned, that both modes conform in their own way to the *imago Dei*.

Tracy suggests that the analogical imagination is demonstrated clearly in the articulated sense of ritual and liturgy native in both Catholic worship and the traditional movement of dramaturgy. Attention to such aesthetic detail does not exist (or is not articulated as systematically) in most Protestant settings, and Trier indirectly suggests this difference in the film. The liturgical dimension of Catholicism, like the structure of drama, places a premium on the sensual and intersubjective participation of the community—the sort of view James Joyce was getting after in his famous (if not exactly salutary) description that Catholicism is the church of "Here comes everybody"—which is not the kind of community practiced by the congregation in the film. At their essence, both drama and liturgy rely on concrete performativity and community participation; and these heavily stylized and ritualized actions possess and convey a deep, embodied sense of sacramentality with which traditional Catholicism is always associated and good drama achieves. Further analogies, such as the Catholic emphasis on God's action (endorsed especially in the epistle of St. James, in which the emphasis is on words *and* deeds) as opposed to the high Protestant emphasis on God's word alone, bear this distinction out and provide further clarity on the topic.[33] This seminal difference provides the content for a key scene in the film, in which Bess returns to the church (after a relatively small trauma that foreshadows the larger one) and walks into the church as a male elder expounds piously about the beauty of "unconditional love" and how he loves the Bible, which has given him such a teaching. Bess staggers into the church dressed in her whore's garb, dizzy with having just been assaulted by brutes. Among the multitude of other prohibitions, Bess, as a woman, is not allowed to speak in service; but Bess becomes the bell that fills the empty space of the belfry, deeply ensconced in the explicitly *prophetic* stage in her mission. She has come too far in her journey to abide by the aridity of social convention, and she speaks her truth unswervingly: the "simpleton" providing, finally, a relevant exegesis of the gospel for all to hear, an exegesis, no less, that accesses the very center of Christian faith:

(*To the pious one*): I don't understand what you're saying *(pause)*.
(*To the congregation*): You cannot love a word. You cannot be in love with words *(pause)*.
You *can* love another human being *(pause)*. That's *perfection*. (*Bess leaves their midst for the last time*)

Unlike her pious interlocutor, Bess's word—in the prophetic sense, God's word, from the "mouth" of God—is subsequently realized and completed in action as she returns to her mission for Jan. The word of unconditional love, of God's kenotic *caritas*, is recapitulated in Bess as she approaches the Golgotha of a broken-down ship in a cold Scottish harbor to offer her last great gift, the donation of her very self.

Bess McNeil: No Longer I Who Live, but Christ Who Lives in Me

Bess's kenotic act illustrates a fundamental transformation. She might say, along with St. Paul: "I have been crucified with Christ; it is no longer I who live, but Christ who lives in me."[34] But it's clear that the deeper nature of Bess's transformation is missed entirely by her community, for, like Jesus, "no prophet is accepted in his native place."[35] Balthasar is very sensitive to such "peak" moments, and his Theodrama radically emphasizes the transparency between performance and participation. Such conceptions reveal a central existential proposition in Christianity and a cornerstone of Pauline theology: conformation in Christ not only is an historical, ideological, or aesthetic proposition, but also is a Balthasarian mantra for modern theology: "The Spirit is empowered to utter a fresh and central answer to every situation."[36] Trier shows that prophetic witness coupled with the turn to dramatic action reveals that participation in Christ's death and resurrection is an ongoing dynamic in Christian life. Conformity to the self-surrender and sacrificial love that marked Jesus' death—and Trier depicts Bess as intimately bound to this event—represents a key element in theodramatic theory:

> The Christian helps to bring about this self-emptying of Christ, and does so in a "galling" service for the redemption of the world. But in this annihilation (which is only to be discharged by the "law of conversion"), the annihilation of self and the depersonalization of the patristic ideal of love have been overtaken. For even here, where nature has attained her end and her truth, the divine life appears as the meaning and fulfillment of everything. But it is precisely the truth that "God is everything" that provides the foundation for the resurrection of the New Eon and establishes the possibility for the fulfillment of the creature, even—and especially—in its ever greater contrast before the ever-greater God.[37]

Above anything else, it is the uniqueness of the Incarnation and the dynamic of the sacramental Real Presence of the Eucharist that speaks specifically to the deeper complexities of dramatic theory and impels us to a deeper respect for dramatic forms. For, in contradistinction to Hegel's conclusions, drama is not subsumed by history and "normalized," a development that Balthasar calls the "mirage of progress."[38] Rather, as in the Theo-Drama of Christianity, the mystery of good drama exists, transcendentally, in a never-ending process. The mystery of Hamlet's procrastination, for example (to take another famous Dane), is never fully resolved, and the play itself is never the same thing twice, especially as it is performed. The same holds true with eucharistic encounter: there is always potential for a deepening, or sometimes there is nothing at all, aridity. This does not diminish the transcendental character of either drama or eucharistic encounter, but it does say something about us, about those who engage in it. *The Spirit is empowered to utter a fresh and central answer to every situation.*

Bess's "teaching in the temple" resonates seismically. As lived speech in a prophetic key, it serves to indicate a significant stage on the road map of Bess's own Passion play. Literary history is rife with examples of the similar flash-points of character growth—the moment when creed meets deed—but few depictions entail the high stakes we see in *Breaking the Waves*. Bess becomes the active *Word*, the figure of Christ in theodramatic action. One such example, albeit minor, can be found in the character of Jim Dixon from Kingsley Amis's *Lucky Jim* (1957), particularly in the moment of his famous "Merrie England" speech. There is a resemblance in that Dixon, like Bess, has nothing left to lose in speaking his prophetic truth. Of course, Jim's speech is raging with humor (and whiskey), but the effect of his having told it redeems and centers him. Tobias Wolff offers a more theologically attuned version in a character that suddenly finds her prophetic voice in his 1981 story "In the Garden of the North American Martyrs." Wolff paints a sharp portrait of Mary, a middle-aged professor of history, who, after being out of the game for a while, is asked to interview for a position at an unspecified northeastern college. Mary's old friend Louise, who has her own self-serving agenda, has set the interview up; and Mary has no idea it is a simply pro forma affair (the job is intended for someone else) until just before she is to give her guest lecture. The rug pulled out from her, Mary finds the strength to speak her truth. She decides to give her lecture anyway, extemporaneously and without her prepared notes. Meanwhile, Wolff endows the setting with the atmospherics of prophetic truth-telling—and with truth-hearing, for the crowd seems hungry to hear some "Good News." He builds rhetorical significance by alluding to the density of need that Jesus encountered while preaching on the banks of the Sea of Galilee: "Behind them the room was full of students, some of whom spilled over into the aisles."[39] Mary begins by reminding the group that they are standing in the midst of an Iroquois cultural landmark, a detail that becomes particularly meaningful as she transitions into a recount of the well-known warrior ferocity of the Iroquois and how they treated the Jesuit martyrs Brébeuf and Lalemont. Wolff then writes us into the area of strange mysterious truth, laying a palimpsest of pro-phet upon prophet—his own voice upon Mary's upon Brébeuf's upon Jesus'—all upon the literary tapestry of a moving theological aesthetic:

> While he was still alive they scalped him and cut open his breast and drank his blood. Later their chief tore out Brébeuf's heart and ate it, but just before he did this Brébeuf spoke to them one last time. He said—
>
> "That's enough!" yelled Dr. Howells jumping to his feet.
>
> Louise stopped shaking her head. Her eyed were perfectly round.
>
> Mary had come to the end of her facts. She did not know what Brébeuf had said. Silence rose up around her; just when she thought

she would go under and be lost in it she heard someone whistling in the hallway outside, trilling the notes like a bird, like so many birds.

"Mend your lives," she said. "You have deceived yourselves in the pride of your hearts, and the strength of your arms. Though you soar aloft like the eagle, though your nest is among the stars, thence I will bring you down, says the Lord. Turn from power to love. Be kind. Do justice. Walk humbly."

Louise was waving her arms. "Mary!" she shouted.

But Mary had more to say, much more, she waved back at Louise, then turned off her hearing aid so that she would not be distracted again.[40]

Clearly, the skilled historian, in an evocation of historical place, in the channeling of the spirit of North American martyrs, becomes herself a martyr. But the scene of her personal victimage—by the hard machinery of academic politics, by the cold dispassion of personal betrayal—is transformed into of redemptive event, a vibrant sacramental moment in contemporary late twentieth century literature.

Sola Scriptura, Sola Fidei

Wolff's short narrative is an exemplary artifact of a Catholic imagination. Just like Trier's Bess, Mary's experience resounds analogically with Christ's passion. For the purposes of this discussion, Wolff sounds a reverberating pitch that might refresh and inform our senses as we return to Balthasar and the hard theology that undergirds aesthetic and dramatic expression. The turn to analogy has always been a move to recognize "similarity in difference"; so let us turn to two avatars of "similarity in difference—Balthasar and Karl Barth—in order to observe the shape of theological difference as two friends engage in a rounded conversation about the analogia entis and what the concept entails for the theological imagination.

Lutheran theologian George Lindbeck has written of a discernible "family resemblance," linking the theologies of Balthasar and Barth on this matter of squaring words with actions and faith with works. Lindbeck asserts that, as good biblical scholars, both Barth and Balthasar are wary of transposing biblical revelation into categories alien to itself, seeking rather to describe the world in terms that are scripturally rooted. The appeal to the Bible by both theologians is, nonetheless, not lacking in intellectual power, for they find there a sophisticated coherence. But one difference emerges, and it flows out of Barth's rejection of the analogy of being in preference for the analogy of faith (analogia fidei). For Barth, on the one hand, scripture can be read narrationally; but the narrative power in this case, from a literary point of view, transmutes itself into a mere allegory, a formal choice that endorses the division of God's world from our own, two worlds separated symbolically by human sin.[41] There exists, then, a partition from God in Barth's schema, which, of course, is consistent with traditional liberal Protestantism and follows from Luther's highly articulated "two kingdoms" theory.[42] For Balthasar, on the other hand, scripture is to be read and received dramatically, as the unfolding of God's story (which is our story) over the course of history. Barth, as a Protestant, emphasizes faith in the scriptural *Word*, and Balthasar carefully builds upon this; but Balthasar, as a Catholic, goes on to reject the *sola scriptura* of Barth's high Protestantism, the fixation on the biblically encased *word* that Barth upholds, in preference for a more metaphysically dynamic and aesthetically *catholic* view. Balthasar locates and qualifies this distinction in the *Prolegomena* of his *Theo-Drama*:

> The analogy between's God's action and the world drama is no mere metaphor but has ontological ground: the two dramas are not utterly unconnected; there is an inner link between them. . . . Thus, by entering into contact with the world theatre, the good which takes place in God's action really is affected by the world's ambiguity and remains a hidden good. This good is something *done*: it cannot be contemplated by pure "aesthetics" nor proved and demonstrated by pure "logic." It takes place nowhere but on the world stage—which is every living person's present moment—and its destiny is seen in the drama of a world history that is continually unfolding.[43]

Balthasar's dramatics seek to demonstrate that it is not only the word but also *action* (and *logic*, as we will see next chapter) that binds divine experience together and makes the second person of the Trinity—indeed, the whole of Christianity—intelligible. Balthasar's aesthetics begins as Barthian in this regard, and Balthasar pays him just tribute in the *Glory of the Lord*;[44] but Balthasar's excursion into Theo-Drama and his willingness to mine sources that preceded the Reformation (which Barth was not, as a rule, disposed or prepared to do) expands the limit of aesthetics to a point at which it becomes quite literally—and quite ironically—iconoclastic. Christ is word, action, and logic, swirling on the stage, gesturing suggestively about beauty, truth, and goodness, not apart from the world, but in it and through it, sacramentally.

We are careful here to avoid any final condemnation of Barth's aesthetics, for no theologian has reconciled aesthetics with scripture so well. It is the cold pietism and the general wariness of art inherent in the Protestant scheme (which Barth's own behavior, as a rabid fan of Mozart, belies) that both Balthasar's and Trier's work indicts. Protestant theologian Gerhard Nebel (1903–1974) comments instructively on the issue:

> Whoever lays store by wide horizons, finely proportioned spaces, heroic lives, manners, the brilliance and abundance of form, the retreat into a mythical world will feel repelled by Protestantism. Luther destroyed the golden chambers of myth and set up an indigent hut in their place. Whoever loves beauty will, like Winckleman, freeze in the barns of the Reformation and go over to Rome. I admit that I, too, have been overwhelmed at times by Winckleman's longing.[45]

Far from self-effacement, Nebel's candid analysis brightly illuminates the juncture between Barth and Balthasar just as they light general distinctions between the Protestant and Catholic imaginations. Barth knew well that Luther's *Theology of the Cross* prohibits any grounded reconciliation between aesthetics and ethics and defers such connections to the heavenly Kingdom; and Barth's preference for the analogy of faith, under the same rationale, precludes the possibility of God being present in any aesthetic format, let alone dramatic creation. Nebel expresses the Protestant view: "But the work of art is by no means ... itself an instance of integral, well-thought creation, since it is not beyond the fall into which every creature plunges. Art however reminds us of creation's 'golden purity' and God's applause for himself."[46] Balthasar concurs with Barth and the traditions of liberal Protestantism enough to grant that God is absolutely dissimilar in this sense; but there is a demonstration of relationship in the Incarnation of Jesus that analogically mitigates God's potential for cold distance as punishment for our presumption in the garden. Furthermore, Balthasar rejects the notion that "golden purity" can be only an "apparition" (as in Nebel) or a "trace element" (as in Derrida) and that representations of profound theological concepts are simply allegorical or symbolic. Such configurations assail the very premise of sacramental theology and the presence on which the theology insists. As such, they are inconsistent with neither the cosmic Christ nor the Christ of the Gospels.

Commercium Admirabile: The Great Reversal

In any event, it is essential to stress that Balthasar (and other *ressourcement* theologians) will join Barth and Nebel in indicting the unarticulated emphasis on beauty, especially the kitsch elements that attend so many conceptions of beauty today. Moreover, as I discussed earlier, "theologizing" the beautiful to inordinate extremes results in the flaw of *aestheticism*, something that Wilde may have practiced before the hard lessons of "Reading Gaol" and *De Profundis* (though, even from the prison cell of *De Profundis*, Wilde paints Jesus as an elegant aesthete!). Aestheticism is a pseudoreligion, of course, and has a rich and variant tradition, especially in literature, in which the religion of art has been practiced by many a colorful character, Waugh's Anthony Blanche being perhaps the most finely drawn, especially in the context of the Catholic framework of *Brideshead Revisited* (1945). Trier is also skeptical about the artistically expensive exaltation of beauty, so much so that he willingly assumes the role of the anti-aesthetic provocateur, proclaiming, in various utterances, "the ugly is a great source of beauty."[47]

This kind of development points to perhaps the most central aspect of Balthasar's *Theo-drama*, one that Balthasar scholar Edward Oakes labels "The Great Reversal," invoking the theological tradition of *commercium admirabile*, which meditates on Christianity's most paradoxical doctrine. In his *Pattern of Redemption: The Theology of Hans Urs von Balthasar* (1997), Oakes heralds the last three volumes of *Theo-Drama* in the strongest terms, as "the apex of (Balthasar's) theological achievement . . . the culmination and capstone of his work, where all the themes of his theology are fused into a synthesis of remarkable creativity and originality, an achievement that makes him one of the great theological minds of the twentieth century."[48] In these volumes, Balthasar turns his focus to God's *kenosis*, and concentrates on Gregory Nanzianzus's great question: "Our task now is to consider that problem which is so often passed over in silence but which—for that very reason—I want to study with all the more eagerness. That precious and glorious divine Blood poured out for us: for what reason and to what end has such an extraordinary price been paid?"[49]

Among many other things, of course, the violence of the cross, the "pouring of the Blood," is meant to establish a community of love, justice, and reconciliation among all people. However, with a gift freely given comes the freedom to reject the gift. The dialectical imagination rightly dwells on this aspect and ponders our refusal of God's deepest overture toward friendship. The "pouring out of the Blood," then, inaugurates the credibility of an anti-aesthetic sense that displays our alienation from God so that God remains radically "Other." The analogical (i.e., Catholic) imagination seeks to find a kind of sacramental linkage in the anti-aesthetic and begins to interpret, parody, and indict our hard-hearted resistance to God's invitation to grace. Such a body of religious art finds an intense beauty in the horrific, violent, and grotesque and finds God acting in all sorts of unexpected settings and modes. Oakes astutely points out that "through the density of this event, all of the previous themes of Balthasar's thought are not just intensified but also converted and upended in the 'great reversal' that took place between God and the dead man Jesus during the Triduum of Good Friday, Holy Saturday and Easter Sunday."[50] Examples of such art throughout the ages—the art that graphically details a scene from the triduum, *Christ Falling the Second Time,* or even from the early church, *St. Sebastian of the Sixty Arrows*—line the walls of museums and fill the pages of guide books. But, in artists such as Trier (and, of course, artists such as Georges Bernanos, Leon Blóy, Paul Claudel, Graham Greene, Flannery O'Connor, and Krysztof Kieslowski) we begin to depart from the spoon-feeding of a ready-made religious identity. Even though it may have served a vital purpose, we are compelled to move beyond the "art as dogma" stage and begin to see alternative, less didactic aesthetic settings for the exposition of theological mysteries. The crucifixion remains the paradox that it has always been—it remains, from the Christian perspective, the greatest work of divine love—but the depth of this mystery requires credible and creative aesthetic modes that testify to this reality as it is lived out by people in time, aesthetic pieces that demand eyes to see the theological trajectories embedded in good art. In this sense, the paradox of the crucifixion gives us license to validate unorthodox theologies of image and narrative that may dwell in bizarre settings and operate by nuance and complication.

Do my remarks suggest that we are more theologically astute than our ancestors? Hardly. But they are meant to reiterate the value that each age requires its own brave language in order to reveal and communicate the vibrancy of Christological reality. Moreover, as Balthasar asserts, the language must always derive from the dynamism of the triune God if it is to have final relevance. As I noted at the outset of this chapter: beauty is ultimately static and illusory without a theodramatic component, without the action of Christ. But Balthasar asserts the sway of an articulate Christology in the first volume of his theological program when he foreshadows the *commercium admirabile*—the "wondrous exchange"—and its implications for aesthetic, dramatic, and, finally, theological interpretation. Nichols comments:

> Kierkegaard, taking up a theme of Luther's Christology, had regarded the Son who was made not only man but "sin" as being, in the humanity which was his in a fallen and guilty world, someone hidden *sub contrario*—beneath their own contrary. That entailed the "crucifixion" of the senses of those who would have like to perceive the glory of God in Jesus Christ in an appealing way. But Balthasar takes just the opposite view. True, the sin of the world obliges God's expressive image to adopt a particular modality—going down into the darkness of the passion, the death, and Hades itself. But so far from abolishing the revelatory character of the sensuous image, the cross and its consequences intensify it, so that it becomes the *supreme* self-expression, to human perception, of God's eternal life.[51]

Balthasar's trilogy, while it presents the transcendentals with a trinitarian logic—as fundamentally dynamic and equal in their dynamism—relies ultimately on the ability of a theodramatic aesthetic to locate and qualify Christ's action in history. Action must provide the center between logic and beauty. Most important, action teaches us truly to see Christ Jesus in the world but also to seek Jesus paradoxically in the depths of His own *hiddenness*. This vision recalibrates and "intensifies" our sense of beauty. As we have observed in the consideration of other narrative and poetic artists, the vision is not always benign. With Trier, we are presently seeing, in stark fashion, just how disturbing it can get.

From the context of ethics and history, Benedict XVI (writing as Joseph Cardinal Ratzinger) comments both thoughtfully and forcefully on the matter:

> People wondered: where was God when the gas chambers were operating? This objection, which seemed reasonable enough before Auschwitz when one recognized all the atrocities of history, shows that in any case a purely harmonious concept of beauty is not enough. It cannot stand up to confrontation with the gravity of questioning about God, truth, and beauty. Apollo, who for Plato's Socrates, was the "God" and the guarantor of unruffled beauty as "the truly divine" is *absolutely no longer sufficient.*[52]

Ratzinger's insight updates the need for developing a renewed understanding of the *commercium admirabile*. The great crime of modern aesthetics, ironically, is the pacification of beauty. We create zones of purity that do not admit that the harsh realities of human frailty and brutal experience are part of our experience, part of the great mysterious drama of being. We can see how we are still complicit in our collective denial of these realities by turning away from the world—whether in the form of gated communities, the spiritual hideout of antidepressants, or the "beauty" pushed in paintings by Thomas Kinkade— and how our various denials contributed to Auschwitz and contribute to the Auschwitzes that exist today. We have not yet comprehended the ethical implications of the "Great Reversal," and the theodramatic sense demonstrates that we are paying a high price for our lack of imagination.

The Golden Heart

However, Trier draws protagonists who possess the countercultural imagination that seeks theological depth. But, as we have mentioned, his vision is anything except benign; and most any sober, critical consideration would admit the prospect that the "heroines" of Trier's *Golden Heart* (*Guld Hjerte*) trilogy are fetishized and exaggerated depictions of women, literary vestiges of the kind of patriarchy that consigns women to dwell in the lurid aesthetic space that exists between sadism and stupidity. These women, much in line with the traditions of darker romanticism (particularly in its *gothic* strand), are depicted as simpleminded pawns enduring the nefarious machinations of male power structures. There is much to this critique, of course (and *endurance*, as a case in point, is a prominent theme in *Breaking the Waves*);[53] moreover, the film stirred many a critic to indict Trier's version of a female hero whose only attributes seemed to be her naiveté and her desire to please. But such critiques may also be too simplistic. Trier comments on his motives:

> I prefer to work with unassailable ideas. And I wanted to do a film
> about goodness. When I was little I had a children's book called
> *Golden Heart* (a Danish fairytale) which I have a very strong and fond
> memory of. It was a picture book about a little girl who went out into
> the woods with pieces of bread and other things in her pocket. But
> at the end of the book, after she's passed through the woods, she
> stands naked and without anything. And the last sentence in the book
> was: " 'I'll be fine anyway," said Golden Heart." It expressed the role of
> the martyr in its most extreme form. I reread the book several times,
> even though my father regarded it as the worst trash you could imag-
> ine. The story for *Breaking the Waves* probably has its origin there.
> Golden Heart is the film's Bess. I also wanted to do a film with a reli-
> gious motif, a film about miracles. At the same time I wanted to do
> a completely naturalistic film.[54]

It is valid to admit that Trier is perpetuating the worst of male artistic hegemony by promulgating yet another "heroine" based on the skewed traditions inherent in the folk fable. But it is perhaps "more valid" to conclude that Trier is attempting to honor the power and dignity of women by writing them as "doubles" or analogies of Jesus. Trier explains: "Bess in *Breaking the Waves* and Selma in *Dancer in the Dark* are supposed to be strong, even though it's a fragility they themselves refuse to accept. The films that I have made have all had to do with a clash between ideal and reality. Whenever there's been a man in the lead role, at a certain point this man finds out that the ideal doesn't hold. And whenever it was a woman, they take the ideal all the way. . . . But let's not talk in terms of men and women. I feel kind of female myself, to a degree."

Trier, of course, is getting at a recovered sense of the human person, one that envisions persons as a fusion of the feminine and masculine. His women protagonists take the idea "all the way" so as to find the palpable reality that is promised within the idea. For Trier, it appears that women are more theologically mature than their male counterparts: they live boldly in faith and behave as if the tenets of Christianity are actually true. Trier, like Catholic theologians and artists before him, tugs on the mystery of personhood and proposes that the essence of Christianity is in its willingness to negotiate opposites. This *complexio oppositorum* is perhaps more theologically astute in that it recapitulates the fully integrated personhood inaugurated and modeled by Christ. Christianity subverts the classic anthropology of gender roles and subverts anthropological *hierarchy*. Christianity, moreover, can be an odd mix of romanticism (the idea that Jesus can be an elegant aesthete in love with the created, an ardent romantic in love with creation) and realism (the idea that Jesus can be a sober pragmatist in his dealing with free persons, "macho," even, to the absurd point of submitting to violence).[55]

However, while *Breaking the Waves* operates on an arc of old-fashioned theological romanticism, it is also laced with enough ambiguity about Bess's consciousness that it challenges conventional theological readings.[56] The widespread critical consensus is that Bess is either mentally deficient or a naïve and childish believer; but while Trier suggests strongly that Bess is innocent,[57] he does not portray her as an idiot, and the film simply does not support such an assessment. A scene with Dr. Ramsay that takes place at the beginning of the last third of the film conclusively demonstrates that Bess is self-reflective, "rational," and sane:

> DR. RAMSAY   I think you've gotten involved in something be-
> yond your control.
> BESS   I don't make love with them. I make love with Jan and save
> him from dying. Sometimes, I don't even tell him. We have a spiri-
> tual compact. God gives us something to be good at. I'm stupid, but
> God gave me this.
> DR. R   What's your talent?
> BESS   I can *Believe*. *(Pause)* Do you always get so involved with
> your patients?
> DR. R   I love you. You're very special.
> BESS   Remove your hands. Don't come here again.

Trier paints Bess not so much as dependent, but as fragile; not so much dim, but resolute and faithful to a vision. As a Christ figure, she is certainly counter-

cultural and alien. She's not *normal*. She's better. She's *good*. A nervously destabilized Dr. Ramsay realizes Bess's truth in hindsight as he testifies at the
inquest that follows Bess's murder. The virile Jan, in the midst of his miraculous
recovery, sits with Bess's sister-in-law, Dodo, weeping in the courtroom:

> Dr. R: I need a glass of water.... *(Pause)* If you asked me to write my
> conclusion again, I wouldn't write psychotic or neurotic, but "good."
>   Magistrate: "Good?" She suffered from being good? Is that what
> you would write?
>   Dr. R: *(Pause)*...No.

He cannot write such a thing, and his failure, he knows, reveals the failures
of culture—the "Free" church, the secular state, the scientific community—
joining together to marginalize Bess. Her murder, like the crucifixion of Jesus,
reenacts the ancient scapegoat mechanism, wherein the slaughter of an innocent "resets" culture and offers a kind of peace between disparate factions
for a time. Bess so bilks conventional therapy that there does not even exist a
category for her behavior, but the truth is inscribed upon all who knew her; and
Trier subtly directs his actors to convey this point dramatically.

Role and Mission: The Dramatic Structure of Being

Another key to validating a theodramatic itinerary that Trier sets for Bess can
be found in Balthasar's theory of *role* and *mission*. If we are to admit that our
experience in the world has meaning and authenticity and that such meaning
is located upon a theological continuum with a beginning (that is, an origin)
and an end (that is, a *telos*), we must come to grips with the dicey issue of
human freedom. Balthasar's solution is both novel and traditional. He finds
the most fruitful explanation for the vicissitudes of human experience and the
challenges of human freedom in the complicated conjunction between *role* and
mission. Balthasar offers a lengthy discussion of the dynamic in his *Prolegomena*. Put simply, *role* is distinguished from *mission* in that *role* is socially
determined and *mission* is divinely bestowed. As a Catholic theist, of course,
Balthasar sees mission as "constitutive of the person, within the mission of
Christ" and asserts that human identity is truly found and discerned in personal mission.[58] Balthasar locates the impetus of this in the trinitarian progression in which the incarnated God is the one who locates and executes a
bold "personal" mission in service of all creation. The mission of Jesus, then,
becomes the model, as the work of René Girard has so conclusively illustrated
(and Balthasar uses Girard in the fourth volume of *Theo-Drama*). Philosophi-
cally speaking, an individual is on the way to being a "person" when he or she
begins to seek, locate, and enact his or her personal purpose. For the "person,"
the step from role to mission is the transcendental step and opens the person
to the wide expanse of being, for "personal mission exists and identifies him
simultaneously in his unique personality and his *a priori* social nature, since

he continues to owe his self being to a human 'thou,' while owing both himself *and* the thou to a divine origin."[59] While most people accept their social roles, whether willingly or not, few people are willing to receive the "manifestation of the divine Trinity"[60] that might disclose the *self-being* and *being-with* of creation, that might disclose the sense of *mission* that Balthasar proposes. When Balthasar observes that "the notion of 'roles' is more prevalent in psychology and sociology than ever before,"[61] he is simply reporting on our temptation to linger under the seductive and reductive umbrella of roles (especially as they are presented today), rather than to look where role might be converted to mission, which, of course, is a matter of transformation and therefore a matter of theological identity.

Balthasar's theological premises—particularly the principles that surround the problem of role—share a major affinity with many theories of postmodernism. One postmodern postulate, established by Heidegger, treats the very beginning of our existence. Heidegger argues that the biggest constraint on our freedom is that none of us has chosen to be born,[62] which creates an original subjectivity in all individuals. However, to my mind, that is neither here nor there. There is a situation that arises soon after birth that provokes much greater constraints on freedom: individuals, once birthed, are born into social structures in which they do not have, and will not likely have, any significant influence or agency. Many other strictures exist in such structures, such as the imperialism of language and culture, which are menaces that particularly trouble the postmodern mind. One response to the oppression of language, as I suggested earlier in this book, is to react by stealing its fire, changing the rules, and thus taming it down to innocuous play, a maneuver perfected by the French literary theorist Roland Barthes. A more sublimated defense-reaction to culture, however, transmutes into more dangerous consequences. As I will discuss next chapter, confusion about language and cultural meaning erodes us from the inside out, as Judith Butler shows, and often foments into psychological or physical violence. But the most insidious example of this kind of structural oppression finds its form in literal ignorance: the fact that most of us may not ever realize this kind of captivity because the hardest chains to break are the ones we do not see.

While profoundly aware of the struggles that accompany (postmodern) existence ("God's struggle for the world, the world's struggle for God"),[63] Balthasar is not prepared to grant final victory to the various mechanisms or structures that wield psychological or sociological force, for, while bona fide and essential, these mechanisms exist and engage only a limited aspect of being, what Balthasar calls the "horizontal axis" of existence. *Role*, on the one hand, exists precisely on the horizontal axis in Balthasar's program and needs to be confronted actively for this reason. *Mission*, on the other hand, engages existence from the *vertical* axis and implies a willing choice to either assent or dissent from its call. Both are essential in *Theo-Drama*, and Balthasar is careful not to set false dichotomies where "horizontal" might mean "material" and "vertical" might mean "spiritual." These kinds of divisions simply do not go far enough; but they do create healthy tensions, and the tension between *role* and *mission* can open the way to a realization of personhood. Without a doubt, understanding personhood is one of the most important missions for Balthasar: "It is when God addresses a conscious subject, tells him who he is and what he means to the eternal God of truth and shows him the purpose of his existence—that is, *imparts a distinctive and divinely authorized mission*—that we can say of a subject that he is a 'person.'"[64] Postmodern theories of subjectivity miss an opportunity on this score; and the exclusion of a more expansive interpersonal language (the kind that theology offers) has resulted in a diminished imagination about possibility and intimacy, both in our interpersonal relationships and in our relationships with the divine. Because of the encroaching gaze of the panopticon, as in Foucault, our reactions become limited to some type of Orwellian "interiorization," and our sense of relationality becomes thwarted. We turn inward and become atomized, and the critic-descendants of Foucault and Lyotard have cataloged this condition very well;[65] but postmodernism, for all of its clarity about the nature and status of human power, has also jettisoned the very theological prescriptions that might address the alienation wrought by such forces. If, as in Foucault, God is simply a "utility" or a textual artifact, then there really is no reason to "act well," as Balthasar puts it; and acting well, of course, is a chief indicator of being human. For this reason, far more than others, the term *post-human age* clangs on the ear with an ominous relevance.

The open sense of *mission* does not erase hardship and suffering, but it does create persons and persons-in-community. For Balthasar, the baptism of role by mission negotiates the two freedoms that we sense in existence: finite freedom (which operates on the horizontal axis) and infinite freedom (which operates on the vertical axis). In the rich person-to-person encounter (in a way not unlike the procession of the Holy Spirit from the Father and the Son), theodramatic action makes space where there was none for the vital third element, that of love: "What unites all these instances of 'genuine love between persons' is precisely the sense of vocation and mission that results from each person's response to the 'brilliance of a loving choice.' In drama, mission and vocation express themselves concretely in the dramatic situation."[66]

As Ed Block astutely observes, the openness to this approach "de-limits" the constraints of both modern and postmodern conceptions of horizon and possibility and once again opens dramatic and narrative art to notions of the transcendent, "ways in which divine involvement is nevertheless operative in the unique particularities in everyday life,"[67] which is always a way of love. Balthasar, furthermore, is keen on expressing that the "loving choice" to be in active relationship with God subsumes all planes of existence: "Christ bursts all dimensions of the purely worldly stage."[68] The relationship does not curtail freedom or individuality, as so many critiques of Christianity posit, but quite the opposite. Balthasar's "co-active" theory of role and mission, which clearly builds on the traditional Catholic idea of *connaturality*, reaffirms the essential tension between external forces and individual freedom played out in relation of horizontal and vertical dimensions, which, according to Block, "does not foreclose upon the possibility of ultimate mystery."[69]

The finite freedom of the individual is contained within the infinite freedom of God.

Finally, Nichols comments that concept of mission is "a key term" for Balthasar and enables him to put forward what "he calls a Christology of consciousness, and on that basis, a Christology of being, two ways, the second deeper than the first, of looking at the work and person of Jesus Christ."[70] The implications of this theory for Trier's Bess are quite profound. The notion of *missio* (literally *being sent*) is of central import to the film, and it is clear that, for all her life, Bess, as *homo viator*, has been waiting for and seeking some great service in the name of profound love. More to the point, Bess's responses demonstrate that the Christian notion that the highest love (*agape*) is itself founded precisely on the receptivity and disposition of such service, that is, upon *kenosis*, the donation of one's entire self for the benefit of the beloved. Her role may have begun as simpleton, as a naïve girl (so her community thought) who was good for cleaning churches and not much more. But when she meets her mission head-on, the open-ended fullness of her personality is disclosed. Turning back to Wolff's tale, it is striking to note a very similar dynamic taking place, both in the protagonist, Mary, and in the historical character who is also invoked in the tale: Jean de Brébeuf. Brébeuf, a Frenchman, wanted to enter the priesthood from an early age, but his health was so bad there were doubts he could make it. His posting as a missionary to the frontier at age thirty-two seemed to be a death warrant, as conditions in the New World were tough for even the most hale of individuals. But his *mission* changed everything. He spent the rest of his life travelling all over New France, and the harsh and hearty climate so agreed with him that the Iroquois, surprised at his endurance, called him *Echon*, which meant *load bearer*; and his massive size made them think twice about sharing a canoe with him for fear it would sink.[71] Balthasar's theory would assert that there was more to Brébeuf's transformation than simple geographical relocation.

These accounts, whether fictive or not, comment persuasively on the mystery of mission. They find their unique sense of both credibility and hope by engaging the analogical imagination, contemplating Jesus as an original model who demonstrated the grace of being *missioned*. As Oakes observes, for us "there is no real sense of mission before Pentecost,"[72] that is, before the the church and the bursting forth of the Spirit. There is no church, of course, without Jesus. The way in which his mission orients and reorders our lives explains Balthasar's final thesis in the "Role and Mission" section of the Theodramatics: "only in Jesus Christ does it become clear how profoundly definitive the 'I'-name signifies vocation, mission. In him the 'I'f and the role become uniquely and ineffably one in the reality of his mission, far beyond anything attainable by earthly means."[73] The point for us is to bring our "I's" as close to our "Thou's" as possible. This, of course, is the great work of being a human person; however, lest he lapse into promethanism (or be accused of Pelagianism), Balthasar also asserts equally that it takes a heavy infusion of God's grace for the I-Thou communion to come off well.

Inscribed on a Body: The Theology of the Empty Space

The hope for the unity of role and mission in a person provides inroads into what I believe to be the most interesting area of Balthasar's "depth" theology. Clearly, for all of Balthasar's conceptual gymnastics, his Theodramatics, in particular, dwells most narrowly on the importance of articulating a valid theology of the body. It has to or else Balthasar's theology jettisons its existential relevance and becomes lost among the ash heaps of theologies of post-Enlightenment idealism, a maneuver that Balthasar is not prepared to make. Similarly, Trier's cinematic articulation of Bess illustrates the theology of Theo-Drama exceedingly well in that it is likewise dependent on theologically sensitive understandings of the "body"—what the body teaches us about finitude and the infinite, personality (ours and God's), and the spiritual impotence of violence—to name a few. The topic is one that obviously flows out of and relies upon our sense of God's incarnational presence. It is therefore a vital inroad to yet a deeper theological texture that might expose uniqueness in the Catholic imagination.

In her recent book, *Postmodern Heretics: The Catholic Imagination in Contemporary Art*, art critic Eleanor Heartney examines the legacy of the Catholic Church and its influence on contemporary art. Presuming her audience might be hostile to the fact that Catholicism is a deeply "embodied" religion, she supports her contention with a brief "delve into theology" and explains:

> Catholic doctrine holds that the human body is the instrument
> through which the miracle of man's salvation from sin is accom-
> plished. As a result, all the major mysteries of the Catholic faith—
> among them Christ's Incarnation, his Crucifixion and Resurrec-
> tion, the Resurrection of the faithful at the end of time, and the
> Transubstantiation of bread and wine into Christ's body and blood
> during the Mass—center around the human body. Without Christ's
> assumption of human form, there could be no real sacrifice, and
> hence, no real salvation for mankind. The Catholic Church has tra-
> ditionally relied upon visual imagery and sensual experience in
> order to convey these truths.
> ... All of this is of course in stark contrast to the Protestant em-
> phasis on biblical revelation as the primary source of God's truth. ...
> Sensual imagery and sensual language are seen as impediments, ra-
> ther than aids to belief. The body and its experiences are things to
> be transcended.[74]

Heartney's insight, far from serving as an excuse or apologia, rightly emphasizes the body as mediator, as site, of transcendental relationship. In stark opposition to Enlightenment tradition, mediation of the real is not located merely in the faculty of the mind or the intellect, but in the body as well. Heartney refers to this more holistic collaboration as "the incarnational consciousness," which, for our purposes, becomes another buzzword in the growing lexicon of the Catholic imagination.

More important, Heartney's idea of "incarnational consciousness" is already anticipated and elucidated by Balthasar and becomes the luminous point that both shuts the door on Enlightenment dualism and facilitates the eschatological finale of Balthasar's theodramatic program. Balthasar finds the full expression of what *body* might entail in the fifth volume of *Theo-drama* by virtue of the fact that the German language possesses two semantically distinct words for *body*: *Körper* and *Leib*. *Körper* is body in the physiological sense, and *Leib* is the expression of the body in its spiritual or *personal* sense. Both aspects constitute our personal being, and Balthasar is very decisive on this point when he insists "that the *dénouement* of the theodrama came through the fruitful sacrifice of the only too material *Körper* of Jesus on the Cross (no Docetism there!), it is from his *Leib* now in heaven, that flow down those energies which can transfigure the image of the trinity on human beings."[75] Our own personal integrity as human persons derives from this relationship, this analogy of Christ's experience to our own, and finds meaning when we attempt to put it all together. Nichols concludes:

> Still, the duality of *Körper* and *Leib* must in no way lead to an Idealism: Balthasar insists on the mortal realism of the physique (if so we may translate *Körper*) nailed to the Cross, without which the spiritual body of the risen Lord was impossible, just as without some share in its suffering of resistance to God our final transfiguration cannot proceed. *Love is hard.* Here the more wounded are in fact more healthy, as philosopher-poets, but also various saints are made to testify.[76]

Trier's portrayal of Bess's journey dramatizes the Catholic heart of Balthasar's Theodramatics in almost every one of its dimensions. The vision, we have detailed, is not benign, and the "major" interpretive communities have either cried "foul" or recoiled in disgust against it. However, if we incorporate the appropriate critical lens, we find the many ways that Trier has rendered a finely drawn post-figure of Christ, a depiction made all the more persuasive and credible, perhaps, by the uneasiness it causes in the communities it means to serve. The final segment of the film is particularly engrossing in that Bess demonstrates conclusively the ownership of her body by submitting to its destruction. This action not only recapitulates the passion of Jesus but also excavates and distills the deepest theological implications that reside in both the historical cycle of Christ's passion and in our mysterious participation in the reiteration of the event ("Set in motion with the departure of Jesus . . . new players act . . . which entails nothing less than an ontological transformation").[77] Trier's contribution to contemporary theological aesthetics cannot be overstated on this score; and the soteriology he offers, while harsh (and largely Anselmian in tone), is faithful to the style of God's own kenotic vision that has manifested itself in so many other ontotheological arenas in which the relationship between love and suffering is of central importance.

This leads us to the most irksome aspect for viewers of *Breaking the Waves*: Bess's *passivity*. While we may not agree with her choices, we can grant that Bess has a sense of embodiment; we can also suspend our disbelief about the fact that she has resigned herself to such a peculiar mission in the first place. However, the fact that she continues it (even though she knows that Jan is not in "his right mind") is objectionable enough to make one get up and leave the theater, as many did. It is the single fact that Bess, in a posture of passive disinterestedness, obediently sustains this bizarre operation that really puzzles critics. Clearly, psychological analogies can be drawn here that would diagnose Bess either as a classically weak-minded groupie drawn irretrievably to a charismatic leader of a cult or as (yet) another nineteenth-century "heroine" held under the thumb of a tyrannical male. However, when viewed against the theological landscape that informs the film, Bess's passive cooperation suddenly strikes a different register—a far more elevated and precise modality—which is a feature that most critics are neither disposed nor prepared to consider. Passivity is one central element that shows us we are encountering a transcendental art. In Trier's film, the expert characterization of Bess's passivity directly links to the profundity of kenotic love that Trier is proposing. His is a cinematic exposition of the way that God relates to us, an exemplum of how God loves us. As Balthasar writes of Jesus in *The Action*: "Obedience . . . is the crucial word. He must become a man in free obedience if his death is to overcome death. At the precise point, moreover, his death becomes the legitimate interpreter of his whole existence."[78] Bess's compliance with the wishes of her beloved interprets her whole existence. Her passive assent to the violence of the world, furthermore, theodramatically connects the action of *Breaking the Waves* to the trinitarian procession, both in the cinematic moment of Trier's film and in the revelatory moment of history (again: *the Spirit is empowered to utter a fresh and central answer to every situation*).

Further analogies can be drawn. In the spirit of almost all of Jesus' male apostles, Jan's rejection of Bess—by publicly endorsing her madness (a madness in which he, if it were valid, would be materially complicit) and by signing her into the state mental ward—is a direct analogy to the events that initiate the historical passion of Christ: the world is mad, God responds. We reject the response. God submits to us totally—even unto death—thus annihilating our more juvenile conceptions of divinity. God then pursues us—even beyond death—to the outpost of our various hells and beyond, which befuddles us further. The only option left for God, it seems, is to capitulate to our culture totally and passively in order to demonstrate the unmitigated protestation of it. As Balthasar observes in regards to what is at stake in the passion of Christ:

> His life is running toward a crescendo that, as man, he will only be able to survive by surrendering control . . . for this surrendering of control to the Father is essential if, in this hour, the single, indivisible event that dogmatics requires is to take place: he must bear the totality of the word's sin (Jn 1:29) being made into sin (2 Cor. 5:21), becoming a curse (Gal. 3:13) by the all disposing will of the Father.[79]

Rejected and abused, Bess becomes "sin," becomes a "curse"; but the critical lens of Theo-Drama provides us with a unique rubric for insight that sees through the apparatus of human violence. The astute viewer is provided with a vital interpretive option and is called to see the golden heart of grace and mission through the rubble of Bess's otherwise meaningless destruction.

In "A Frost Lay White in California," William Everson meditates well on this brand of complicated, kenotic theology and renders into poetry what is so difficult to express in prose, a wailing lover-God who loves creation beyond, even, the outposts of dignity:

> "Never Forget," cried God, "I am your slave!"
> Call me and I come.
> Curse me, I cannot quit.
> I have never renounced. Do you know what I am?
> I am your woman.
> That is my mouth you feel on your heart,
> Breathing there, warming it.
> I am more. I am your dog.
> That is my moan you hear in your blood,
> The ache of the dog for the master. I am your dog woman.
> I grieve a man down,
> Moan till he melts.[80]

Everson navigates the complexity of self-donation by honoring its terrible logic and describing its overwhelming ferocity. In God's great love, God becomes a "slave," a dog to be kicked and spurned. Everson echoes the theological vision proposed by Isaiah, that of the suffering servant who is not only unrealized by the world but also rejected, abused, and summarily banished.[81]

Oakes facilitates a further interpretation of this great mystery. He dwells upon the "immense stress" that Balthasar places on this crucial moment in *Theo-Drama*, which, according to Oakes, constitutes his single greatest innovation to the tradition: the passive death of God. Balthasar's innovation takes the form of a Theology of Holy Saturday, one that informs the events of the passion and the resurrection of Jesus Christ and one that recovers a more theologically comprehensive treatment of the triduum. God-in-Christ, beginning with the events of late evening on Holy Thursday, transforms into the *passive* mode. The death of Jesus does not conclude with the crucifixion; Jesus' Holy Saturday descent into hell (i.e., *Sheol* in scripture) is a continuum of his death on the cross and further reveals the extreme profundity of his salvific mission. Balthasar's controversial theory astutely shows that Jesus does not enter hell in glory (as some Catholic tradition insists); rather, Jesus enters the dark realm with the same degree of puzzlingly passivity with which he endured his *via dolorosa*. The Glory of the Lord, to put matters most starkly and precisely, hinges on the extremity of this historical action because the action of Holy Saturday proclaims the constitution, procession, and method of God's glory, or, as Rowan Williams declares: *"Holy Saturday leads us to the very be-ginning of creation."*[82] The moment of Holy Saturday, as Balthasar shows so persuasively in *Theo-drama*, penetrates all existence and reveals the central mystery of the divine mission: "In this way (and only thus), he (Jesus) becomes the creaturely prototype and sacrament of the omnipresence and total self-giving of the triune God."[83]

By following the paradox of Jesus' radical submission where it leads, Pope Benedict (again writing as Joseph Cardinal Ratzinger) builds on Balthasar's Theology of Holy Saturday, asserting the magnitude of God's action:

> Christ himself, the truly Just One, is in his very innocence he who undergoes suffering and abandonment even unto death. The Just One descended into Sheol, to that impure land where no praise of God is ever sounded. In the descent of Jesus, God himself descends into Sheol. At that moment, death ceases to be the God-forsaken land of darkness, a realm of unpitying distance from God. In Christ, God himself entered that realm of death, transforming the space of non-communication into the place of his own presence. This is no apo-theosis of death. Rather, God has cancelled out and overcome death in entering it through Christ.[84]

Ratzinger continues, reiterating Balthasar's controversial claim (and the tradi-tion that sired it) that God *actually* dies: "The God who personally died in Jesus Christ fulfilled the pattern of love beyond all expectation, and in so doing justi-fied the human confidence which in the last resort is the only alternative to self destruction. The Christian dies into the death of Christ himself."[85] Our ability to begin to understand this great mystery, as Oakes illustrates, becomes dependent not only on our imagination but also on our facility with grammar:

> The pious imagination of the past held that the verb descended when applied to Christ (he descended into Hell: Apostles Creed) was an intransitive verb in the *active* voice (as in he descended a staircase); whereas Balthasar insists that it must be understood passively (as in the ball descended the staircase). . . . The radicality of Balthasar's ap-proach is that Christ's descent is, must be, totally passive, the descent of the dead to the dead.[86]

Christ does not descend in glory to rescue souls from hell, as so many traditional images depict; Christ *actually* dies so as to be in *actual* solidarity with the dead. The Son's act of surrender, furthermore, is an act done in absolute freedom, a *mission* within the divine *hypostases*.[87] It is the Holy Spirit who, also in freedom, allows the performance of Its own mission (as *vinculum amoris*, as ligament of love, between Father and Son) to maintain the integrity of the Revealer and the Revealed as God-in-Christ lay in the tomb of hell, the deep impression of God's self on all eternity, awaiting the Resurrection.[88] In this way, as Balthasar posits in *Mysterium Paschale*:

> Jesus was truly dead, because he really came as a man as we are. . . . In
> the same way that, upon earth, he was in solidarity with the living, so,
> in the tomb, he is in solidarity with the dead. . . . Each human being
> lies in his own tomb. And with this condition Jesus is in complete
> solidarity.[89]

Ratzinger seems to arrive at the same conclusion, albeit from a slightly different route:

> The answer lies hidden in Jesus' descent into Sheol, in the night of the
> soul which he suffered, a night no one can observe except by entering
> this darkness in suffering faith. . . . For the saints, Hell is not so much
> a threat to be hurled at other people, but a challenge to oneself. It is a
> challenge to suffer in the dark night of faith, to experience commu-
> nion with Christ in solidarity with his descent into the Night. One
> draws near to the Lord's radiance by sharing his darkness.[90]

Romanticism, Realism, and Hope: The Miraculous Gift of Love

The consequence of a personal solidarity with God, especially in the very
"death" of God, can be nothing other than hope. Ratzinger's forceful commentary illustrates precisely what is at stake:

> Hell is so real that it reaches right into the existence of saints. Hope
> can take it on, only if one shares in the suffering of Hell's night by the
> side of the one who came to transform our night by his suffering.
> Here hope does not emerge from the neutral logic of a system. . . .
> It must place its petition in the hands of the Lord and leave it there. . . .
> The idea of mercy . . . must not become a theory. Rather, it is the
> prayer of suffering, hopeful faith.[91]

Jesus descends (or, rather, is descended) into hell, into the preternatural empty
space, in order to fill it with his presence. In this sense, it is fair to claim that it is
not on Pentecost that the church is founded, not even on the day of the rolling-
back-of-the-stone-that-reveals-the-empty-tomb (even though both events baptize
the promise and the fecundity of the postmodern empty space), but on Holy
Saturday. For the poetic minded, Holy Saturday annihilates death and recalibrates human horizon. For the more pragmatically minded, the whole Easter
triduum is endowed with a logic that gains credibility precisely as it inverts. In
this sense, even for the most logical positivist, the extremity of Easter—the
embodied resurrection that follows Holy Saturday (and our various personal
Holy Saturdays)—should at least encourage the *possibility* of living in hope.
The kenotic gift that premises both of these states ought to inspire us to live in
love, which is clearly what both Balthasar and Trier counsel as the best way to
look at Christianity: the belligerent, unfailing, unconditional love that God has

for us, a love that is a truly miraculous and unique gift. Trier is after such provocations; and he concludes *Breaking the Waves* in such a radical style that it invites us to interpret these claims with the appropriate theological gravity. Trier comments:

> It's about taking the miracle seriously. Dreyer's film about Jesus was supposed to end with the crucifixion, but he stressed that he wouldn't mind having it ending with the resurrection, that is the miracle. It was just more practical to end with the crucifixion. As a general rule, Dreyer goes for the miracle.[92]

By sounding the bells out from thin air ("there's nothing on the radar"), Trier goes for the miracle as well. His shameless and romanticized aesthetic exaggeration becomes effectively legitimated in its conjunction with the theological subtext of the film. In fact, it is at this point that the text of the film is out of the closet as an overtly theological exemplum. Trier proclaims a fundamental truth of Christianity, a confession of faith and the power of faithful vision. Clearly, like Dreyer, he is not after "some sort of abstraction"[93] but insists on the *real presence* of the bells—the actuality of bells ringing that are a musical hosanna to celebrate Jan's recovery, the actuality of bells ringing as a formal ratification sign of Bess's loving self-donation upon her beloved for all time. In this sense, Trier is again employing decidedly Catholic imagery, a dramatic version of the miraculous sacramentality of human experience. As O'Connor once quipped about the Eucharist: "If it's a symbol to hell with it"; Trier is making as bold a claim: "a miracle shouldn't have to be credible in relation to reality, for then it's not a miracle."[94] A miracle, as Balthasar demonstrates, is the Glory of the Lord, a formal, finite expression of the absolute.

The key in the extremity of Trier's vision (insisting on miracles, upping the ante at every turn) is that of Theo-Drama. It is not so much an affront to realism, as most critics of the film complain, but a radical challenge to believers: Christianity is and has ever been a radical proposition. To deny its miraculous character is to deny Christianity as a valid and relevant theology. Trier is suggesting, precisely, an ontological ground for exposing one face of Christianity in his portrayal of a mentally ill character that turns out to be the healthiest and "truest" person out there. Furthermore, Trier is challenging the default interpretive machinery that we employ in our approach to aesthetic and dramatic art by reclaiming ground for the religious critic. Trier is speaking quite loudly and without equivocation that Christianity is always and ever countercultural. Dramatic art serves human meaning by suggesting palpable inroads to the miraculous revelation of transcendental truth.

A disposition toward theological aesthetics helps us *see the form* of "He (who) is before all things and in him all things hold together."[95] To behold the immutable radiance that is impressed upon form inclines us toward Theo-Drama and aids us in seeing the action of God. We behold the multivalent stages on which God acts in the world and how we, in our various roles and missions, participate in this dynamic action. We will now examine how the combination of aesthetics and dramatics is *both* premised upon *and* culminates in God's logic. Let us then turn to chapter 5 to fix again upon Balthasar and the nature of his theological program, to explore how his *Theo-Logic* informs the theology of literary and aesthetic expression.

5

Therapy

No Creature Stands Alone before God

Funny is not the opposite of serious, it is the opposite of not-funny.
—G. K. Chesterton, 1920

True humor springs more from the heart than from the head; it is not contempt, its essence is love.
—Thomas Carlyle, c. 1840

There are two kinds of people in the world: those who divide the world up into two kinds of people and those that don't.
—Dom Joseph Warrilow, 1986

Love does not come to man 'from outside' because the human spirit is tied to the senses, but because love exists only between persons, a fact that every philosophy tends to forget.
—Hans Urs von Balthasar, 1963

God's Logic: Revelation and Participation

J'espere en Toi por nous.

—Gabriel Marcel

The sensitivity to the theological content embedded in narrative art "makes room" for a needed renaissance in both aesthetic making and aesthetic theory. Balthasar's theodramatic theory, as one example, establishes the significant contribution that art provides for meaning-making in a language (and, of course, an imagination) that critical theorists in today's culture, with their emphasis on political action and *praxis*, will find more palatable. As Balthasar asserts,

"All knowledge of God is mediated through the contingency of the world. . . . If we did not have this implicit recognition of God's transcendence, we would never be able to draw any inference from this world to God."[1] Dramatic art, as one such mediation, has always demonstrated a keen understanding for the contingent nature of human experience and continues to serve as one of the many "analogies" of understanding, one of the many media that makes meaning more legible. Trier's portrayal of Bess, from this perspective, creates a fresh context for Christian understanding—that is, for understanding the mystery of Christ's action in our own historical context—and so serves us as a culturally perceptive approach to post-figuring the never-ending event of Christ, as the revealed location of meaning, at the dawn of the new millennium.

As I have consistently posited throughout my entire discussion, both aesthetic making and dramatic action have, by their nature, a sacramental quality about them. Following Balthasar's articulation of theological aesthetics, an informed consideration of the transcendentals reveals the way that art can be an *expressio*, a "language" of divine *presence*. Both the aesthetic artifact and dramatic performance can provide an articulated image or sense experience that, at once, manifests, points to, but also *conceals* some aspect of the divine. An artistic experience, at the very moment it "speaks" (say in a painting or a film), also conceals its fullness. Dramatic performance, to draw out the phenomenon perhaps more rustically, is like a thrusting fist in malleable clay: the impression is remarkably strong and enduring, but the removal of the fist also leaves a gap, that is, it leaves a residue of presence, an impression whose absence now becomes missed or even mourned. George Steiner dwells on this phenomenon most acutely in his *Real Presences* (1989), and his analysis of the "empty space" that attends the artistic experience has proven to be a profoundly prophetic account of the uneasy relationship that has escalated among philosophy, aesthetics, and theology:

> The density of God's absence, the edge of presence in that absence, is no empty dialectical twist. The phenomenology is quite elementary: it is like the recession from us of one whom we have loved or sought to love or of one before whom we have dwelt in fear. The distancing is, then, charged with the pressures of a nearness out of reach, of a remembrance torn at the edges. It is this absent "thereness," in the death-camps, in the laying waste of a grimed planet, which is articulate in the master texts of our age. It lies in Kafka's parables, in the meanings of Golgotha in Beckett's *Endgame*, in the Psalms to no-one of Paul Celan. It is the reverse of Kierkegaard's phrase, where the helper is no longer the help, but one still resonant with recent reading, that the futile light flashes on the execution of Joseph K., that Beckett's Malone lurches into nullity.
>
> It is only when the question of the existence or non-existence of God will have lost all actuality, it is only when, as logical positivism teaches, it will have been recognized and felt to be strictly nonsensical, that we shall inhabit a scientific-secular world. Educated

opinion has, to a greater or lesser degree, entered upon this new freedom. For it, emptiness is precisely and only that. General sentiment may follow; or it may, most threateningly, aspire to religious fundamentalism and *kitsch* ideologies.[2]

Steiner suggests that the "absence" of God produces at least a double bind. The ascendance of science as intellectual lingua franca has produced, moreover, at least two negative by-products: an atrophy of wonder and a diminished capacity for engaging a bona fide religious imagination. At the same time, the relegation of God-talk by the intelligentsia to the realm of pious superstition or mere folklore has created an unproductive backlash of theological anti-intellectualism from some quarters and has, in turn, produced manifold occurrences of both religious fundamentalism and kitsch ideologies. These are significant developments; and the negative assessment of the age forecasted by Steiner clearly conjures another prophetic voice, that of the Irish poet W. B. Yeats, who laments in verse a major symptom of modern rupture: "the best lack all conviction while the worst are full of passionate intensity."[3]

Balthasar, while monitoring this situation closely, is not as pessimistic as Steiner. Balthasar has done well to illustrate that the phenomenon of presence—how the deep impression that God makes in the world—does not, paradoxically, terminate in a kind of limbo or in an abyss of an empty space, as the majority of postmodern theory suggests. It flowers out, rather, a surge of multifaceted spiritual expression made manifest in speech, creative making, and action. As a specifically Catholic theologian, Balthasar exhorts us to *see the form* and encourages us to delimit our vision by remaining open to the freedom and variety of God's gracious presentation. However, this is not to say that postmodern scholars have it all wrong and are misguided in their focus on *aporia* and *khora* (on gaps, the traces left behind, and the unnamable surplus of meaning), for they certainly are not. A concern with the lacunae that makes its mysterious abode in existence and experience underscores the theological tradition that the world is ruptured; and questions about "traces" of meaning stem from authentic wonder at this sense of loss and, whether consciously or not, seek after a whiff of understanding, an inkling of restoration. Too often, however, it appears that we have not yet to come to grips with the deep theological reality these gaps signify; or, if we have, we are not prepared to admit that the nature of the gaps demands that we recalibrate and revise our basic theological assumptions so that we might step out from the safe trenches of our belief. Our view may well hold that God has vanished from the world stage and that we are alone; but have we thought seriously about what the "vanished one," to use critical theorist Michel de Certeau's term, might be after in this theological arrangement?[4] What might be the logic of this erasure? What, if anything, purports to "take its place"? If we have not considered these questions or revised the scope of our imagination, we have obstructed essential avenues that help us make sense of the world. Steiner, for his part, believes that we have reached this point—that postmodern critics, in their strip-mining of the theological properties inherent in language and aesthetics, have become, by their own devices, "metaphysically tone-deaf."[5]

Balthasar is especially mindful of the ruptures that attend the now institutionalized machinery of postmodern thought and culture. However, in the same spirit of postmodernity, he offers a sustained critique of the logic that has produced such structures, but with one difference: Balthasar does this so as to reorient our view and refix our gaze on a theological center. God's logic, though it may manifest itself variably and constructively in the world, ultimately cannot be equivocated with human logic. As the capstone of his trilogy, Balthasar's three-volume *Theo-Logic* is devoted to presenting this position systematically—indeed as the very truth of the cosmos. As such, the work serves as the finale to his innovative consideration of the transcendentals. *Theo-Logic*, then, is a vastly complex work; it seeks, in each volume, to examine truth (in different modalities)—*The Truth of the World, The Truth of God, The Spirit of Truth*—and, for this reason, unlike *Theo-Drama*, it tends to be a deeply cerebral treatment of theological subject matter. This is especially the case on volumes 2 and 3 of the work; and it essential to note that, while these volumes were finished well after Balthasar finished both his aesthetics and dramatics (in the 1980s and not long before Balthasar died), the first volume was written in 1946, well before he began his magnum opus. Beginning his large trilogy *in media res* is yet another indicator of Balthasar's trilogistic panache. His formal choice endows his entire program with a sense of narrative structure, the alpha and omega of a great theological plot.

A brief survey in current scholarly discourses will indicate that it is notoriously presumptuous (or, at minimum, naïve) to make absolute truth claims in any format. Yet *Theo-Logic*, for all of its cross-volume certainty that truth is found in God and formed in Christ, also supports the incomprehensibility of truth.[6] As we observed earlier, truth dwells not in the sludge of slow dualisms, as Balthasar has taken great pains to demonstrate at every opportunity, but rather in the vigorous "circumincessive relation" of the *imago Trinitatis*.[7] Truth is as nimble as Christ, to invoke again the theological poetics of Hopkins. Following the theology of Richard of St. Victor (d. 1179), Balthasar proposes our direct collaboration in the trinitarian enterprise, in which trinitarian theology is specifically linked with human encounter and human community.[8] This configuration suggests that theological truth is a relational concept and that it demands openness and participation, or, as Balthasar posits: "The 'I,' giving itself to the 'thou,' becomes really itself for the first time, the two being realized in a 'we' that transcends their egoisms."[9] More important, Balthasar recognizes—following the model of subsistent relationships within the Trinity along with the history of God incarnate recounted in the gospel—that truth reaches out to others, that truth is love: "There is an order here: love presupposes knowledge, while knowledge presupposes being . . . the very existence of truth, of eternal truth, is grounded in love."[10] In volume 1 of the *Theo-Logic*, Balthasar offers both a philosophical and lyrical account of this proposition; and whereas volumes 2 and 3 often seem like a high-wire act in philosophical theology, volume 1 is an immediately accessible and practicable tract. In its judicious consideration, appreciation, and application of the broad disciplinary spectrum, *The Truth of the World* reads much like a pioneering piece in critical theory. Moreover, Balthasar's attention to practical issues in the social sciences, such as subject formation, interpersonal relationships, and the ethics of love, serves as an early if unexpected artifact in postmodern discourse. For this reason, my focus in applying Balthasar's *Theo-Logic* to narrative art in this chapter will derive mainly from volume 1, *The Truth of the World*.

As a classically trained scholar, Balthasar knows that philosophy and theology always draw life from each other; however, as Nichols identifies, the gospel ultimately "purifies rationality."[11] The Event of Jesus crushes all categories of understanding, *a priori*, *a posteriori*, and beyond, and asserts, in real time and space, the supratemporal truth that Christ is norm.[12] The gospel, then, with its uniquely historical sensibility, illuminates and recovers rationality. In this spirit, the "Catholic thinker," according to Balthasar, will "describe the truth of the world in its prevailing worldly quality (*Welthafigtkeit*) without thereby excluding the possibility that the world thus described contains elements of directly divine, supernatural provenance."[13] Of course, for Balthasar, the *practical* means that brings to light this wide expanse of truth remains located in our ability (and, of course, in our desire and our willingness) to understand and engage the analogical potential of the transcendentals. For the purposes of this chapter, like the chapters that precede it, *practical* means employing a select piece of narrative art in order to facilitate the presentation of significant aspects of Balthasar's *Theo-Logic*.

Language, Imagination, and Lodge's *Therapy*: The Theological Significance of Persons in Relation

My own conscience is quite clear. The three of us are the best of friends. We're going off together for a little autumn break. To Copenhagen. It was my idea. You could call it a pilgrimage.

—David Lodge, *Therapy*

Such is the final movement of David Lodge's 1995 novel, *Therapy*, the text that hosts the literary application of this chapter. Whereas Lodge concludes his novel with a not-so-subtle endorsement of the trinitarian imagination, Balthasar, however, begins *The Truth of the World* with a kind of eulogy that mourns the philosophical pathology that occludes such an imagination. As if waking the dead (in the Irish sense of the term), he laments the chasm that has cleaved the space between philosophy and theology (he writes that the philosophical discourse of the twentieth century is "entrenched in the intra-worldly" and that theology "floats on its foundation of air")[14] and links the alienation between the two disciplines to the dependency upon the machinery of "violent" dualisms that underpin and describe modern philosophy. By Balthasar's reckoning, the extremity of this division reaches its apotheosis in the person and work of Friedrich Nietzsche (1844–1900), who, following Kant, described the transcendentals as "categories" of thought, not of being. Balthasar, in direct contradiction to Nietzsche, asserts: "The transcendentals are not categories. Categories have finite content and so can be de-fined against one another. The transcendentals, by contrast, are all pervasive and, therefore, mutually immanent qualities of being as such."[15] Balthasar humorously admits that his assertion risks "a drubbing from Nietzsche"[16] and that Nietzsche would take him to task for commingling the transcendentals too wantonly ("It is unworthy for a philosopher to say, 'the good and the beautiful are one'; if he has the audacity to add 'so is the true,' he should be soundly beaten").[17] And Nietzsche, who clearly prefigured the postmodern temperament, makes a list of valid points in his refusal to grant the veracity that the ancient metaphysical scheme of the transcendentals invokes. The true, good, and beautiful are certainly nice concepts, but we are in our rights to ask, "Have we seen them lately?" Does the action of the world support the fantastic assertion that there is such a thing as transcendental truth? Can we not cast aside childish things and match our ideas about "God" with the maturity of our scientific and technological developments? Certainly, we may pay a kind of lip service to "God," but there is not the broader reality on which the transcendentals are premised: there is not much of "the practice of God" going on. God, at least in the way Christianity describes God, really is dead. Who would want such an impotent, unimaginative God anyway?

As we have seen, however, it is not quite so simple. In the time that has elapsed since the philosophical assassination of God in the nineteenth century, theologians, academics, and thinkers of all stripes have been scrambling about in an attempt to reconfigure ontological structures with respect to this grand erasure. What Nietzsche and his camp sought to declare was noble enough— that human beings had power. The power he proclaimed, furthermore, can be viewed as an inevitable and just repudiation of Hegel's indefatigable idealism that had, hitherto, governed continental philosophy. It also served as necessary critique against the narcotizing influence of believing in Christianity, especially as an emotional crutch. However, while Nietzsche understood the importance of realism and the necessity of considering humankind in its fleshy and evanescent context(s), he failed to understand the teleological implications of human beings in relation. This is profoundly important to note in that it locates a precise break with another soaring figure from nineteenth-century idealism, Soren Kierkegaard (1813–1855), who is a central figure in Lodge's narrative and a key theologian in Balthasar's structural conception of the religious imagination.[18] Nietzsche's task was to liberate the person from the chains of an illusion within which persons were held, with the tenets of philosophy and religion (especially Christianity) as taskmasters. But he neglected to understand the mysterious irony that humans are most fully empowered when they turn to one another in community and, furthermore, that human culture, as "creaturely," originates and participates materially in the trinitarian community of God. Nietzsche, while sympathetic to the "radical inwardness" that Kierkegaard proposed, altered it significantly by refixing the trajectory of "inwardness" firmly upon the human sphere. Nietzsche diagrammed the world not as a trinitarian community but as a collection of self-sufficient egos.[19] This represents a major philosophical transvaluation and is an explicit rejection of the kind of community that Kierkegaard's Christianity, even with its emphasis on individualism, entails. But persons, we witness time and again, are not so easily atomized. Since the death of God was meant to liberate us, why is it that we continue to encounter the same (and, more often, worse) psychospiritual problems that plagued our ancestors? As we assert our personal agency vigorously in the world, how is it that we also are struck dumb by the void(s) that our assertions of power creates? What about the sharp increase in cases of depression?[20] What about despair? One answer seems to be that God is not so easily "offed" and that substituting mechanical alternatives in the place of authentic theological reflection leads to self-destruction and to nihilism. Balthasar condemns Nietzsche's logic, his "hollowing out of the transcendentals," and writes: "Neither goodness, beauty, or truth is exhausted by any definition; the multi-dimension reality of the transcendentals can never be flattened out by any kind of reduction, and there is no way to capture the mystery either of their existence or their essence in a formula. Of course, the ultimate ground of the mysterious character inherent in the knowable is disclosed only when we recognize that every possible object of knowledge is creaturely, in other words, that its ultimate truth lies hidden in the mind of the Creator, who alone can speak the eternal name of things."[21] Such is the province of *Theo-logic*.

Today's culture is still reeling from the snuffing out of God, but this onslaught, in the end, has demanded new clarity in our discourses and has provided sharp and textured responses in a variety of academic disciplines. The conversation between theologians and critical theorists, as I suggested at the outset of this book, has livened up and produced a wealth of keen humanistic insight into the matter. Much of this conversation, as we have posited, has to do with language (and theology has always been aware of power of words); but a renewed interest in both linguistics and semiotics has come to characterize our efforts to discuss theology in environments that are often hostile to it. Postmodern theory, as we have shown, is also deeply concerned with language and signs and demonstrates the fact that how we choose to discuss theoretical concepts can be as important as what we say about them. For example, shall we call an individual simply an "individual" or rather a "subject," an "ego," a "self," a "soul," a "unit," or a "person"? Shall we call what is not an individual a "group," a "body" (whether figuratively, literally, or even mystically), a "menace," a "state," a "church," a "collective," or, mysteriously, an "Other"? The nomenclature we employ will certainly color our remarks because—and criticaltheory is wise in this regard—language is performative. Language discloses and reveals, as George Steiner proposes, "a substantiation,"[22] that is, how we view ourselves substantively. Language performs being, performs presence, and, most important, describes relationship.

The Catholic Imagination (D): Outposts
of the Trinitarian Imagination

Sometimes from a high point on the road, you could look down on the Camino
ribboning for miles ahead, with pilgrims in ones and twos and larger clusters
strung out along it like beads as far as the horizon, just as it might have looked
in the Middle Ages.

—David Lodge, *Therapy*

We arrive now at an important place in our pilgrimage: the point at which we
begin to end this discussion. Like the pilgrimage in Lodge's *Therapy*, Balthasar's
theological program concludes in the illumination of the mystery of relationship, in the declaration that relationship pumps the very heart of God. The
logic of God asserts that all existence originates and participates in the structural vibrancy of the trinitarian dynamic. More important, perhaps, Balthasar
is more concerned with demonstrating that the *imago Trinitatis* unfolds upon
the world stage, and, that with the gift of human freedom (which contributes to the rich structure of existential drama), comes the challenge to assent or
reject the form of existence. Balthasar terms this phenomenon as essentially
"aesthetic" and assesses it "as something properly theological, namely as the
reception, perceived with the eyes of faith, of the self-interpreting glory of
the sovereign free love of God."[23] As Balthasar demonstrates in *Theo-Drama*,
the mission of humankind is not so much to stand back and clinically observe this proposition but to enter into it—as a statement of identity, imagination, and will—in order to participate in it. As Balthasar concludes, following, again, Henri de Lubac, "it is the essence of the gift of freedom to be able to
choose one's own highest value, thereby realizing oneself for the very first
time."[24] This choice, Balthasar continues, isolates the call to personhood and
situates personhood precisely in the realm of relationship: "For being a person
always presupposes a positive relation to some fellow person, a form of sym-
pathy or at least a natural inclination and involvement."[25] Such a configuration
of individuality challenges the notion of postmodern subjectivity, as we will
observe in Lodge's novel as it interrogates the theological potential of Kierkegaardian existentialism that quietly informs our age. It also recovers the unique sense of mission that is predicated upon human persons: "subjects"
might be consigned to an intramundane struggle, but "persons" are uniquely
engaged in a transcending *telos*, an eschatological journey within the trinitarian
community of God.

    To be sure, this journey, while serious, does not have to be devoid of com-
edy and humor; and a theological consideration of narrative art reminds us
that, while experiencing tragedy or wallowing in ambiguity might divide human community and isolate persons, comedy can function as a unifying force,
or, as William Lynch writes, "Comedy is perpetually reminding the uprooted
great man that in some important sense, he once was, and still is, a bit of

a monkey."[26] Furthermore, a healthy concept of humor discloses the position that the ideas of joy and reconciliation are fundamentally trinitarian and eschatological in nature, as Dante, the de facto patron of theological aesthetics, does so well to commemorate in his *Divine Comedy* (c. 1321). The central hinge of this chapter, then, is to examine the erasure of God that I spoke of above and to juxtapose this erasure against David Lodge's vastly comedic (and theologically astute) novel *Therapy*.[27] Lodge does very well to illustrate that the erasure of God significantly affects contemporary conceptions about "subject formation" and "people in relation"; but he makes this claim with a theologically aesthetic flair by constructing a narrative that moves through the tripartite stages of Kierkegaardian theological formation and by illuminating the shrouded vitality of humor inchoate within Kierkegaard's system. Humor, after all, because it is premised on incongruities between things as they are and things as we hope they would be, is the main premise that initiates Kierkegaard's "absurd" leap of faith. The "stages" of Lodge's novel mirror the existential progression of the well-known Kierkegaardian "stages" (the *aesthetic*, the *ethical*, and the *religious*); but more important, for the purposes of this discussion, the stages propose a direct analogy with the transcendentals, which illumines one of the many reasons that Balthasar admired Kierkegaard and that Kierkegaard is a major figure in Balthasar's work—so much so that Nichols calls Balthasar "the new Kierkegaard."[28] The analogy, quite obviously, is extended further when we consider how the Kierkegaardian stages apply directly to the "phases" of Balthasar's tripartite theological program. For this reason, I will develop a reading of Lodge's novel that navigates this thrice-tiered terrain, juxtaposing Kierkegaard against Balthasar at each literary phase of the novel in order to demonstrate how a careful consideration of *Therapy* will provide both an aesthetic and dramatic route to making sense of *Theo-Logic*.[29]

Finally, in order to illustrate the broad theological chasm that can exist within the "same" critical school (or, more likely, to illustrate how postmodernism, finally, resists one theological definition), I will engage in one last discourse with postmodernism. I will begin my reading of the novel with a look at two postmodern critics who come from wildly different philosophical and theological stances—the cultural theorist (and now, more than ever, religious literary critic) René Girard, and the literary critic Judith Butler, who specializes in theories of power and subjection. I will conclude the chapter by incorporating the work of a third figure, the Jewish personalist theologian Martin Buber (1878–1965), who, as another important interlocutor for Balthasar, will aid closing this work fixed on the appropriate theological signature: love.[30] One may ask, "Why this unlikely trio?" The answer is twofold: (1) the Theo-Logic that Balthasar proposes, with its fixation on the warm *circumincession* of the divine Trinity, is an intimate subtext in every source, and (2) the mysterious logic of this "personalist" God who is ever turning toward us resides precisely in the notion of "turning," that is, in our ability to see and participate in the divine dance (*perichoresis*) of God. In their respective visions of subject formation, all three (along with Balthasar and Kierkegaard), place a heavy—if dissimilar—emphasis on the phenomenon of "the turn." And Lodge does as well, for the motivation of the existential odyssey of his protagonist is nothing if not an urge to return. And while we may realize, like O'Connor, "that conversion is the hardest thing to write about,"[31] the compression of many sources upon our topic will demonstrate just how prolific and interdisciplinary the phenomenon of conversion tends to be.

The People Next Door

When she asks me where I get these ideas from, I tell her magazines and books, and she's quite satisfied.

—David Lodge, *Therapy*

One of René Girard's many contributions to the repository of cultural and literary theory is his work on *mimetic desire*. In Girardian jargon, mimetic desire is practically synonymous with *mimesis*: "mimesis evokes desire, desire constitutes mimesis."[32] Mimetic desire, according to Girard, is an unconscious and biologically rooted tendency to imitate others. As "interdividual"[33] beings, our ontological identity (as a subject, as a person) is constituted by the "other." As a subject struggles "to be," he or she runs headlong into a series of "model obstacles" (i.e., parents, siblings, institutions). The subject, out of jealousy, desire, and the like, imitates the model-object, whereby the subject, in a phased ontological progression, gains personality. In watered-down, Freudian terminology, the mimetic dynamic can be worded thus: "Since dad has mom, I must want mom, too," or even, later on in one's development, "Hortense has a shiny new BMW. A BMW is what I need." The ultimate result of mimetic desire, in most cases, is rivalry—the desire to supplant dad or to be like my "successful" neighbor, Hortense. This rivalry, furthermore, when exhausted by its journey along the ontological path, usually ends up in violence. The subject becomes prone to the extreme possibilities of suicide and "murder" (of the "model-obstacle") or other more psychospiritual forms of violence such as schizophrenia, the assumption or escape into a new identity, or the descent into the mundane world of vanity and despair, to name a few.

Although Girard has been vocal in his insistence that mimetic desire tends toward violence and is potentially destructive,[34] his fundamental view is that the phenomenon is neither bad nor good. Rather, it is "structural" and therefore neutral—in the same way that Kierkegaard's aesthetic stage is neutral or in the way that Balthasar's transcendental beauty, as self-evident and normative, is neutral. Since mimetic desire (and, indeed, a preoccupation with the aesthetic) is so deeply rooted in humanity, it is simply a behavioral pathology proper to humans. Mimesis, moreover, is an element of many philosophical systems and has been contemplated through the ages. An essential component of Girard's mimetic theory, however, is the existence of a "good mimesis." According to Girard, mimesis normally converts to (often unbridled) desire and tends toward violence; and humanity, left to its own devices and self-created structures, seems to leave the mark of violence at every turn. A critical reading of a variety of mythopoeic literature, humanity's wellspring of remembrance, will testify to the millennia-wide blight of violence (and particularly, for Girard, of "scapegoating") that has often characterized human culture.[35] Girard, as both an anthropologist and a convert (to Catholicism), sees a way to conflate the psychological structure of mimesis with the historical manifestation of God in order to propose a unique anthropology of the cross. In this way, the blight of violence is thwarted first by the Incarnation of God but then, most decisively, by the *kenotic* action of the cross: "By dissipating all this ignorance, the Cross triumphs over the powers, brings them into ridicule and exposes the pitiful secret of the mechanism of sacralization. The Cross derives its dissolving capacity from the fact that it makes plain the workings of what can now only be seen—after the Crucifixion—as evil."[36]

A new mimesis is disclosed specifically through the Cross and, of course, in the ways Jesus addressed a thriving system of blame, scapegoating, and violence on his way to the Cross. According to Girard, since "violence is the controlling agent in every form of mythic or cultural structure . . . only a non-violent deity (i.e., Christ) can signal his existence to mankind only by becoming driven out by violence—by demonstrating that he is not able to remain in the Kingdom of Violence."[37] In his departure from these structures, Christ "frees us from their dominance"[38] or at least shows us *how* to be free. The appearance of Christ in the world, then, as O'Connor's Misfit pines in *A Good Man Is Hard to Find*, decenters the world and changes its trajectory ("Jesus thown everything off balance").[39] Christ becomes the new model, and the opportunity for mimetic liberation is born.

But Girard is careful to stick to his postmodernist guns. Mimesis, he concludes, is, finally, an indeterminate phenomenon: it "is 'undecidable,' in the sense that it is decided in common with the model," who may or may not be *seen*: "a good model will make our mimesis good (Christ) and a bad model will make our mimesis rivalrous."[40] Christ, then, for Girard, is the "good mimesis" or the "good contagion"[41] that can inspire and model nonviolent mimesis for those who are open to the gospel message. This imitation of Christ results in an ultimate "turning" in a subject, a revolution or, in short, a *conversion*.[42] The subject becomes emancipated in this Girardian "Conversionary Mimesis"[43]— he or she turns inward and toward and is turned around yet again by the model of human love, the Christ.

Clearly David Lodge's postmodern hero, Laurence Passmore, can be read in one way as a prime example of Girardian mimetic desire. Laurence (or "Tubby," as he is more often called in the text) especially manifests aspects of the phenomenon early in the novel, in his "aesthetic stage." Tubby precariously bobbles on an injured knee (or what he calls his "internally deranged knee")[44] and makes his way through modern bourgeois society. Tubby, responding to years of cultural conditioning, operates like a curious ape with a checkbook. He has always done what he "should" with his life and has pursued the dreams of any card-carrying member of the consumerist middle class. Tubby takes stock:

Under the "good column" I wrote:

1. Professionally successful
2. Well-off
3. Good health
4. Stable marriage
5. Kids successfully launched in adult life
6. Nice house
7. Great car
8. As many holidays as I want[45]

Yet with all of these creature comforts and emblems of success, Tubby "feels unhappy most of the time."[46] It is not (necessarily) that what Tubby has or seeks to attain has no value or is crass, inappropriate, and makes him unhappy; it is that he cannot gain authentic happiness from owning these things. In fact, like many in our radically consumerist culture, Tubby is being consumed by the very things he himself consumes. In any event, something is missing. He hungers after these things because his urge to be like others has been validated by a half-century of clever advertisements and other weapons of psychological mercantilism. Such methods appeal not to the free and loving promotion of persons but, in their stoking of our unfocusable desires, to exposing the "gaps" in our lives. It is no accident that Tubby has created a sitcom called *The People Next Door*, for Lodge depicts Tubby as a character who is forever looking over his shoulder to see how the Joneses (or the Davises, in his sitcom) fill the holes. Take, for example, his "Richmobile"—an automobile (a Lexus, the text clearly indicates) that is finely engineered, rated favorably by automotive experts, and is actually a car that Tubby likes and one that he can afford to buy. For weeks he drives by the dealer and smiles at the car but only decides to purchase it when another consumer actually buys the model that he wanted (Tubby perceives) from right out under him: "A couple of days later, I drove past the showroom and the car was missing.... Someone else had bought my car. I couldn't believe it. I felt as if my bride had been abducted on our wedding eve. I said I wanted the car. I had to have the car.... To cut a long story short, I ended up paying £1000 over the list price to gazump the chap who had just bought my car."[47] After Tubby buys the car, he rarely drives it for fear it might get scratched. The only time the car takes on any significance, beyond an object to be desired by the fellow motorists he passes on the M1, is when he imagines his old girlfriend, Maureen Kavanaugh, sitting in the passenger seat next to him,[48] which signifies, when this occurs later in the novel, two things: (1) a break— both with bad mimesis and disordered aestheticism—and (2) an arrival at a healthier stage in his ontological growth. The car becomes a rightly ordered object for Tubby and takes on a sacramental quality in that it becomes a carriage that "coincides with itself."[49] The car, then, recovers a "right" relationship: it provides comfort to true pilgrims. Moreover, the "conversionary mimesis" that Girard describes becomes enacted in Tubby when he finally *parks* the Richmobile and begins to *imitate* the pilgrims who represent a "right" relationship with the transcendent. He walks with them in community and solidarity. Pilgrim see, pilgrim do: environmentally sound, good for cardio-vascular health, and a boon to reviving an important friendship.

Balthasar read Girard, and in volume 4 of his *Theo-Drama* (*The Action*), he devotes a long section to examining the contribution Girard makes, particu-larly in the area of theological anthropology. Balthasar salutes Girard's original approach to theological studies: "Girard's is surely the most dramatic project to be undertaken in the field of soteriology and theology generally."[50] He also appreciates Girard's engagement with literary sources: "Note particularly his considerable use of great drama, especially Greek drama: he quotes practically all the plays of the three great tragedians; but he also cites Shakespeare, Cor-neille, and scenes from Cervantes and Dostoevsky."[51] Clearly, Balthasar rec-ognizes a deep kinship with Girard, especially in the way that Girard engages in cross-disciplinary study for the purposes of theological understanding. But Balthasar is also critical of the ultimate implications of Girard's work, and he lists a few of them in *The Action*. The first critique is that Girard's theories of *mimetic desire* and the scapegoat mechanism curtail, foreclose upon, or elim-inate altogether the reality of human freedom. The next is that, while Balthasar applauds Girard's theological anthropology, he ultimately thinks Girard is, in fact, *too* anthropological in his approach—Girard eschews traditional meta-physics and his "closed system," according to Balthasar, and impinges upon the possibility of transcendence. Finally, Balthasar is worried that Girard's transferal of the world's guilt onto Jesus is only a myopic "psychological un-loading" and lacks the sturdiness of ontological grounding.[52]

Still, Balthasar recognizes Girard's psychological acuity and concludes that Girard's work "has rendered us a service,"[53] particularly in tracking our basic motivations as persons. Tubby's mimetic desire and his preoccupation with aesthetic comfort, then, have resulted in a type of violence of which Girard speaks. In Tubby's case, it is a spiritual and psychical violence. Somehow, the bourgeois method that Tubby imitates and the material trappings that his de-votion to the method has produced have resulted in what appears to be a vast cultural wasteland, in which many individuals traipse about in a drugged-up haze of vanity, malaise, and quiet desperation. Even Tubby's attempts at therapy and reparation are colored by mimetic repetition. He turns from acupuncture to psychoanalysis, from aromatherapy to alcohol, sex, and drugs—a monkey-see-monkey-do consumer shopping for the latest trend in the gleaning-of-what-afflicts. Yet nothing can satisfy him, he is one of St. Augustine's "restless" ones, and he dangles in the abyss. But we will return to him later because, I say again, returning is the thing.

The Internally Deranged Knee

Turning and turning in the widening gyre
The falcon cannot hear the falconer;

Things fall apart; the center cannot hold
Mere anarchy is loosed upon the world.
—W. B. Yeats, "The Second Coming"

Judith Butler's theory of subjection and subject formation clearly owes a debt
to the nineteenth-century pioneers of existentialism, Kierkegaard and Nietzsche. It also plays an important part in the tradition of work, configured first
for the modern age by Hegel and then carried on by Freud, Melanie Klein,
and others; and it also bears a trace resemblance to Girard's mimetic theory.
In Butler, there is a mimetic pathology, but there is no "good" subjection *per se*.
Instead of the opportunity for relief from the system brought on by the transcendent, Butlerian subjection is premised on a series of individual "prohibitions and foreclosures"[54] and results in a hermetically sealed psychic life
symptomotized largely by the dread of powerlessness. As with Girard, subjects
in Butler are formed through a series of "turnings" (or "tropings," as Butler has
it)[55] against roughly the same topography of classic object relations; but in
Butler, there is no possibility for relief, no chance for Girardian "conversionary
mimesis." Subjects, in Butler, are initially formed by external forces: "The
power that first appears as external, pressed upon the subject, pressing the
subject into subordination, assumes a psychic form that constitutes the subject's self-identity." The form that psychic power takes "is relentlessly marked
by the figure of turning, a turning back upon oneself, or even a turning on
oneself."[56] The turns, clearly, are aimed inward and the whole process is characterized by an *inwardness*; but the subject that Butler has in mind becomes, by
turns, increasingly insulated, just as the subject in the epigraph that frames
this section becomes insulated: Yeats's famous falcon who turns in on himself
in a foreclosed and abandoned gyre,[57] unable to hear the rescue chant of the
falconer.

The product of Butlerian subjection is often melancholy and despair. The
subject, after a series of inward turns, is left at the center with no relief:
"The turn from the object to the ego produces the ego, which substitutes for
the object lost. . . . Thus, in melancholia not only does the ego substitute for
the object, but the act of substitution *institutes as a necessary response* to or
'defense' against loss . . . (it is) the resolution of a tropological function into the
ontological effect of the self."[58] Perhaps what happens in Butler, and in those
systems that seek to create a false dichotomy between psychology and ontology,
are only half turns, are only one-winged falcons that flail and thrash about.
The first tropological moment is the precise spark that inaugurates the system
of Butlerian subjection. Subjects react to the external forces by turning inward.
They mimic and then appropriate the power that was brandished on them and
begin to do a little brandishing of their own: they look outward, they turn
inward.[59] They desire the universe of the other but are barred from this possibility by the philosophical constraints intrinsic to the view of *being* they propose. Their desire for wholeness, then, becomes negatively transmuted. This
plethora of incomplete and baseless turns creates, then, an excess of being, and
the internally deranged system cannot accommodate this vibrant swell. What

we have, then, is a sense of loss; and what remains, outside the inward spiral, is necessarily mourned.

The close consideration of Butlerian subject formation reveals tensions that get to the heart of issues in postmodern criticism, and the nihilism that accompanies Nietzsche's philosophy hits full stride in Butler. The Butlerian "turn" endorses, in its exclusion of the kenotic outpouring of the trinitarian model as a legitimate psychological option, the deep sense of nihilism inaugurated by Nietzsche's work. The hardscrabble effects of this shift in personal formation can be both subtle and nefarious: from the waning frequency of authentic encounters between persons, to the unconscious preference for disembodied relationships that the age of technology so amply provides. The turn that Balthasar proposes, however, because it is based upon and participates in the kenotic outward turn modeled in the trinitarian procession, endorses the lush abundance of human encounter, community, and relationship. One key to understanding the difference has to do again with language. Butler, on the one hand, uses the more mechanical term *subject* for individuals; Balthasar, on the other hand, while he speaks in the parlance of the age, ultimately prefers *person* ("In the first place, the subject, considered a person, has the freedom . . .").[60] The distinction is very significant and its importance cannot be underscored enough. Balthasar presages this ascendancy of this *subject* in *The Truth of the World*, and the following passage anticipates and clarifies the flaw (as far as the theological imagination is concerned) in Butler's *Psychic Life of Power*:

> It is not true then, that in order to attain self-knowledge, the ego, acting out of some sort of freedom, sets a non-ego over against itself, in order to regain itself from some other's point of view. If the ego had this kind of freedom, it would be divine from the very outset, but then it would have no need of a non-ego in order to cometo self-consciousness. In fact the contrary is true: the most marked index of the finite subject's creaturehood is the fact that it is already serving before it awakens to itself as subject. It awakens in the act of service, and henceforth it will awaken to itself in the measure that it serves in an attitude of self-forgetfulness. . . . A subject, as personal, free, and sovereign interiority, is far from being a mere *tabula rasa*, on which one can inscribe whatever happens to come to mind. . . . Because the subject is spiritual and self-conscious, it can freely determine itself. . . . This is because even the gaze with which God looks upon his creatures is not only the judging gaze of justice but also the loving gaze of mercy.[61]

Balthasar makes an important distinction. The kenotic "person" is ever prone to the "full" turn; the opposite is true for the psychologized "subject." Within the insulation of subjectivity, the freedom to "encounter" is occluded by a misguided conception of the personal ego. If the "ego" does not sense and enter into the divine *circumincession*, it is liable to descend into alienation and isolation. Still, as Balthasar suggests, this ego is never conclusively beyond God's love.

While Balthasar is critical of the subject formation that Butler has in mind, a fair consideration of it becomes useful when examining the second phase of Tubby's growth in *Therapy*, the so-called ethical phase of the novel,[62] during which Tubby assumes the mantle of the postmodern hero, adrift in empty spaces. Clearly, the type of "inwardness" that Butler promotes is also superficially akin to the kind promulgated by Kierkegaard, but, teleologically, the two views are markedly different. For Kierkegaard, the ethical sphere may give birth to inwardness; but, in its purest terms, the ethical stage is more about making sense of obligations that are external to the person than it is it is about delighting in a palpable sense of individual subjectivity. Full-blown inwardness is a theological location and is therefore reserved for Kierkegaard's religious phase. Still, something about the mystery of inwardness is learned in the ethical stage:

> When he has finished with China, he can take up Persia; when he has
> studied French, he can begin Italian; and then go on to astronomy,
> the veterinary sciences, and so forth, and always be sure of a reputa
> tion as a tremendous fellow. Inwardness has no such compass, and
> cannot arouse the astonishment of the sensuous man; inwardness
> in love does not consist in consummating seven marriages with
> Danish maidens, and then cutting loose on the French, the Italian,
> and so forth, but consists in loving one and the same woman, and
> yet being constantly renewed in the same love, making it always new
> in the luxuriant flowering of the mood.[63]

Inwardness, according to Kierkegaard, or at least the fruit of inwardness, is ripened by degrees. Once inwardness is "attained," however, it resists such rational descriptions. It becomes a phenomenon that is inexhaustible and perpetually fresh, its wisdom a matter of profundity, not novelty. We may draw an analogy here about the love between persons that springs from inwardness (in the fashion described by Kierkegaard above) and the way a mystic might approach a relationship with the Absolute. The passage also reveals a primary difference between the theological and psychological imaginations: to put it in polemical terms, one has a sense of faith and resignation and sits in beloved awe (or fear and trembling) before the transcendent; the other has a sense of isolation and abandonment and sits anxiously before an abyss nursing a detached psyche.

The truth for Tubby, more likely, is somewhere in the middle. But Lodge suggests that Tubby's psychological unease stems from the fact that he has failed to "play well" with others: "Whatever truth there might be in her complaints about my self-centeredness, moodiness, abstractedness, etc., etc. (and admittedly my inattention to the news about Jane's pregnancy was an embarrassing lapse) they didn't amount to grounds for leaving me."[64] Tubby's complaint, written in the confessional space of his personal journal, leads to other keen insights about the age in which we live. Clearly, Butler has read Kierkegaard, and Butler's theory of subjectivity would be meaningless without him; yet, whereas Kierkegaard makes his famous leap of faith, Butler's work seems not to make this option available. An empty space in Butler is the absence of the transcendent dimension. In any case, Tubby realizes he needs to make a resigned change. He decides, in the middle of the novel, that his exercise in Girardian mimetic desire has resulted in a kind of spiritual emptiness and has influenced a series of destructive, isolating turns. He consciously jettisons the toxic mode of these behavioral phenomena and begins seriously to rethink his personal development. Tubby becomes aware that he is some type of pilgrim on a road toward ultimate meaning, or at least on a road to Copenhagen, a thought that is itself a surefire sign of "ethical" thinking.[65] He begins to *choose*.

It is precisely in Kierkegaard's Copenhagen that Tubby reaches the nadir of his turning, the turning point of his U-shaped narrative. The reader begins to perceive a distinct shift in Tubby's personal *via*, a sense of hard grace, perhaps, being insinuated into his existential journey. In the Copenhagen sequence of the novel, he is clearly out to have a well-orchestrated existential event. Tubby's itinerary of Kierkegaardian haunts takes on the patina of a late modern consumerist style that believes that philosophical insight may be purchased quickly and cheaply. But what he initially envisions happening and what he ends up achieving are two very different things. He imagines that he will have lusty aesthetical romps with his young intern in between his contemplations of the ethical teachings of a great philosopher. But the reality of his situation is at once more humorous and more meaningful, something of a *felix culpa*, as far as his personal growth is concerned. Tubby disqualifies this possibility, it seems, simply by entertaining it: "The beautiful Samantha shamelessly offered me all the delights of her sumptuous body, I couldn't take advantage of it."[66] A beautiful, almost lyrical irony, to be sure, but Tubby's aridness of spirit and his unwillingness to perform indicate his "location" in Kierkegaard's ethical stage, which is a stop that guidebooks rarely mention. It is also uncertain, in Tubby's case, if his refusal of the tryst is a teleological suspension of the ethical (as Kierkegaard would posit), but certainly it is an abstention that strikes the reader both as absurd and downright funny. In any case, it becomes clear that sashaying between the two Kierkegaardian modes does not mix and that Tubby has his crotch wedged upon the fence that divides the aesthetic from the ethical realms. Tubby turns inward and rejects encounters that previously defined him. We begin to see more clearly the Butlerian inwardness described above: "My frantic, idiotic sexual odyssey after Sally walked out, trying desperately to get laid in turn by Amy, Louise, Stella, and Samantha, was my attempt at wild dissipation. But when it failed, religion was not a viable alternative for me. All I could do was wank, and write."[67] Tubby's attempts at external "dissipation" are transformed into wounds upon his ego (in line with the "Butlerian" schema), and he retreats from other people. His entire experience in Copenhagen can be classified as an introspective meeting with melancholia and inward spiraling. While Tubby "does not hurt others,"[68] he becomes atomized in the vacuum of his own ego, an isolation that Lodge delivers to the reader in an ingenious juxtaposition of mirth-provoking proportions. In the compartmentalized space of his hotel room, Tubby becomes the true psychological man: cut off from self and community, in a "dreary city,"[69] and on the phone with a woman he does not love but who is one wall away. He masturbates in front of pay-per-view pornography—and there can be no greater example of unexamined inwardness and disconnection than the solipsism of making disembodied love to images of women on television. Tubby can sink no lower: a final visit to Kierkegaard's grave signals the death of his old self, and a late-night flight home prepares his return to the world of others, his homecoming.

Back to Hatchford Five Ways and My First Breast

O sages standing in God's holy fire
As in the gold mosaic of a wall,
Come from the holy fire, perne in a gyre,
And be the singing masters of my soul.
                                   —W. B. Yeats, "Sailing to Byzantium"

The religious phase of the novel is initiated by an internal call in Tubby to *return* to his roots and sort out what has gone wrong. This process, quite common to those who have lost their way, seems to have simple directions: go back home and go from there. The metaphorical implications of this kind of turn, this turning toward home (i.e., the idea that God is "home"), furthermore, suggests the advent of Kierkegaardian inwardness in Tubby as a literary character and completes the application of the Kierkegaardian trajectory in *Therapy*. That Tubby suddenly drops everything and has a sudden religious conversion is too simplistic a reading of the novel; it is clear, however, that Lodge has given us a credible rendering of a spiritual return and psychological renewal in his depiction of a middle-aged, middle-class protagonist who goes back home in order to make amends and to rescue himself.

A judicious turn to Martin Buber complements our discussion of "the turn" and helps describe Tubby's narrative pilgrimage and the phenomenon of moving from an ethical to a religious dimension. Buber calls the urge to recover the straight path *teshuvah*, which, while it entails repentance, literally translates as "to return." Buber could have had Tubby in mind when he describes what the pilgrim must do: "This is the intent of the teaching of the return: that everyone alone and from his own depth *must strive for divine freedom and unconditionality. . . .* Nothing already accomplished by another can facilitate his own deed, for all depends on the shattering force of his own action."[70] Tubby initiates his own quest for rescue. He returns to where he first "got lost," to the five corners at Hatchford and to the ghosts of girlfriends past. This quest for recovery and clarity is not merely an ethical act of what he "should" do; in fact, to view this type of return—this attempt at reparation and the stanching of old spiritual wounds—as an ethical gesture is utterly false. For *teshuvah* is a religious act; in truth, it is "the religious act, for it is God's revelation through man."[71] Buber, then, like Kierkegaard, insists upon the preeminence of both introspection and volition in matters of religious conversion.

Balthasar admired Buber's work immensely, and the interpersonal intimacy promoted in *Theo-Logic* can be seen as both an incorporation of and homage to Buber's influential work *Ich und Du* (1923). While Balthasar is critical of Buber in that Buber's conception of the I-Thou encounter creates a scenario in which "theological speech becomes impossible to distinguish from anthropological speech,"[72] Balthasar also uses Buber's I-Thou construction multiple times in his own writing and appropriates the analogical vitality of Buber's grammatical *taxis*, especially as a resource in comprehending more fully the inherent mysteries of the trinitarian dynamic. Balthasar holds that the I-Thou structure derives from and points to a third reality, a "mysterious more," as Balthasar terms the phenomenon.[73] When the *I* and *Thou* turn to each other in mutual intimacy—in dialogue—the result is a pantheon of fecundity:

> The criterion of truth thus lodges partly in the I and partly in the Thou.
> It can be attained as a whole only in the movement of dialogue.
> The criterion within the I lies in the evidence of *cogito ergo sum*, in
> the actual experience of being and consciousness.... And yet each
> epiphany of this evidence occurs only when the spirit goes outside of
> itself in order to record its personal word in objective work in the
> world, in objective conversation with the Thou outside of itself....
> The truth of this world remains suspended between these two poles.[74]

Balthasar spends the last third of *Theo-Logic* meditating on how triadic structures owe their structural existence to dyads (such as the *I and Thou*) and reiterates the idea that this relationship describes the central movement of his analogical thinking:

> The creature's participation in God and God's revelation is thus
> analogous to the relation between the worldly expression and what
> it expresses, between matter and spirit. In the inner-worldly analogy,
> the two poles seem to be bound by a mediating third—sensory intu-
> ition or imagination, which lifts matter into the domain of spirit,
> tough without yet spiritualizing it, and, at the same time, enables
> spirit to become enrooted organically and physiologically in matter.[75]

Given the nature of this study, it is intriguing to point out that once again Balthasar locates the faculty of the imagination as one of the mysterious elements that expresses the relationship between matter and spirit.

Balthasar finds lasting kinship with Buber in that both men fix their theological gaze upon *encounter* and *love*. Under this perspective, we begin to recover the more boundless terrain of the trinitarian dynamic and see how the triadic structure of human relationships reveals something very important about the universe. In this regard, examples abound; we are struck by the astute language that the early Franciscans used to invoke the Trinity ("In the name of

The Lover, The Beloved, and Love"); we are mindful of the mystical theology of John of the Cross, who draws triadic analogies among the theological virtues of Faith, Hope, and Love and the human faculties of intellect, memory, and will; we behold creative ways in which postmodern critcal theorists, such as Julia Kristeva, conceive of the trinitarian dynamic and how it might express the topography of the psychospiritual realm: "The Trinity itself, that crown jewel of theological sophistication, evokes beyond its specific content and by virtue of the very logic of its articulation, the intricate intertwining of the three aspects of the psychic life: the symbolic, the imaginary, and the real."[76]

The Trinity, particularly as Kristeva shows us, is a relevant resource for the postmodern pilgrim, especially as a way to imagine personality and relationship. Most current notions about subject formation and personality development tend to valorize (and also isolate) the individual: "to be a human is to see myself in opposition to everybody else." Buber identifies this tendency as a classic condition of what he calls the "I-it" relationship. In the "I-it" state, our view of God—and by extension, our view of the human community—is eclipsed, and the objects that obstruct our vision of God are, tragically, of our own making. Moreover, the "I-it" phenomenon as a sociological description, even in Buber's day, was in full bloom. If in the early twentieth century the "I-it" was the default location of culture, how much more descriptive is it now in an age that has elevated the consumerist ethos to a form of religion? When our fundamental relationships are fueled by the desire for money, social status, or other transferable commodities, when we choose to relate with one another out of fundamental self-interest, we are dwelling in the "I-it" universe. We eclipse God and so consign ourselves, by our own agency, to a fate that excludes God. The challenge, of course, is to defy the anthropological gravity of the "I-it" vacuum and to be in genuine relationship with one another and so with God. In Buber, this phenomenon is accomplished and represented by authentic persons relating with one another in an authentic community—the "Shalom Yahweh" of traditional Judaism—a relationship that links the present moment with eternity:

> The I of the basic word I-You is different from the that of the basic word-It. The I of the basic word I-It appears as an ego and becomes conscious of itself as a subject (of experience and use). The I of the basic word I-You appears as a person and becomes conscious of itself as subjectivity (without any dependent genitives). Egos appear by setting themselves apart from other egos. Persons appear by entering into relation with other persons.[77]

Buber at once predicts and refutes the Butlerian subject—the subject who is formed by the turning away from objects and whose ego is "produced" in this turning. The subjects produced by the narrowness of psychical (and entropic, which is yet another variety of turn) turnings seem to have no hope except to be disjointed and disconnected egos. By limiting the scope of the turn, by "bending back, on the other hand, turns God into an object," as Buber holds.

"It appears to be a turning toward the primal ground," Buber continues, "but belongs in truth to the world movement of turning away."[78] Persons, as illustrated in Lodge's depiction of Tubby, are formed by their desire to turn outward to others, to be in relation with others. It is in this turning that we remember our original state: we remember (even if it is a trace) our original relationship with God and "turn" toward it. Buber is decisive here: "It is in the return that the word is born on earth; in spreading out it enters the chrysalis of religion; in a new return it gives birth to itself with new wings.[79] It is in this type of turning that we transcend.

The type of turning that is here described resonates intimately with the passage from Yeats that frames this section. The excerpt, from "Sailing to Byzantium," can be read as a poetic version of the phenomenon of *teshuvah*. The falcon in "The Second Coming" was abandoned in an isolated gyre and things fall apart; in "Byzantium," there is an additional element introduced, the figure of a *perne*, which is a spool formed by the interpenetration of two whirling cones or gyres.[80] The poet asks that the sages whirl down from the "holy fire" so that their spinning motion is united with his own soul and becomes its "singing master." The difference between Yeats's two poems is the precise difference between two postmodern views of the person: one view is fragmentary and situates the subject as detached from the whole, a lone spool; the other view seeks communion while affirming the dignity of the individual, a spool in relation, if you will. Buber's philosophy, then, serves as a counter-friction to schismatic views of the person, views "that are based on the gigantic delusion that spirit occurs in man. In truth it occurs from man—between man and what he is not. As the spirit bent back into itself renounces this sense, the sense of relation, he must draw into man that which is not man, he must psychologize world and God. This is the psychical delusion of the spirit."[81] Spirits bent thus impede our path to God and cause an eclipse. Buber stokes our memory of God and recalls our primary relationships. The "spirit" that is not delusional is in concert with the person; the "spirit" from Buber's point of view actually is the person, for Buber's theology is also critical of the Cartesian split. The spirit is ordered toward convergence: in the individual person, in community, in God.

Ultimately, we do not see this type of relationship in Kierkegaard, which reveals again the variety of perspectives that exist within the theological imagination. Whereas Kierkegaard, Buber, and Balthasar are in concert on the issue of choice and resignation, they are at odds over the questions of mediation and grace. Buber exhorts us toward community in our religious quest, in which community becomes an important sign of holy mediation. Balthasar appropriates Buber's dynamic personalism and envisions it as an example of divine *perichoresis*, the divine dance of trinitarian participation realized by a procession of love. In this schema, God inaugurates the vitality of mediation and conciliation by the very structure of Godself, that is, by the triune nature of God. But Kierkegaard insists upon the dualistic structure of "either/or," that *we* choose to live in mediation or *one* chooses to live in the tension of the eternal paradox of the absurdity of belief:

The thing becomes far more difficult when one would ask about the religious in the strictest sense of the word, in which case the explanation cannot consist in infinitizing man through immanence, but in becoming aware of the paradox and holding the paradox fast every moment. Paradox... is essentially conditioned by the fact that a man is in existence.... And what then follows? Nothing, nothing at all.[82]

To speak of this phenomenon in terms of the novel is to speak in terms of *grace*; and we come to the point at which Lodge, quite conclusively, steers us away from a simple Kierkegaardian philosophical/literary application. In the conclusion to the novel, Tubby chooses the "radical communitarian" option, thus departing markedly from the acute subjectivity and inwardness inherent in the Kierkegaardian pathology.[83] This, of course, represents a significant break—both theologically (for reasons I adduced above) and narratively (because the parallel story between Tubby and Kierkegaard ends on the road to Santiago). Tubby's "religious" phase, moreover, is mediated specifically through the trinitarian turn to community, which, of course, to follow the prospectus of the I-Thou encounter that Buber lays out, finds that both its motivation and its by-product is love. I don't think Lodge suggests that Tubby arrives at a graceful tension between immanence and transcendence, but his "slow, looping dawdle along the Camino"—his pilgrimage along the path of St. James—is certainly a start. Tubby's experience is clearly no Damascus experience (and Lodge, as a realist, is not interested in lightning-bolt conversions); but Tubby's odyssey discloses a profound spiritual truth about the uniqueness of human need. Balthasar, again, is insightful about the human *pathos* inherent in this mysterious progression: "Because the full truth can be attained only in love, only the lover can have the real eye for it. He alone is ready to disclose himself truly and thus bring to completion the movement in which the truth of being comes into existence."[84]

Central to Buber's vision—and what Tubby finally intuits is necessary in his own life in ways that are finally un-Kierkegaardian—is the idea of convergence, or what Buber calls *encounter*. Encounter, Buber proposes, is truly authentic and meaningful when the will of the person is mission oriented and unencumbered by caprice: "The capricious man does not believe and encounter. He does not know association; he only knows the feverish world out there and his feverish desire to use it,"[85] which clearly would describe Tubby in his aesthetic mode—out for larks and transient mollycoddles at feverish clips, an "unhappy hoper" aloof, even, from the advertisement of himself.[86] However, as Tubby transitions into his religious phase, a phase that is colored more by human *encounter* than it is by isolated *subjectivity*, Tubby drops all of the whimsy of popular therapy, and as a result, his entire person becomes focused on "Maureen in all her specificity. Maureen. My first love. My first breast."[87]

Lodge emblematizes Tubby's growth imaginatively by mining the irony of Maureen's breast. As an adolescent, Tubby adored her breasts: "How I longed to see them, and to suck and nuzzle them and bury my head in the warm valley

between them,"[88] but his inability to see Maureen's anatomy as anything beyond an "object of attachment," coupled with his incapacity to behold the per-
son-behind-the-breast, sets him (as it has many others) upon the "I-it" course.
As a young man, he does not see Maureen at all, just her body. However, as a
pilgrim approaching the *camino* of the religious stage, Tubby encounters
Maureen's breast with a more developed understanding. Between these encounters much has transpired in the lives of each character. Maureen has battled
breast cancer and has lost one of her own, lost something of her very self. When,
on their pilgrimage together, the couple first share an intimate bedroom encounter, Tubby reacts to the missing breast: "It was a shock, of course"; but then
he immediately "unbuttoned the front of her nightdress and kissed the puck-
ered flesh where her breast had been."[89] This gesture was both "the nicest thing
anybody ever did" for Maureen and an indication that, just as Maureen's chest
has been transformed, so, too, has Tubby's ability to relate to people in transformed ways. Tubby's new sense of Maureen is no less "embodied," but his
vision of Maureen is converted and focused upon more than the mere synec-
doche (i.e., the breast) of her personhood. Tubby's encounter with Maureen—
who personifies his original sense of intimacy and community—discloses the
dramatic realism inherent in a credible spiritual journey and serves as a good
example of an I-Thou encounter. By encountering properly, Tubby, it seems,
becomes a man recalled to himself, or as Buber has it:

> Now he no longer interferes, nor does he merely allow things to
> happen. He listens to that which grows, to the way of Being in the
> world, not in order to be carried along by it but rather in order to
> actualize it in the manner in which it, needing him, wants to be
> actualized by him—with human spirit and human deed, with hu-
> man life and human death. He believes, I said; but this implies: he
> encounters.[90]

Tubby's return to Maureen results in both an inadvertent pilgrimage to
Santiago de Campostela and a credible literary depiction of an encounter with
grace. The encounter, as Buber suggests, does not turn out the way that Tubby
necessarily intends it to, but it turns out for the best since it originates from
authentic good will. Tubby does not interfere, nor does he merely allow things
to happen. As Tubby muses, "The true pilgrim was the religious pilgrim, religious in the Kierkegaardian sense. To Kierkegaard, Christianity was 'absurd'—
if it were entirely rational, there would be no merit in believing it. The whole
point was that you chose to believe without rational compulsion—you made a
leap into the void and in the process chose yourself."[91] Tubby, then, in his
embrace of the *return* (and the implications for community that the "return"
entails) invites righteousness upon himself. A cloak of faith quietly descends
over his entire existence—past, present, and future, aesthetic, ethical, and
religious—and brings peace. "My own conscience is quite clear,"[92] says Tubby,
a conscience that opts to journey in warm human fellowship, to Copenhagen

and beyond, with Maureen and Kierkegaard, strolling upon a knee now cured of its internal derangement.

In *The Varieties of Religious Experience* (1902), William James links such moments of psychological growth directly to the mystery of transcendence. While James is careful not to assert any specific theological program, he states strongly that religious experience always seems to entail the kind of paradox that Tubby experiences in *Therapy*: surrender leads to freedom, vulnerability leads to strength. James observes:

> There is a state of mind, known to religious men, but to no others, in which the will to assert ourselves and hold our own has been displaced by a willingness to close our mouths and be nothing in the floods and waterspouts of God. . . . The time for tension in our soul is over, and that of happy relaxation, of calm deep breathing, of an eternal present, with no discordant future to be anxious about, has arrived.[93]

A fair amount of twentieth-century psychology has genealogically linked the kind of "peak experience" Tubby undergoes to the nebulous realm of "religious experience"; but most theorists, in ways that are significantly more conservative to those of James, are reticent when it comes to naming precise theologies that might define or describe such peak experiences more narrowly. Again, we are confronted with issues in grammar and imagination. What is *Pelagianism* to the theologian may be *self-reliance* to the social historian. As religious critic Ed Block points out, a psychologist such as Abraham Maslow might term Tubby's experience a "Cognition of Being." Balthasar (and others disposed toward a theological imagination) would not necessarily strike such terminology from the equation but would add that such cognition is not merely a mechanical event proper to all humans: cognition, rather, is the physiological route of divine *revelation*, both an act and emblem of divine grace working through finite structures to imprint upon and influence the consciousness of the human person.

The Catholic Imagination (E)—Seeing the Form and Con-Forming to the Seen: At Home in the Trinity

It is a wonderful thing to see a first-rate philosopher at prayer. Tough-minded thinking and tenderhearted reverence are friends, not enemies. We have for too long separated the head from the heart, and we are the lesser for it. We love God with the mind and we love God with the heart. In reality, we are descending with the mind into the heart and there standing before God in ceaseless wonder and endless praise. As the mind and the heart work in concert, a kind of "loving rationality" pervades all we say and do. This brings unity to us and glory to God.
—Kierkegaard, *The Prayers of Soren Kierkegaard*

As Pelagian as *Therapy* might appear to the critic with theological sensibilities, a close reading of the novel will reveal how divine grace propels the narrative at almost every turn. *Therapy*, of course, is also an excellent novel to read against theories in psychology, especially in its lighthearted parody of our attempts to grow as persons, even against the curious machinery of the psychology industry. But the novel, in a unique and pointed way, transcends the psychological realm and becomes a reasonable study on the possibility of grace in our own postmodern context. Of course, as discussed last chapter, grace may make its presence known in a dramatic hierophany—a flash of lightning, the music of bells ringing inexplicably above the North Sea that "breaks the waves"—but a more credible account of grace finds that grace expresses itself inexhaustibly in everyday things—the smell of bread baking, a conversation with an old friend. Lodge offers such a vision in his novel, and his approach of tracking grace through the world of finite things—objects, structures, and personal relationships—reveals his realist sensibility as sacramental artist.

My hope in this chapter was to stress how a posture of *turning toward others* can be a posture that analogically links human persons to the trinitarian *perichoresis*. As Buber wisely demonstrates, it is precisely in a dialogic, outward turn that we place ourselves in position to develop the authentic encounter between the *I* and *Thou*. The ingredients for completing this process, of course, are graciously supplied by God. Balthasar interprets this phenomenon as the "truth in the world" and locates it also in the dialogical "empty space" between the *I* and *Thou*, a space that is "neither a mere being nor a mere becoming."[94] This is the place of the "inconclusible movement" of God, the place that, because it is the location of dialogue and relationship, is also the location of palpable, incarnated truth. Balthasar expands: "Truth without life, without dialogue, would immediately cease to have any meaning: it would be an unveiling, but no longer an unveiling for anyone, a word that no longer would be heard or answered, a light that could no longer shine because of lack of air."[95] The open turn to the other, in fact, reveals Theo-Logic. More important, it reveals that God's logic is love, that "God is Love."[96] Balthasar concludes:

> Once again, then, we see that the sense of truth as a whole is *love*. We have seen that the unveiling of being transcends the I in order to attain the completion of the Thou. We have seen, then, that the *logos* becomes the *dialogos*, which is to say, a communication that can never be closed again.[97]

As an expert theologian of the Trinity, Catherine LaCugna has an important place in this discussion, and her insights help tie the various strands of this chapter together. Her extraordinary work *God for Us: The Trinity and Christian Life* (1991) revitalizes the logic of the trinitarian imagination by recovering the early roots of trinitarian doctrine. More important, LaCugna demonstrates the enduringly practical dimensions of conceiving our faith in God as a loving community of persons. She writes:

God is interactive, neither solitary nor isolated. Human beings are created in the image of the relational God and are gradually being perfected in that image (*theōsis*), making more and more real the communion of all creatures with one another. The doctrine of the Trinity stresses the relational character of personhood over and against the reduction of personhood to individual self-consciousness, and also emphasizes the uniqueness and integrity of personhood over and against the reduction of personhood to a product of social relations. Thus it can serve as a critique of cultural norms of personhood, whether that of "rugged individualism" or "me first" morality.[98]

The free gift of God's loving, Lacugna continues, is precisely the concept that informs the way we ought to imagine our "selves," for as "the supremely personal font of all existence, God is turned toward another."[99] This turning, again, is kenotic, unmerited, and inexhaustible because God is love; and his love, as the prophet Joel sings, "is unrelenting."[100] LaCugna concludes:

God begets the Son from this Love, God breathes forth the spirit from this Love, God creates everything to exist eternally from this Love.... God does not have to be loved in order to love. This is not the situation of the creature who learns to love in response to being loved. God is Love itself and the origin of Love, that is to say, God is the origin of existence.[101]

Because love is the fullest expression of theological intelligence, it occupies the very heart of Balthasar's theological program. Love is its beginning (i.e., its aesthetic beauty), its middle (i.e., its dramatic action), and its end (i.e., both its Theo-Logic and its *teleo*-logic). Love is our *exitus* and our *reditus*, our *proodos* and *epistrophe*. Love stands strong between all of our polarities: the universal and particular, the essential and existential, *doxa* and *praxis*, past and present. Love is, as Balthasar encourages, our simple sturdy truth, "the ground that accounts for truth and enables it to be." And love, he continues, is God: "To be sure, God is eternal truth and by this truth, all other things are true and meaningful. But the very existence of truth, of eternal truth, is grounded in love."[102] The urge for return, then, is the urge toward loving relationship. Some will call it "karma" or "closure," and others will deem it a reconciliation, a moment of the "Shalom Yahweh," a *kairos* expression within "the kingdom of God." I think the urge to return is both the memory and the hope of who we are as persons who dwell with one another. It reveals our innate sense of journey, that we are eschatologically oriented and that our relationships constitute a shared sense of *telos*, a shared mission together in the body of God.

Finally, as literary critic Paul Fiddes reports, "The idea that human persons are created to participate in the relational life of the triune God has become quite widespread in recent theology, owing a good deal to the recovery of the thought of the early Eastern Fathers of the Church."[103] Certainly this is true; but it is a fact that Balthasar (and the theologians of *ressourcement*) has both known and guarded dearly through the turbulent days of modernism.

The trinitarian imagination was always a most healthy philosophical option in that it befuddles the polarities of the Enlightenment dualist. Moreover, it accounts well for the empty space that piques the interest of postmodern scholars. Fiddes provides a most constructive assessment of the re/turn to Trinity, employing the language of the age:

> This space opened up for created beings is felt to be the nothing or empty place of apophatic theology, and the nameless *khora* of such thinkers as Heidegger, Derrida, and Kristeva, because there are no infinite subjects present making the relations and dominating presence. But this emptiness is at the same time a fullness, a *pleroma*, because the space is surrounded and inter-penetrated by active *perichoretic* movements of giving (sending, responding, and opening), and passive movements of receiving (being glorified, being sent, and being breathed out).[104]

Balthasar's entire theology, then, provides us with a great service. Its trinitarian heart, exposed at so many turns, but chiefly through the transcendentals, is able to do what the Catholic imagination has always sought to do: negotiate opposites. The Catholic imagination, then, is one version of a broader theological vision, one that conceives of the large integrity of the cosmos while "making the mysterious space for creaturely spontaneities."[105] The Trinity, finally, asserts its own identity upon us: the loving gift of true community. Balthasar concludes:

> In the community that comes into being through the son's eternal *communio*, everyone is utterly open and available to each other, but this openness is not like the total perspicuity of states or situations; instead we have free persons freely available to each other on the basis of the unfathomable distinctness of each. What is offered to the other is thus always an unexpected and surprising gift.[106]

And this is God's challenge to us: to use our imaginations in order to see, to act, to know, and to love.

6

Coda

On the Theological Imagination

He knew the precise psychological moment when to say nothing.
—Oscar Wilde, 1890

Let the kind reader refrain from weighing every one of my words
with a gold-scale. Let him rather pick a nugget here or there, if he
comes across one.
—Hans Urs von Balthasar, 1986

My foray into the possibility of a Catholic imagination has been fruitful. Balthasar's creative engagement with the transcendentals demonstrates how a judicious methodology that emphasizes analogical
relationships can reveal much about the trinitarian mystery of God.
It is perhaps refreshing that Balthasar does not reiterate an approach
that conceives of analogical relationships from the "top down," as
traditional trinitarian theology does; rather, Balthasar moves from
the historical event of Jesus, from the paschal mystery that is recorded
in the Gospels, in order to illuminate the cosmological mystery of
trinitarian relationality. From a very immediate, context-based sense,
we are challenged to apprehend a dynamic of God's action that invites us to faithful acknowledgment and intimate participation at
the same moment that it demands submission to the radical incomprehensibility of God's purpose.

We have also found that Balthasar's program challenges us not
only to first "see the form" in the world, but also to see the beautiful, the good and the true at work in a broad array of narrative art.
At the same time Balthasar's unique theological method provides
us with some practical directives that aid in formally elucidating
the presence and veracity of such a vision. Clearly, the Catholic

imagination does not have a monopoly on such tendencies, as I have endeavored to show; but it is also clear that artists of a Catholic temperament return to these ways of imagining the world—of imagining God—in order to draw meaning from imagination, to find a coincidence in opposites, and to find *similarity in difference*. In many cases, such a return is facilitated effectively by the turn to many disciplines, that is, by a turn to interdisciplinarity, for interdiciplinarity seeks to demonstrate and endorse *the great symphony of truth*, to use Balthasar's term, and to provide a stage for "conceptual interpenetration."[1] By the same token, interdisciplinarity also discloses the gaps and angles at which "truth" is dissonant, or rather the places where the great mystery of what-is-true clangs loudly in its very discordance or whose presence shines brightly, even, in its very absence.

It is perhaps more important to note, especially in regard to the context in which we find ourselves, that my examination of the Catholic imagination has helped recover the legitimate place of a "theological imagination" in the critical study of literary and narrative art. In my attempt to explore tendencies of a Catholic imagination, I have found that it is precisely this restoration of theological imagination to discourses in meaning that will aid in reestablishing "a theology of criticism," that is, the kind of criticism that cultivates a more inclusive array of epistemologies. A reappraisal of the theological imagination is essentially a call to scholarly balance, a call to reorient our interpretive gaze upon substantive meaning in addition to the transmission of meaning. We have also found through this exercise that postmodernism, while preconceived by many to be a threat to theological meaning, actually may aid in the enterprise of constructing careful and credible theological analyses. Postmodernism, with its careful critique of entrenched philosophical assumptions and reiterated codes of meaning, can provide both critics and theologians alike with the tools that assess, challenge, and celebrate the theological imagination as it is depicted today. More important, perhaps, postmodernism is helping develop a vital—and interdisciplinary—theology of language.

A famous genealogy is fastened to studies in the imagination, one that becomes, all of a sudden, beyond the scope of my discussion. Hume, Kant, Hegel, and Coleridge, among many others, have all commented broadly on the imagination as a human faculty and on the imagination's role in human "knowing." In many instances, these philosophers developed the theological potential of the imagination (especially in Coleridge's case, who, as a poet and theologian, as a practitioner of theological aesthetics, deserves special praise here), but in most cases, the imagination has been traditionally distrusted as a defining source of theological and philosophical knowledge. Balthasar's program, though, for all its abstract and conceptual language, relies specifically on the practicality of imagination and portrays it as a cognitive faculty that aids in presenting the "actual." The well-tuned imagination is occupied with "seeing the form" of God, a paradoxical process that entails both deeper disclosure and deeper concealment.[2] But the imagination is also the faculty that seeks and contemplates concealment, the sense of "remainder," or what Balthasar calls the "something more," without which "there would be neither knowing nor anything to be known."[3] This "mysterious more" is what enables the human person to sense deep beauty and follow it to philosophical and theological meaning. The imagination, according to Balthasar, "is what alone enables us to appreciate works of art"; it "reveals itself as so rich that it satisfies (our) entire need for truth."[4] In order to see what is there, the imagination helps us navigate discourses that insist on grounded ontology between those that are more airborne and speculative.

The imagination is vigilant. It remains thirsty for expression. The imagination demands that we work with it and listen to it, that we develop a relationship with it. As Lynch scholar Gerald Bednar proposes:

> Art is for humanity what nature is for God. Imagination frees a person
> from subjectivity by the creation of art whereby the self becomes
> objectified, real, and in relation to concrete reality. Imagination lib-
> erates the person from the confines of the self. Through acts of
> creative imagination, a person becomes real. It is there that a person
> 'imitates' God, or participates in the divine, most closely.[5]

It is precisely in this sense, this call to participation with the beautiful, that the imagination continues to reveal its theological orientation. Bednar suggests further that this relationship (following the late Enlightenment philosopher Friedrich Schelling [1775–1854]) has both an erotic and procreative quality about it, in that the imagination is primarily a form of love. The imagination is connatural with the author of love, with the Creator, and therefore reaches out in relationality so as to invite creativity and participation.[6] According to Bednar, the imagination "bears all the freedom, as well as all the responsibility, of love";[7] and love, as Balthasar illustrates so persuasively in *Theo-Logic*, is indivisible from truth: "Love is inseparable from truth.... Love is not something lying on the farther side of truth. Rather, it is the element in truth that guarantees it an ever-new mystery behind every unveiling."[8] Imagination connects love and truth; imagination provides for the very ontology of love. We must conclude, then, after all concepts fall so quickly by the wayside, that love provides the center for both the Catholic imagination and the theological imagination. Love guarantees a posture of openness that is ready to receive every new revelation of God's great unveiling, every gracious outpouring of God's great love.

Balthasar offers one compass for the theological imagination. My examination of select examples of art under his influence and methodology illustrates how artistic expression works through the finite in order to reveal the credibility of a unique critical vision. My conclusion is that interrogating the Catholic imagination through the lens of Balthasar's tripartite program has revealed its three most essential tendencies, tendencies that derive, however broadly, from the analogical attributes that each transcendental reveals: the Catholic imagination is *incarnational*, *sacramental*, and *trinitarian*. Jesus, as the incarnational "form" and kenotic outpouring of God's own imagination, is the one who uniquely invites us into the divine dance of God. This invitation to love sacralizes the great drama of our otherwise mundane existence in the very same motion that it creates a broad metaphysics of community and relationship. In order to "see this form," a cultivated sense of beauty is vital in every instance. The form of beauty initiates the journey that is both our longing and our home. The ethics of beauty demands that we enter all situations in justice, honesty, and peace. The logic of beauty is both its origination and objective of love, the love that is always prepared for authentic encounter. A cultivated sense of beauty is but one way we can know that we are truly living.

So the final word rightly belongs to beauty, belongs to the poetic imagination that, without translation or qualification, sees how unfathomable beauty dwells among us. To see the nature of beauty most clearly, we must become, as Marianne Moore advises in her poem "Poetry" (1935), "literalists of the imagination"; to participate in the grace of beautymost faithfully, we'd do well, as Denise Levertov counsels in "On Belief in the Physical Resurrection of Jesus" (1981), to enter into its mystery—into the miracle of Christ's incessant Eucharist—with the totality of our being:

> It is for all
>   "literalists of the imagination,"
>   poets or not,
> that miracle
>   is possible,
>   possible and essential.
> Are some intricate minds
>   nourished
>   on concept,
> as epiphytes flourish
>   high in the canopy?
>   Can they
> subsist on light,
>   on the half
>   of metaphor that's not
> grounded in dust, grit,
>   heavy
>   carnal clay?
> Do signs contain and utter,
>   for them
>   all the reality
> that they need? Resurrection, for them,
>   an internal power, but not
>   a matter of flesh?
> For the others,
>   of whom I am one,
>   miracles (ultimate need, bread
> of life) are miracles just because
>   people so tuned to the humdrum laws;

gravity, mortality—
    can't open
       to symbol's power
unless convinced of its ground,
      its roots
        in bone and blood.
We must feel
   the pulse of the wound
      to believe
that "with God
  all things
    are possible,"
taste
  bread at Emmaus
    that warm hands
broke and blessed.[9]

Notes

CHAPTER I

1. Graham Ward, *Theology and Contemporary Critical Theory* (New York: St. Martin's Press, 1996), ix.

2. For an excellent discussion about literature as a prime model of thought and consciousness, see David Lodge, *Consciousness and the Novel: Connected Essays* (Cambridge, MA: Harvard University Press, 2002).

3. While this examination is not primarily an historical study, history is still a vital part of it. There is a genealogy to the Catholic imagination that needs to be recognized as a subtext, and the Catholic literary revival of the early twentieth century is of particular import in this regard. The movement began primarily in France in the years between the world wars and was characterized by its antimodernist/antipositivist bent. Poet/philosopher/bordello resident Leon Blòy (1846–1917) was essential to the early formation of the revival (and later Blòy became particularly instrumental in the conversion of the great neo-Thomist philosopher Jacques Maritain and his wife, Raissa). Playwright/poet Paul Claudel (1868–1955) was also a significant figure. The movement was always interdisciplinary but reached literary heights in the 1930s with the work of Georges Bernanos (1888–1948), François Mauriac (1885–1970), and the Franco-American Julien Green (1900–1998). The French-Catholic revival became a flash point for a larger Catholic revival that had worldwide influence in the later decades of the twentieth century.

4. Pierre Rousellot, *The Intellectualism of St. Thomas*, trans. James O'Mahoney (New York: Sheed & Ward, 1935), III.

5. As Maritain writes: "Let us rouse ourselves, let us stop living in dreams or in the magic of images and formulas, of words, of signs, of practical symbols. Once man has been awakened to the reality of existence and his own existence, when he has really perceived that formidable, sometimes elating, sometimes sickening or maddening fact that I exist, he is henceforth possessed by the intuition of being and the implications it bears with it" (Jacques Maritain, *Approaches to God* [New York: Collier, 1954], 18).

6. *TL 1*, 235.

7. William Lynch, *Christ and Prometheus: A New Image of the Secular* (Notre Dame: University of Notre Dame Press, 1970), 23.

8. *GL 1*, 125.

9. "As it was used in the thirteenth century, 'transcendent' means an aspect of reality which extends beyond categorical divisions . . . is part of reality before it is separated into categories . . . is a property common to every existent" (Francesca Aran Murphy, *Christ, the Form of Beauty: A Study of Theology and Literature* [Edinburgh, T & T Clark, 1995], 216). Murphy also points out a vital distinction that is relevant to my thesis: while for the scholastics the transcendentals regulated reality, for Kant, by contrast, they regulated thought only.

10. Balthasar devotes over three hundred pages to "subjective evidence" in the first volume of *The Glory of the Lord*: "We can already see how unsatisfactory those theologies are which, by a process of abstract isolation, disengage the Christian act of faith from all elements of insight and understanding and then proceed to analyse it in purified form" (*GL 1*, 139)

11. See S. L. Greenslade, ed., *Early Latin Theology* (Philadelphia: The Westminster Press, 1954), 10.

12. Editor's introduction, *Renascence* 52, no. 1 (Winter 1996): 6.

13. Augustine, *De Musica*, book 6, cited in Albert Hofstadter and Richard Kuhns, eds. *Philosophies of Art and Beauty* (Chicago: University of Chicago Press, 1964), 199.

14. Denise Levertov, *Poems 1960–1967* (New York: New Directions, 1983), 73.

15. Catherine Pickstock, *After Writing: On the Liturgical Consummation of Philosophy* (Oxford: Blackwell, 1998), 262–63.

16. *TH 20*, 90–91.

17. *GL 2*, 127.

18. Henri de Lubac, "A Witness of Christ in the Church,"in Hans Urs von Balthasar: His Life and Work, David Schindler (ed), (San Francisco: Ignatius Press, 1991), 272.

19. Aidan Nichols, *Say It Is Pentecost* (New York: Catholic University Press, 2001), 211.

20. Hans Urs von Balthasar, *Truth Is Symphonic: Aspects of Christian Pluralism*, trans. Graham Harrison (San Francisco: Ignatius Press, 1990), 7–8.

21. *TL 1*, 140.

22. Ibid., 144.

23. See Frank Burch Brown, *Religious Aesthetics: A Theological Study of Making and Meaning* (Princeton: Princeton University Press, 1989), 4.

24. *GL 1*, 80.

25. Dante, *The Divine Comedy, Paradiso*, XXXIII, 145, trans. Dorothy. Sayers and Barbara. Reynolds (London: Penguin, 1962), 347.

26. See Balthasar, *Explorations in Theology: The Word Made Flesh* (San Francisco: Ignatius Press, 1989), 206.

27. G. K. Chesterton, *Orthodoxy* (San Francisco: Ignatius Press, 1995), 190. The first edition was published in 1908.

28. Balthasar, *Test Everything: Hold Fast to Everything That Is Good*, trans. Maria Shrady (San Francisco: Ignatius Press, 1989), 51.

29. Gerard Manley Hopkins, "As king fishers catch fire . . ." from *The Selected Poems and Prose of Gerard Manly Hopkins*, ed. W. H. Gardner (Middlesex: Penguin, 1953), 51.

30. Gerard Manley Hopkins, *The Sermons and Devotional Writings of Gerard Manley Hopkins*, ed. C. Devlin, S.J. (1959), cited in Balthasar, *Studies in Theological Style: Lay Styles*, vol. 3, *The Glory of the Lord: A Theological Aesthetics*, ed. John Riches, trans. Andrew Louth, John Saward, Martin Simon, and Rowan Williams (San Francisco: Ignatius Press, 1984), 385.

31. Balthasar, *Test Everything*, 48.

32. *TL 1*, 147.

33. Ward, *Theology and Contemporary Critical Theory*, 2.

34. Ibid., 10.

35. See Luke Ferretter, *Towards a Christian Literary Theory* (New York: Palgrave McMillan, 2003), 28. In his 1968 essay *"differance,"* Derrida insists that the notion of difference is fundamentally different than negative theology even though "the detours, locutions and syntax in which I will often have to take recourse will resemble those of negative theology, occasionally even to the point of being indistinguishable from negative theology" (ibid., 19). In 1968, Derrida was a self-avowed atheist. In the years before his recent death, he did not declare his theological location in such final terms—much to the delight, we can speculate, of his late mother who, in some kind of oblique parody of the relationship between Augustine and his mother, Monica, was ever afraid to ask young Jacques if he still believed in God because she was afraid he'd say no. In 1991, Derrida mused aloud that his mother "must have known the constancy of God in my life called by other names and that he has 'an absolved, absolutely private language' in which he speaks to God all the time" (John Caputo, *The Prayers and Tears of Jacques Derrida: Religion without Religion* [Bloomington: Indiana University Press, 1997], xvii–xviii).

36. *Khora* is a place that "eludes all anthropo-theological schemes, all history, all revelation, all truth" (Jacques Derrida, *Khora*, trans. Ian McLeod, in *On the Name*, ed. Thomas Dutoit [Stanford: Stanford University Press, 1995], 124). *On the Name* is a compiled text of three essays and does not exist in France.

37. John Guare, *Six Degrees of Separation* (New York: Vintage/Random House, 1990), 118.

38. Caputo, *Prayers and Tears of Jacques Derrida*, 35–36.

39. To paraphrase Augustine's logic on divine representation, the logic that Derrida takes up: Augustine holds that if God is a word, then he is spoken. But if it is said that God is unspoken, then he is ineffable. Yet, the message of the Incarnation is that God is something, but who can speak this word? No one can but he who is the word. So, God is a word that speaks itself.

40. Lucy Gardner and David Moss draw out further connections between Balthasar and postmodernity. In their essay "Something Like Time; Something Like the Sexes—an Essay on Reception," Gardner and Moss dwell on further linguistic comparisons that generate when we read Balthasar and Derrida together. How are our words, gestures, and giving of signs, "the textuality of life," related to the Word of God and the spirit of the writer (Lucy Gardner, David Moss, Ben Quash, and Graham Ward, *Balthasar at the End of Modernity* [Edinburgh: T & T Clark, 1999], 69–138).

41. *GL 1*, 527.

42. Graham Ward, "Kenosis: Death, Discourse, and Resurrection" in *Balthasar at the End of Modernity*, 55.

43. Ibid.

44. Paul Giles, *American Catholic Arts and Fictions: Culture, Ideology, and Aesthetics* (Cambridge: Cambridge University Press, 1992), 23.

45. Ibid., 30.

46. *TD* 2, 320.

47. *TL* 1, 138.

48. Paul Fiddes, *The Promised End: Eschatology in Theology and Literature* (London: Blackwell, 2000), 254.

49. David Schindler, *Heart of the World, Center of the Church*: Communio, *Ecclesiology, Liberalism, and Liberation* (Edinburgh: T & T Clark, 1996), 210.

CHAPTER 2

1. Henri de Lubac, "A Witness of Christ in the Church,"in *Hans Urs von Balthasar: His Life and Work*, David Schindler (ed), (San Francisco: Ignatius Press, 1991), 272. It is difficult to overstate Lubac's influence on Balthasar. In Balthasar's last years, he would write a definitive study of Lubac's contribution to twentieth-century theology and ecclesiology. The rest of the quote is interesting so I include it: "This man is perhaps the most cultivated of his time. *If there is a Christian culture, then here it is!* Classical antiquity, the great European literatures, the metaphysical tradition, the history of religions, the diverse exploratory adventures of contemporary man and, above all, the sacred sciences, St. Thomas, St. Bonaventure, patrology (all of it)—not to speak just now of the Bible—none of them that is not welcomed and made vital by this great mind. Writers and poets, mystics and philosophers, old and new, Christians of all persuasions—all are called on to make their particular contribution. All these things are necessary for his final accomplishment, to a greater glory of God, the Catholic symphony."

2. Aidan Nichols, *The Word Has Been Abroad: A Guide through Balthasar's Aesthetics.* (New York: Catholic University of America Press, 1998), 3.

3. Paul Fiddes, *The Promised End: Eschatology in Theology and Literature* (London: Blackwell, 2000), 5–6.

4. Ibid., 9.

5. Ignatius of Loyola, *The Spiritual Exercises of St. Ignatius*, trans. Luis Puhl, S.J. (Chicago: Loyola University Press, 1993), 49.

6. Nichols, *The Word Has Been Abroad*, xiii.

7. Balthasar scholar David Yeago comments instructively on this concept, the idea that Jesus Christ is Word made flesh is the *universal concretum et personal*: "The advent of Jesus Christ in all its contingency is the arrival on the scene of the 'finally valid *Logos*' which surpasses, completes, and encompasses every other bestowal of meaning.' There can be for theology no more general "logos," no more universal, external standard of truth and meaning, to which Christian thought is accountable; the internal logic of the eventof Jesus Christ is itself the final criterion. Thus, any interpretive reciprocity between Christian revelation and human culture must finally be asymmetrical: it is nature which receives its meaning from grace and finds truth in grace, not vice-versa" ("Literature in the Drama of Nature and Grace, 103). Karl Barth would agree entirely with Yeago's observation; however, it is Balthasar who saw the aesthetic ramifications of the Incarnation most clearly and recast it as another form of the analogy of beauty: the *Logos* made manifest is an historical event; it is also a continually gracious event, a sacramental alive and at work in an aesthetic "artifact."

8. As Nichols reports, Balthasar issued a statement after he made his decision that discloses his rationale: "I took this step, for both sides a very grave one, after a long testing of the certainty I had reached through prayer that I was being called by God to certain definite tasks in the Church. The Society felt it could not release me to

give these tasks my undivided commitment.... So, for me, the step taken means an application of Christian obedience to God, who at any tithe has the right to call a man not only out of his physical home or his marriage, but also from his chosen spiritual home in a religious order, so that he can use him for his purposes within the Church. Any resulting advantages or disadvantages in the secular sphere were not under discussion and not taken into account" (Aidan Nichols, *Nem Blackfriars* 79, no. 923 (1998), 7. [1998]).

9. Nichols, *The Word Has Been Abroad*, xix.

10. St. Paul writes of Phoebe: "I commend to you Phoebe our sister, who is (also) a minister of the church at Cenchrae, that you may receive her in the Lord in the manner worthy of the holy ones, and help her in whatever she may need from you, for she has been a benefactor to many and to me as well" (Rom. 16:1–2). Balthasar, to my knowledge, has not written on Phoebe (not enough have), who seems to be one of the several scripturally endorsed female clergy on record. Whether or not Paul would have endorsed a female clergy (Garry Wills suggests that Paul would make such an endorsement in his recent book *What Paul Meant* [New York: Viking, 2006]), Paul's approach to feminine spirituality and the contributions to the church that women have made (and can make) are unique and radical, especially when we consider the context in which he wrote. Again, I cite Balthasar's advanced Marian theology, in which the "fiat" of Mary means everything to the faith life of humans; but Balthasar has also written intimate portraits of the mystics Therese of Lisieux and Elizabeth of Dijon, portraits that amplify the unique power of feminine spirituality in the context of ecclesiological potential.

11. Henri de Lubac, "Un témoin du Christ dans l'Église: Hans Urs von Balthasar," in *Paradoxe et Mystère de l'Église* (Paris: Aubier-Montaigne, 1967), 185.

12. Werner Löser quoted in *America*, October 16, 1999. Available: http://web .archive.org/web/20010501181954/www.findarticles.com/cf_0/m1321/11_181/ 56201143/p3/article.jhtml?term.

13. John Allen, "Debating Karl Rahner and Hans Urs von Balthasar; Interview with David Schindler; Appointments in the Roman Curia; Archbishop Laurent Monsengwo of Kisangani," *NCR* 3, no. 7 (November 2003). Available: http:// www.nationalcatholicreporter.org/word/word112803.htm.

14. Werner Löser quoted in *America*, October 16, 1999. Available: http://web .archive.org/web/20020907134545/www.findarticles.com/cf_0/m1321/11_181/ 56201143/p1/article.jhtml.

15. *TH*, 23.

16. Stratford Caldecott, "An Introduction to Hans Urs von Balthasar," *Second Spring* (November 2001). Available: http://www.catholiceducation.org/articles/ religion/re0486.html.

17. As Lutheran theologian George Lindbeck astutely observed in a 1994 interview: "It's strange to think that von Balthasar, not least in view of his critique of Marian maximalism, was once thought of as on the far left instead of on the far right, where some try to locate him now. *Ressourcement*, it seems, leads to the margins—or to martyrdom. The miracle of the Council is that the conjunction of forces was such that an authentic return to the sources could, for a moment, capture the center" (*First Things* 48 [December 1994]: 47).

18. *LAC*, 114–15.

19. Peter Casarella, "The Expression and Form of the Word: Trinitarian Hermeneutics and the Sacramentality of Language in Hans Urs von Balthasar's Theology," *Renascence* 48, no. 2 (Winter 1996): 118.

20. Balthasar, *Test Everything: Hold Fast to Everything That Is Good*, trans. Maria Shrady (San Francisco: Ignatius Press, 1989), 51.

21. Balthasar, "The Fathers, the Scholastics, and Ourselves," originally published in 1939 as "Patristik, Scholastik und wir: *theologie der Zeit*" (Ensiedeln: Johannes Verlag, 1939), 51.

22. We are careful here to avoid any condemnation of the faculty of reason. I reiterate: it is the inordinate emphasis on reason that Balthasar's work indicts. Equally, Balthasar (and other *ressourcement* theologians) indicts an overemphasis on beauty, for that would flow into the flaw of mere *aestheticism*, something that Wilde may have practiced before "Reading Gaol" and *De Profundis*. Pope Benedict XVI, writing as Joseph Ratzinger, comments thoughtfully on the matter: "People wondered: where was God when the gas chambers were operating? This objection, which seemed reasonable enough before Auschwitz when one recognized all the atrocities of history, shows that in any case a purely harmonious concept of beauty is not enough. It cannot stand up to confrontation with the gravity of questioning about God, truth, and beauty. Apollo, who for Plato's Socrates, was the 'God' and the guarantor of unruffled beauty as 'the truly divine' is *absolutely no longer sufficient*" (Joseph Cardinal Ratzinger, "The Beauty and Truth of Christ," *L'Osservatore* Romano (6 November 2002), quoted in James Schall, "The Whole Risk for a Human Being: On the Insufficiency of Apollo," *Logos* 7, no. 2 (Spring 2004): 14. Balthasar concurs: Beauty is ultimately static and illusory without a theodramatic component. The trilogy, though it presents the transcendentals with a trinitarian logic—as fundamentally dynamic and equal in their dynamism—relies ultimately on theodramatic aesthetics. Action is the center between logic and beauty. Action teaches us to truly see Christ Jesus in the world. I'll return to Ratzinger's insight in chapter 5.

23. Balthasar, *My Work: A Retrospective* (San Francisco: Ignatius Press, 1988), 22.

24. Balthasar, "The Fathers, the Scholastics, and Ourselves," 31. One caveat must be proposed, however, as it would be foolish to conclude that *ressourcement* wouldn't tend to a romanticized view of history. Theologian Brian Daley is acute on this point, as he pines on the matter in the introduction toBalthasar's book on Maximus: "The dangers inherent in this kind of historical-theological study are obvious. Even scholars willing to acknowledge the magnitude and interpretive brilliance of this book, especially in reviews of its second edition in 1961, suggested weaknesses in von Balthasar's approach: the questions he asks of Maximus are modern questions, set by situation of French and German Catholic theology in the mid-twentieth century, and the picture of Maximus he draws is, in the end, an incorporation of substantial and authentic elements of Maximus's thought into the proportions and shadings of Balthasar's own theological enterprise." (Daley quoted in Balthasar, *Cosmic Liturgy: The Universe According to Maximus the Confessor* [San Francisco: Ignatius Press, 2003]), 16–17. Balthasar himself was fully aware of such dangers, and, even though he exhibits a timeless intimacy with patristic sources, disclaimers about the fallibility of historical investigation are threaded through his work. Rather than sit on his hands and wave farewell to the horizon of history, Balthasar continually engages it, continually participates and dialogues with it.

25. Balthasar, "The Fathers, the Scholastics, and Ourselves," 31.

26. David S. Cunningham, "The Transfiguration of Time," *Sojourners* 23 (December 1994–January 1995): 40.

27. *TL 1*, 272. Emphasis mine.

28. Balthasar, *The Threefold Garland*, trans. Erasmo Leiva-Merikakis (San Francisco: Ignatius Press, 1982), 8.

29. Colossians 1:17.

30. Balthasar, *Threefold Garland*, 8.

31. Flannery O'Connor, "Greenleaf," in *Collected Works* (New York: Library of America, 1988), 522.

32. Ibid., 523.

33. Balthasar, *Threefold Garland*, 8–9.

34. Henrici, quoted in John Peter Pham, "The Logic of Revelation" (book review), *Crisis* (October 2001). Pham has done well to nail the number down exactly and reports: "The bibliography assembled by Balthasar's literary executor, Cornelia Capol, catalogues 119 books, 532 articles, 114 contributions to other books, 110 translations (mostly into German) of both ancient and modern authors, 103 forewords and after-wards to books by other authors, 93 major book reviews, and 13 critical editions of various writers." Available: http://www.crisismagazine.com/october2001/book4.htm, or see Cornelia Capol, *Hans Urs von Balthasar. Bibliographie 1925–1980* (Einsiedeln, Johannes-Verlag 1981.)

35. Balthasar, *Bernanos: An Ecclesial Existence*, trans. Erasmo Leiva-Merikakis (San Francisco: Ignatius Press, 1996), 17, quoted in Leiva-Merikakis's introduction to Georges Bernanos, *The Heroic Face of Innocence* (Edinburgh: T & T Clark, 1999), ix.

36. Ibid.

37. *GL 2*, 168.

38. Oscar Wilde, "The Soul of Man under Socialism." Available: http://witcombe .sbc.edu/modernism/artsake.html.

39. G. K. Chesterton, *The Illustrated London News*, 12/25/09, in *Collected Works* (San Francisco: Ignatius Press, 1987), 447.

40. See. *GL 2*, 315, 335, 340–43, 348–60.

41. Ibid., 22. Cited in Nichols, *The Word Has Been Abroad*, 66.

42. Nichols, *The Word Has Been Abroad*, 68.

43. Casarella, "The Expression and Form of the Word," 131.

44. Christophe Potworowski, "An Exploration in the Notion of Objectivity in Hans Urs von Balthasar," *Renascence* 48, no. 2 (Winter 1996): 142–43.

45. Andrew Greeley, *The Catholic Imagination* (Berkeley, CA: University of California Press, 2000), 1.

46. Thomas Groome, *The Catholic Imagination: Eight Gifts for Life* (San Francisco: Harper, 2002), 82.

47. For further reading on the renaissance of studies in the Catholic imagination, see Ross Labrie, *The Catholic Imagination in American Literature* (Columbia: University of Missouri Press, 1994) and Kenneth D. Whitehead, ed., *The Catholic Imagination* (South Bend, IN: St. Augustine's Press, 2003). Labrie discusses thirteen Catholic writers chosen for their intellectual and artistic achievement and active practice of Catholicism and "focuses" on Catholic themes. Along with Daniel Berrigan and Thomas Merton, subjects include Orestes Brownson, Paul Horgan, Robert Lowell, Flannery O'Connor, and Mary Gordon. Born before Vatican II (which Labrie labels the "great divide" for Catholic writers), all share an "underlying unity of outlook" missing in the "increasingly fragmented" post-conciliar church. Labrie analyzes a representa-tive sample of each writer's work in light of the individual's particular interpretation of Catholic teaching. The study is useful as a kind of reference but does not add anything theologically compelling to conversations about the Catholic imagination. In particular, Labrie misses the opportunity to draw connections between post-Vatican II Catholic writing and the ascendancy of the critical commitments of postmodernity. He also fails to include Balthasar in his discussion. The Whitehead piece is a collection

of essays (assembled from a conference held at Creighton University in 2002. It is interesting to note here that Creighton has a fully dedicated "Catholic Imagination Project," which is part of the university mission). The collection, which seeks to locate the Catholic imagination from a cross-disciplinary perspective—architecture, music, literature, cinema—is unique in that the focus of each essay is primarily theological.

48. Paul Giles, *American Catholic Arts and Fictions: Culture, Ideology, and Aesthetics* (Cambridge: Cambridge University Press, 1992), 28.

49. Ibid.

50. Ibid., 195.

51. See *GL* 1, 241–57.

52. *TD* 2, 320.

53. Joseph Martos, *Doors to the Sacred: A Historical Introduction to Sacraments in the Catholic Church* (Ligouri, MO: Ligouri, 2001), 54.

54. For an excellent discussion on the relationship among the analogy of being, philosophy, theology, and narrative art, see Denis Donoghue, "The Analogical Imagination after *Christ and Apollo*," *Religion and Literature* 32, no. 3 (Autumn 2000): 1–22.

55. Michel de Certeau, "How Is Christianity Thinkable Today?" in *The Postmodern God* ed. Graham Ward (Oxford: Blackwell, 1997), 148. Certeau wrote extensively on Cusanus and his idea of "coincidence of opposites" and added to the discussion by means of his own work.

CHAPTER 3

1. The description of the opposing viewpoints, of course, is simplified and overly general; but it will serve well enough for the purposes of this chapter.

2. Jacques Maritain, *Creative Intuition in Art and Poetry*, Bollingen Series 35 (New York: Sheed & Ward, 1960), 80.

3. A very brief paraphrase of both Foucault's and Derrida's main philosophical planks, to be sure. There are, of course, other versions of *postmodernism*, some of which this book will address. Postmodernism viewed through the lens of Karl Rahner or David Tracy, as will show, has a decidedly different trajectory.

4. Paul Giles, *American Catholic Arts and Fictions: Culture, Ideology, and Aesthetics* (Cambridge: Cambridge University Press, 1992), 366.

5. Ibid.

6. Flannery O'Connor, *The Habit of Being*, ed. Sally Fitzgerald (New York: Farrar, Straus and Giroux), 216.

7. I'll mention this here as a promissory note of things to come: O'Connor has the tendency in her fiction to promulgate orthodox theology by drawing figures and characters who have gotten the theology exactly and diametrically wrong.

8. Walker Percy, *The Message in a Bottle* (New York: Farrar, Straus and Giroux, 1997), 116.

9. "Poetics of Incarnation" is Albert Gelpi's phrase. He employs it as the guiding rubric to "accessing" the poetry of William Everson in *The Dark God of Eros: A William Everson Reader*, ed. and introduced by Albert Gelpi (Santa Clara, CA: Santa Clara University Press, 2003), xv.

10. The "bodily" tendency toward unity that Paul espouses is also taken up elsewhere, most notably in Romans 12. Essentially, a most basic exegesis points to transcendental unity.

11. Given the tenor of his theology, one begins to see why Denys identifies with the Dionysius of Acts 17. One persuasive reason is the imaginative *kerygma* that

characterizes Paul's preaching to the Athenians: "He made from one the whole human race to dwell on the entire surface of the earth, and he fixed and ordered seasons and the boundaries of their regions" (Acts 17:26). Creation in this light refutes instantly the paganism and multiplicity of the Greek pantheon while at the same time endorsing the creative variety of God's Divine Wisdom.

12. Acts 17:28. All scripture references are from *The New American Bible* (New York: The Confraternity of Christian Doctrine, 1986.)

13. That is, *integrity* in the transcendent, totalizing, and unitive sense. As St. Paul writes: "I, then, a prisoner of the Lord, urge you to live in a manner worthy of the call you have received, with all humility and gentleness, with patience, bearing with one another through love, striving to preserve the unity of the spirit through the bond of peace: one body and one Spirit, as you were also called to the one hope of your call; on Lord and one faith, one baptism; one God and Father of all, who is over all and through all and in all" (Ephesians 4:1–6).

14. That is, the tendency to distill, to nominate; the tendency to describe mystery as mechanism or the transcendentals merely as philosophical categories.

15. *GL* 2, 107.

16. Ibid., 108.

17. Clarity about the relationship among sacramental theology, epistemology, and aesthetic theory is central to this discussion. Balthasar writes: "The concrete method that he (Denys) has in view is not a method of thought, but an always experienceable encounter, something that takes place in the presence of the mystery of the living God, known through faith. And therefore the often mentioned 'third step' beyond affirmation and negation, the transcendence, not a cognitive 'method', but the proof that there is, beyond anything that a creature can affirm or deny, only the objective superabundance of God, so that the last word of 'mystical theology' can only say that God is not only beyond all affirmations, but beyond all negations too" (*GL* 2, 206). Clearly, one "Third Step" Balthasar refers to would be the Incarnation, the salvific outpost of God's *procession*. This outpouring inaugurates the incarnational imagination and is the link between God's analogical procession and our anagogical return, especially in mystical theology. I note that it is equally incumbent upon any commentator on the analogical imagination, especially one in the postmodern milieu, to consider the full span of analogy: "David Tracy, rereading Aquinas through Rahner and Derrida, likewise stressed the tensive power of the negative implicit within Thomistic conceptualizations. The differences and the dissimilarities between the world and God are, Tracy asserted, equally as significant as those similarities upon which the analogical traditions in Catholic theology have traditionally insisted. It is the power of difference, Tracy declared, that prevents the idea of analogy from degenerating into a domesticated sense of philosophical coherence" (Giles, *American Catholic Arts and Fictions*, 366).

18. *GL* 2, 208. While I agree with Balthasar on this point, mainly because Denys's theology is located biblically and oriented toward the Trinity and because Denys says that "the Greeks had made an impious use of the divine in relation to the divine, trying by means of the wisdom of God to destroy the fear of God" (ibid.), a case can be made that Denys was being theologically creative and thus contextualizing his arguments in Platonic and Neoplatonic language for the service of Christian truth. By using language that had currency in his time, Denys illustrates his rhetorical skill. It becomes a mother tongue to facilitate the presentation of Christianity. It becomes analogical; his approach also reiterates the importance of contextual sensitivity and therefore exposes further his own (major) contributions to analogical thinking and forecasts an abundance of twentieth-century academic discourse.

19. See particularly Catherine Pickstock, *After Writing*, in which Pickstock, with a rather ingenious thesis, beats the more vapid and unmoored aspects of grammatology with its own stick. Pickstock, like many others, indicts the vivisecting nature and legacy of the Enlightenment project; but she locates ontological fissures (that show up in language, for example, aporia that exist between *sign and signified*) in willful repudiation of history. "Among the many powerful aspects of this work, or 'essay', as the author likes to call it, is the scrupulously detailed critique of postmodern culture as contradictory, deceptive, and necrophiliac. More powerful still, in the face of such morbid reality, is the work's vigorous optimism that the 'linguistic' turn" can itself 'be turned around' or converted (*convertere*: to turn back)' so as to restore the sign to its life-giving signified and to reweave death into the fabric of life" (David Williams's book review of Pickstock's work in *Religion and Literature* 31, no. 2 [Summer 1999]: 114). Among the many ways that philosophy is consummated in liturgy is by the focal point of the liturgy itself, the act of consecration. The historical words of Jesus are uttered in the context of the mass. The words of Jesus, which refer to the sign of bread and wine become identical (in *amanuensis*) to what they signify, Himself the signified Christ: "identifying with his dead body in advance of its absence or death by pointing to something outside of himself, thus claiming death as an act of giving" (Pickstock, *After Writing: On the Liturgical Consummation of Philosophy* [Malden, MA: Blackwell Publishers, 1998], 263; emphasis added).

20. Erasmo Leiva-Merikakis, *Love's Sacred Order* (San Francisco: Ignatius Press, 2000), 12.

21. Flannery O'Connor from "The Catholic Writer in the Protestant South" in *Collected Works* (New York: Library of America, 1988), 856. Whereas, in Neruda's *La Palabra*, I was interrogating the postmodern tendency to overembody reality, O'Connor is critiquing the modernist tendency to "angelize" (or "psychologize" it). The trinitarian imagination negotiates such opposites as these.

22. That language as a theological aesthetic tends toward community is perhaps the central point that distinguishes Catholic (i.e., trinitarian) imagination from most Protestant (dialectical) modes of interpretation. The distinction, of course, is not always so cut and dried, as David Tracy's seminal work *The Analogical Imagination* demonstrates. Tracy shows how the Christic imagination vacillates between analogical and dialectical modes, calling, generally, the analogical "Catholic" and the dialectical "Protestant." Donald Gelpi examines how Peirce's work exposes this logic in a different way, showing how Peirce's pragmatism "turns" toward community, whereas the modernist Catholic theologian, Bernard Lonergan, following Kant, turns toward the subject (see Donald Gelpi, *Peirce and Theology, Essays on the Authentication of Doctrine* [Lanham, MD: University Press of America, 2001), 4. Percy, of course, would be interested in these distinctions as his work embodies them aesthetically.

23. Walker Percy, in a manuscript released by *Facts*, Washington: National Endowment for the Humanities (May 3, 1989): 1. Quoted in Karl-Heinz Westarp, "Message to the Lost Self: Percy's Analysis of the Human Situation," *Renascence* 44, no. 3 (Spring 1992): 217. Balthasar holds a similar view: "Truth can be found only in a floating middle between appearance and the ting that it appears. It is only in relation between these two things that the empty mystery becomes full" (*TL 1*, 138).

24. See *LAC*, 55. Balthasar's concluding description of God's "organization" is one that Percy would certainly embrace and apply to his own philosophy of language: "Only because he is over the world is he in it. But being over it does not deprive him of the right, the power, and the Word, to reveal himself to as eternal love, to give

himself to and to make himself comprehensible even in his incomprehensibility" (*LAC*, 150).

25. I have mentioned that theological "fallen-ness" is central in both Percy and O'Connor. Francesca Murphy points out that a more recent scholar, Michael Edwards, similarly locates the embrace of philosophical egocentrism in Edenic fall, which supports, ironically, the postmodern suspicion of language and meaning. Edwards's "Christian Poetics" is particularly interesting, as Murphy observes: "His diagram circles the arch between Fall and ultimate redemption. He suggests that language itself, the vehicle of the story, is fallen. It can no longer achieve the perfect mirroring of reality with which pre-lapsarian language was gifted" (Francesca Aran Murphy, *Christ, the Form of Beauty: A Study of Theology and Literature* [Edinburgh, T & T Clark, 1995], 6).

26. George Steiner, *Real Presences* (Chicago: University of Chicago Press, 1989), 129.

27. Walker Percy, *Lancelot* (New York: Farrar, Straus and Giroux, 1977), 147.

28. Ibid., 145.

29. O'Connor, *Collected Works*, 803.

30. Percy, *Lancelot*, 146, 276.

31. Ibid., 275.

32. Ibid., 276.

33. Albert Gelpi, commentary on an earlier draft of this chapter, 11/2004.

34. Walker Percy, *Lost in the Cosmos: The Last Self-Help Book* (New York: Farrar, Straus and Giroux, 1983), 103.

35. Again, postmodernism, for all intents and purposes, was born in the 1940s. Emmanuel Levinas, one of the founding philosophers of postmodernism, asked a very good question: "Why the six million"? When it seems there is nothing happening from the "top-down" (i.e., "Where is God?"), it seemed justifiable to Levinas to scrub the project and look at an epistemology that proceeds from the bottom up.

36. Namely Levinas (1906–1995), a rabbinical scholar, and Michel de Certeau (1925–1986), a Jesuit priest. There are others, of course.

37. Roland Barthes, *Image Music Text*, trans. Stephen Heath (London: Fotana, 1977), 147, cited in Luke Ferretter, *Towards a Christian Literary Theory* (New York: Palgrave-MacMillan, 2003), 1. Ferretter continues on to locate Barthes's perspective in Marx, Nietzsche, and Freud, who, all three, were suspicious of theology.

38. Walker Percy, *The Thanatos Syndrome* (New York: Farrar, Straus and Giroux, 1987), 132, 143.

39. William Lynch "Theology and Imagination," in *Thought*, 29, no. 112 (Spring 1954): 66.

40. Leiva-Merikakis, *Love's Sacred Order*, 12.

41. *GL* 2, 148.

42. Denys in *The Mystical and Celestial Hierarchies*, trans. Friars of the Shrine of Wisdom (Surrey: The Shrine of Wisdom, 1928), 38. The italicized and parenthetical emphases are mine.

43. Flannery O'Connor, *The Habit of Being*, ed. Sally Fitzgerald (New York: Farrar, Straus and Giroux), 116.

44. Leiva-Merikakis, *Love's Sacred Order*, 13. Bold emphasis is mine.

45. Mark Delp, "On the Concept of Motion according to Pseudo-Dionysius" (master's thesis, Graduate Theological Union, 1989), 30.

46. Augustine, "De Musica," book six, in *Philosophies of Art and Beauty*, ed. Albert Hofstadter and Richard Kuhns (Chicago: University of Chicago Press, 1964), 185–86.

47. The Plotinian system, though, is more sympathetic to mediating factors such as matter and creation, but ultimately, in its assent to the One, it denies the salvific uniqueness of Christ. Still, Plotinus is close to the Christianity when he "rails against the Gnostics' claim that they alone among 'living creatures' have a special relationship with the intellect, 'that their soul is immortal and divine but that the whole heaven and stars have no share in the immortal soul' " (Margaret Miles, *Plotinus on Body and Beauty* [Oxford, UK: Blackwell], 118).

48. William Lynch, S.J., *Christ and Apollo, The Dimensions of the Literary Imagination* (New York: Sheed & Ward, 1963), 150–51.

49. Michel de Certeau is particularly useful here as a post-structuralist who has translated the postmodern lexicon into a language that corresponded with the "reality of Jesus." Graham Ward knows Certeau's work well and writes: "Certeau explores the way in which 'every figure of authority in Christian society is stamped by the absence of that which founds it.' The event which 'authorizes' Christianity and which it is always 'not without' implies an 'irreducible *plurality of authorities*,' none of which can function without the others; 'it leaves behind only a multiplicity of signs: an historical network of interconnected places rather than a hierarchical pyramid.' The heterogeneity of Christian authorities can be seen within the canon of Scriptures ('they are a collection of texts which do not say the same thing') as well as in a boundary drawn between the canon itself and the subsequent authorities ('the closing of the New Testament makes differences possible and even preserves the necessity of such differences')" (Graham Ward, *The Postmodern God* [Oxford, UK: Blackwell, 1997], 138).

50. Denis Donoghue, *Adam's Curse: Reflections on Religion and Literature* (Notre Dame: University of Notre Dame Press, 2001), 91.

51. Lynch, "Theology and Imagination," 65. According to Arthur Kinney's research, O'Connor underlined this comment in her own copy of Lynch's article, along with quite a few others. Another enlightening passage of Lynch's that O'Connor underlined is: "Only, we must take a more positive stand towards the elements of total predecision which make each of us the kind of explorer of the world of symbol and being that we are. We must all of us decide that our dogmas are instruments of exploration into the real, and the latter does not give up its secrets to those who have no instruments. Surly the new image will take on the analogical shape of the old, but that does not allow any man to say in advance what the next piece of history, the next fact, the next image will be that confronts him, or what the analogical shape or rhythm it will be given" (Lynch quoted by Kinney in *Flannery O'Connor's Library: Resources of Being* [Athens: University of Georgia Press, 1985], 179–80).

52. The "reunion" of sign and signified is an epistemological, ontological, and, as I suggested in a footnote above, an ultimately Christological transaction. I will go as far as Maritain and say that the mind can comprehend "being as such" but cannot mentally encompass it. As Francesca Murphy puts it, in her paraphrase of Maritain and his meditations on being: "We cannot possess it as a concept. We can only know this notion through it analogues" (53). It is as much knowledge as "mystery" can allow, and it supports the notion of transcendental referent, which is, I believe, the ontological (i.e., *sacramental*) junction that links sign and signified.

53. Denys, *Mystical and Celestial Hierarchies*, 38.

54. Denys, *The Divine Names*, trans. C. E. Rolt (London: MacMillan, 1920), 19.

55. *GL* 2, 164. *Proodos* and *epistrophe* are the Greek terms for *exitus and reditus*, which are the Latin terms for *procession* and *return*.

56. G. K. Chesterton, "The Everlasting Man" from *Collected Works* (San Francisco: Ignatius, 1986), 2:148.

57. Murphy, *Christ, the Form of Beauty*, 200.

58. Denys, *Mystical and Celestial Hierarchies*, 27.

59. In his own way, the Czech novelist Milan Kundera can be seen to subscribe to the beauty that moves Denys's hierarchy. His novel *The Unbearable Lightness of Being* flirts with the temptations of nihilism and anarchy but in the end assents to the "Yes" of being. To see in coincidence, not meaninglessness, but transformation into existential and narrative beauty is a kind of partnership with the Absolute. In so doing, the protagonist, Tomas, enters into the paradoxical relational mystery: in capitulating to the Beauty that is behind being (and this is key for anybody who reads Balthasar), the heaviness that characterized Tomas's life before his willing capitulation gives way to a further beauty—realization of an unbearable *Lightness* that, in turn, sustains Tomas in his married life, in his life in community, and ultimately in his death, which speaks to the those who read Denys. In O'Connor, though, the assent or turn to the absolute is initiated (or is seemingly coerced) by violence. The moment of grace in O'Connor is the well-known "advent of a gracious catastrophe" to a character that, because he (or she) is (so) fallen (but never so much as to be unworthy of grace), he requires distorted measures of sacramentality to remind him of his need to turn toward the true, his need to aspire to God.

60. Henri de Lubac, S.J., *Catholicism: A Study in Dogma in Relation to the Corporate Destiny of Mankind* (New York: Sheed & Ward, 1964), 124.

61. See Murphy, *Christ, the Form of Beauty*, 17–20. Murphy here is distilling a major element of Balthasar's theology: "Heaven and earth together create the Theo-drama. . . . But the play is in His hands. His acts are reiterated, not created, by our narrating. In myth, being is proportioned, or related, to the finite human mind: the drama of revelation unfolds the actions of God who is the fullness of being." (Murphy, *Christ, the Form of Beauty*, 18.)

62. Arthur Kinney, *Resources of Being, Flannery O'Connor's Library* (Athens: University of Georgia Press, 1985), 18. Kinney notes further that O'Connor both underlined and made a marginal arrow to Mounier's phrase.

63. See Paul Elie, *The Life You Save May Be Your Own* (New York, Farrar, Straus and Giroux, 2004), 242.

64. Delp, "On the Concept of Motion," 18.

65. Murphy, *Christ, the Form of Beauty*, 52.

66. *GL* 5, 624.

67. *GL* 2, 139.

68. Alejandro Garcia-Rivera, *The Community of the Beautiful* (Collegeville, MN: The Liturgical Press, 1999), 80.

69. Ibid., 82.

70. Raymond Gawronski, S.J., *Word and Silence: Hans Urs von Balthasar and the Spiritual Encounter Between East and West* (Grand Rapids, MI: Wm. Eerdmans, 1996), 52.

71. As I discussed in an earlier footnote, this is a central organizing principle in conceiving of God "structurally." Balthasar follows Nucholas of Cusa's idea of *De Non-aliud*—God is so other that God is non-Other (who, of course, is following Denys)—when he says: "Only because he is over the world is he in it. But being over it does not deprive him of the right, the power, and the Word, to reveal himself to as eternal love, to give himself to and to make himself comprehensible even in his incomprehensibility" (*LAC*, 150).

72. Denys, *The Divine Names*, V.I, 816 b., cited in Luke Ferretter, *Towards a Christian Literary Theory*, 22.

73. Ferretter, *Towards a Christian Literary Theory*, 23.

74. Gawronski, *Word and Silence*, 53. Gawronski is quoting Balthasar, *GL 2*, 182. Derrida, for his part, seems to be saying something similar. Eckhart scholar Rebecca Stephens comments instructively:

> The answer lies with the Derrida of today, not of thirty years ago. In *How to Avoid Speaking*, and *On the Name*, he has reconsidered the natures of the practices. This revisiting of negative theology is his first, his earlier words are admitted now to be "too negative," too "brief, elliptical and dilatory." Like the negative theologians of the fourteenth-century, Derrida's intellectual position has frequently been attacked by fellow-philosophers he has likened to inquisitors. *Différance*, and Derrida, can now be read as the friends of religion, in the same way as can Eckhart. But not friends to those who are wary of change: *différance* does not set itself against faith, it seeks to shake up the language of faith so that the passion and the belief are freed from any expectations. The earlier, emphatic, denial that negative theology and deconstruction have anything to say to each other has been superseded Derrida now accords a translatability to either method: in what Caputo has termed a "generalised apophatics," it is recognised that they both express a desire for something other than the created, tangible, present world, *a passion for the impossible*. When Derrida discourses "on the name," or dreams of the wholly other, about whom we do not know how to speak, he expresses a universal desire: the impossible and the practice of addressing it have many names. He now imagines himself as a negative theologian, as everyone can and should be: so that nothing can be trusted that tries to get along without negative theology, that is not at least "contaminated by negative theology." (Available: http://www.op.org/eckhart/Essay.html)

75. Garcia-Rivera, *Community of the Beautiful*, 81. He in turn is quoting from Denys, *The Divine Names*, in *Pseudo-Dionysius: The Complete Works*, Classics of Western Spirituality, ed. John Farina (New York: Paulist Press, 1987), II. 140AB.

76. *GL 2*, 168. Balthasar is drawing directly on Denys's *The Divine Names*. This "Both/And" conception of the divine life is ultimately *anagogical* and, therefore, absolutely mysterious and religious.

77. William Everson from "The Blood of the Poet" in *Dark God of Eros: A William Everson Reader*, intro. and ed. Albert Gelpi (Santa Clara: Santa Clara University Press; Berkeley: Heyday Books, 2003), 176.

78. Ibid., 66.

79. Ibid.

80. Albert Gelpi, from the introduction to *Dark God of Eros*, xxxvii. Gelpi concludes his introduction stressing Everson's "integral vision," which clearly is very complementary to *revelation and concealment*. Commenting on a stanza from an earlier poem ("The South Coast"), Gelpi writes: "The Spirit's delight in generation, the flesh's declaration of Spirit: the double helix of erotic mysticism. Moreover, the delicate pun on clarus/light in the final turn of 'declares, / Delights' transmutes language into vision and vision into language: the double helix of the poetics of Incarnation."

81. Ibid., xxix.

82. Gelpi also comments on this phenomenon: "In the encounter with God incarnate, gender distinctions become blurred, inverted, doubled . . . as Antoninus

discovered, erotic mysticism moves in two complementary or reciprocal modes, like the cones on a gyre or in the double helix that marks all animate life" (ibid., xxxii).

83. Ibid., 103.

84. In fact, "Rose" was a particular human person: Rose Tawnlund. Gelpi reports that "Everson saw the incarnate revealed in her fusion of *eros* and spirit" (Gelpi, a marginal comment on an earlier draft of this chapter, 11/2004).

85. Ibid., "The Raging of the Rose," all passages, 102–10. There is a list of scripture that also make use of *revelation and concealment*. As the dynamic is para-doxical, it accesses the radical mystery of divine expression. Second Corinthians will serve as one small example: "When I am weak, I am strong" (2:10).

86. Gawronski, *Word and Silence*, 52.

87. Ibid., 53.

88. Marion Montgomery rightly assesses O'Connor's developed sense of the notion of freedom to her refined understanding of Thomistic thought:

> The point is not so esoteric as it may sound in our taking recourse to
> St. Thomas through (Etienne) Gilson. And it is a point absolutely central to
> Flannery O'Connor's understanding of her own calling to be a realists of
> distances, as it is to our concern to understand her sacramental vision. What
> the scholastic point means by extension to the artist and his art is that man, in
> every instance of his action, is operating as a creative agent and participat-
> ing in his own existence, but at a secondary level. It is the refusal to accept our
> own being at a secondary level that is the well-spring of Sartrean existential-
> ism, a philosophy as old as the fall from grace in the garden. Though man may
> be given a freedom through which he may easily suppose himself the first, the
> sole or primary cause of his free actions of creation, his reason will tell him at
> last that he is *himself* a given and that even his freedom is given. In this view
> there can be no such thing as the self-made man, only the self-unmade man.
> Foe whatever the nature of his action as maker, man is always operating *upon*
> givens *with* givens *from* his own givenness. (Marion Montgomery, "Flannery
> O'Connor: Realist of Distances" in *Realist of Distances: Flannery O'Connor
> Revisited*, ed. Karl-Heinz Westarp and Jan Nordby Gretlund [Aarhus: Aarhus
> University Press, 1987], 232)

89. Karl Rahner, *The Rahner Reader*, ed. Gerald A. McCool (New York: Seabury Press, 1975), 226.

90. Flannery O'Connor, from "Revelation," *Collected Works*, 653.

91. So central is her concern with *disposition*, for example, that she mentions the word five times in ten pages: "as long as you have a good disposition, I don't think it makes a bit of difference what size you are. You just can't beat a good disposition" (ibid., 634); and in regards to Mary Grace: "She was obviously the lady's daughter, although they didn't look anything alike as to disposition, they both had the same shape of face and the same blue eyes" (ibid., 637). O'Connor's systematic juxtaposi-tions of the word, especially given her famous penchant for verbal economy, support the significance.

92. Ibid., 636.

93. In a letter to Maryat Lee, O'Connor writes about the idea of Ruby receiving the beatific vision just after the story's publication: "Sure you right. She (Ruby Turpin) gets the vision. Wouldn't have been any point in the story if she hadn't. I like Mrs. Turpin as well as Mary Grace. You got to be a very big woman to shout at the Lord across a hog pen. She's a country female Jacob. And that vision is Purgatorial.

Purgatory and I don't reckon (your niece's) Presbyterian instincts operate on
the middling planes of glory" (Flannery O'Connor, *The Habit of Being*, ed. Sally
Fitzgerald [New York: Farrar, Straus and Giroux], 577; Flannery O'Connor, *Collected
Works*, 654).

94. O'Connor, *Collected Works*, 637.

95. Ibid., 644.

96. Charles Péguy, "Hope," in *God Speaks: Religious Poetry* (New York: Pantheon,
1945), 66.

97. O'Connor, *Collected Works*, 633.

98. Ibid., 639, 650.

99. Ibid., 633, 639, 637, 638.

100. Ibid., 644, 645.

101. Ibid., 648.

102. Kinney, *Resources of Being*, 7.

103. O'Connor, *Collected Works*, 652.

104. Ibid., 653.

105. Ibid., 654.

106. Paul Fiddes, *The Promised End: Eschatology in Theology and Literature* (London: Blackwell, 2000), 18. I think it's meaningful to note the epigraph from T. S. Eliot's
Little Gidding that begins Fiddes's study:

> What we call a beginning is often the end
> And to make an end is to make a beginning
> The end is where we start from.

Eschatology is proving to be a promising area of relationship between continental philosophy (i.e., postmodernism) and theology. The grammar is there;
it's only a matter of clarifying the metaphysics.

107. The Christology is striking and is the culmination of years of a sharp intellect pitting the claims of modern philosophy against those of revelation. Again,
the objectivity of Christ as Lord is the *expression* of the form that *impresses* itself upon
us. We are the evidence of Christ in the world because we have encountered Christ
graciously; we are in graced relationship with Christ, in communion and community.

108. See O'Connor, *Collected Works*, 653.

109. Northrop Frye, *Anatomy of Criticism* (Princeton: Princeton University Press,
1971), 141.

110. O'Connor, *Collected Works*, 652–53.

111. Gawronski, *Word and Silence*, 55. Gawronski, in turn, is quoting Balthasar
from *GL 2*, 177.

112. O'Connor, *Collected Works*, 654.

113. Gabriel Marcel, *On the Ontological Mystery* (La Salle, IL: Open Court Publishing, 1984), 41–42.

114. The question, we have demonstrated, is ultimately one of *ontotheological*
orientation. At one extreme, according to Nicholas Lash, "is that assured Prometheanism (more widespread in the nineteenth century than at the end of the
twentieth) which sees in the suppression of the very *question* of God the opening up of
new vistas of human possibility and which therefore regards the death of God as
pure benefit for humankind." At the other extreme, according to Lash, is a cause for
deep sorrow: "(Nietzsche's) announcement of the death of God has been construed,
equally straightforwardly, as a matter of regret. Atheism is the deep disease and
darkness of our modern world, the source of manifold oppression and moral anarchy"

(Nicholas Lash, *Easter in Ordinary: Reflections on Human Experience and the Knowledge of God* [Notre Dame: University of Notre Dame Press], 199).

CHAPTER 4

1. Aidan Nichols, *No Bloodless Myth: A Guide through Balthasar's Dramatics* (Washington, DC: Catholic University of America Press, 2000), 3–4. I use *narrative* and *dramatic* more or less synonymously in this chapter.

2. *TD 1*, 32–33.

3. Ibid., 125. Edward Oakes notes also in *Pattern of Redemption* (New York: Continuum, 1997) that "one of the most striking aspects about the Theodramatics is that such a perspective seems to never have occurred to anyone before. And it is not as if the very terminology of theology has not always been deeply indebted to the theater" (p. 221).

4. *TD 1*, 126.

5. Nichols, *No Bloodless Myth*, 23.

6. *TD 1*, 314.

7. Nichols, *No Bloodless Myth*, 25.

8. Plato, *The Laws*, trans. Trevor J. Saunders (London: Penguin, 1970), 74.

9. *TD 1*, 138. Balthasar is quoting Plato from *Nomoi* VII, 817b, trans. Trevor J. Saunders (London: Penguin, 1970).

10. Watt argues that drama, as both an ancient and evolved form, has always been implicitly aware of the power of dialog; it was only after the great democratic revolutions of the eighteenth century when we begin to see similar developments in the novel. Watt further argues that is precisely the turn toward democracy that marks the advent of the multivocal, multicharacter novel and that the urge toward democracy was as much a political as an aesthetic development. Read Ian Watt, *The Rise of the Novel* (Berkeley: University of California Press, 1957).

11. *TD 1*, 125.

12. Ibid., 128.

13. Oakes, *Pattern of Redemption*, 217.

14. Balthasar is deeply concerned with the traditional Christian idea of *role* and *mission*. His *Theo-Drama* devotes much space to visiting the concept and midwifing it in to the modern and postmodern stage. As Balthasar rightly asserts, the idea that role as finite and personal destiny could unite a person in the infinitude of divine commission "was no longer available in Romanticism's theater of the world" (*TD 1*, 1). Romanticism's embedded value of the sanctitiy of personal liberty blurred the lines between divine inspiration and personal power. It is striking to note then that, like Balthasar, Trier is after a recovered sense of romanticism: one that reasserts the value of freedom with the spark of desire for intimacy with the absolute. Trier negotiates this splendidly by weaving a narrative in the nineteenth-century style, framed by chapters that are subtitled under Romantic landscapes, against the harsh realism of broken families, communal rejection, and other human sorrows. All of this is postmodernity's cinematic answer to modern *cinema verité*, a bountiful meeting between substance and technique.

15. *TD 1*, 262–63.

16. Whether it be "persons in relationship" or "persons in community," inter-subjectivity seems to be postmodern shorthand for the philosophy of *personalism*, a vibrant theological/philosophical school of thought that reached the zenith of its popularity in the mid 1950s. Early adherents were Martin Buber and E. S. Brightman. Other key thinkers were Gabriel Marcel and John MacMurray. Pope John Paul II also

numbers among the cohorts of other philosophers/theologians formed in the personalist tradition.

17. *TD 1*, 128.

18. The phenomenon of paradox pervades the thought of Lubac so extensively as to be a kind of element of his being. It shows up consistently in his writings, of course, but for a brief but systematic presentation of his view on the relationship between the Christian experience and paradox, see Maritain, *A Preface to Metaphysics* (New York: Sheed & Ward, 1939).

19. *TD 1*, 322–23.

20. As we've established, Balthasar's work is threaded with the presence of postmodern concern. *Theo-Drama* addresses the stakes (in this case, difference and deferment of meaning) and the implications of the movement explicitly, and there is no better indication of Balthasar's sophistication with issues in postmodernity than the following passage. Its length merits more than a footnote, of course, but fits best here. Most important, it significantly situates *Theo-Drama's* relevance to discourses of post-modernity:

> If God is to deal with man in an effective way and in a way that is intelligible to him, must not God himself tread the stage of the world and thus become implicated in the dubious nature of world theatre? And however he comes in contact with this theatre—whether he is to take responsibility for the whole meaning of the play or is to appear as one of the cast (in which case one can investigate his connection with the other *dramatis personae*)—the analogy between God's action and the world drama is no mere metaphor but has ontological ground: the two dramas are not utterly unconnected; there is an inner link between them. Theologically speaking the ambiguity of the "world theater" does invade the clarity of God's saving action, but how far is the latter obscure by the former? Or are we to say when God's action submits to the rules of the world stage it becomes invisible and can no longer be verified as a distinct action? On the human stage he "plays" through human beings and ultimately *as* a human being; does that not mean that he goes completely incognito behind the human mask? Is he only to drop this mask in death, when the play reveals who the actor in reality was (This man was truly the Son of God" Mt 27:54)? And surely only a human being can die, is not God really truly dead? Thus by entering into contact with the world theatre, the good which takes place in God's action really is affected by the world's ambiguity and remains a hidden good. This good is something *done*: it cannot be contemplated in pure "aesthetics" nor proved and demonstrated in pure "logic." It takes place nowhere but on the world stage—which is every person's present moment—and its destiny is seen as the drama of a world history that is continually unfolding. (*TD 1*, 19)

21. At her burial, the minister declares, "Bess McNeil, you've earned your place in hell." It's not certain how he justifies this claim, since even the most severe reading of Calvinism reserves questions of salvation to God alone. NB: since there are several differences between the film and screenplay, quotations from the dialogue in the film will be cited without page numbers. The screenplay *Breaking the Waves* (London: Faber and Faber Limited, 1996) is available, but I've decided to cite in terms of the finished film.

22. In a 1996 interview with C. B. Thompson, Trier reports: "I was baptized a couple of years ago together with my daughter—which didn't turn me into a good

catholic, you definitely couldn't call me that. I mean I just got divorced" (from *Poltiken* (Denmark), 5 July 1996, cited in *Lars von Trier*, ed. Jan Lumholdt (Biloxi: University of Mississippi Press, 2003), 108.

23. *TD 1*, 75.

24. Nichols, *No Bloodless Myth*, 18–19.

25. *TD 3*, 245.

26. *TD 1*, 101

27. Given the importance of bells in *Breaking the Waves*, it's tempting to make a shorthanded reference to the aesthetics of Catholicism as "smells and bells." A playful pun on "bells" and sacramentality occurs when one of Jan's bibulous groomsmen, Terry, asks, "Don't you ring a bell when people get married?" An elder answers sharply, "We don't need bells to worship God." Terry muses and then replies, "That's no fun." The conflict is played out even further between these two characters (Terry and the unnamed church elder). At the reception, Terry, sitting across the table, eyes him as if at a streetlight, a young upstart challenging an old man to a drag race. Terry takes a pint can of beer, opens it, drinks it in one go, eyeing, all the while, the elder playfully (if petulantly), and then crushes the can with one hand and lets out a big bold laugh. The elder, whose expression has been ever fixed on Terry in granite sobriety, responds by methodically placing a pint glass in front of him, pouring a glass of lemonade, drinking it in one go, and then smashing the glass with one hand. The scene ends with the elder stoically removing shards of glass from his bleeding hand. Terry is not unaffected by this experience. His face exudes a confused and newfound respect.

28. John Knox, "A Vindication of the Doctrine That the Sacrifice of the Mass Is Idolatry" (1550), from *Selected Writings of John Knox: Public Epistles, Treatises, and Expositions to the Year 1559* (London: Westminster John Knox Press, 1974), 166.

29. Stig Bjorkman, *Lars von Trier*, trans. Alexander Keillor, *Sight and Sound* 4, no. 11 (November 1996). Available: http://www.industrycentral.net/director_interviews/LVT01.HTM.

30. Trier notes in the Bjorkman interview that he went so far as to set his *Dancer in the Dark* in Washington State without ever having set foot there. This stands to reason, as Trier doesn't fly. As he admits, he has "control issues" (another informative fact that may explain the beauty of his conversion), which have caused certain scandal. When he won the director's award for *Breaking the Waves* at Cannes, for example, he had to turn around after journeying halfway. The Cannes community did not know the details and read it as a snub.

31. Ann Kibby, *The Interpretation of Material Shapes in Puritanism: A Study of Rhetoric, Prejudice, and Violence* (Cambridge: Cambridge University Press, 1986), 45, 49.

32. David Tracy, *The Analogical Imagination: Christian Theology and Aspects of Pluralism* (New York: Crossroads, 1981), 408.

33. The exhortation in James 1 ("Know this, my dear brothers: everyone should be quick to hear, slow to speak, slow to wrath, for wrath of a man does not accomplish the righteousness of God.... Be doers of the word and not hearers only, deluding yourselves. For if anyone is a hearer of the word and not a doer, he is like a man who looks at his own face in the mirror") and others like it have long been held as "Catholic." The implication that it is faith (merely "hearing" and "reading" the word) alone that saves is where the two traditions separate. James likens the preponderance upon the word alone (a development that has become doctrinal in some quarters as *sola scriptura*) to a kind of theological narcissism James worries about scenarios where the"action" demanded by words (i.e. the Gospel need for the "doers") is encroached upon by the preference for contemplative self-reflection (i.e merely "hearing" of

the word). To be so divided between words and deeds creates an unhealthy tension, The result a kind of spiritual stasis wherethe needs of both the individual person and the community become compromised.

34. The passage is from Galatians 2:20–21, a critical meditation on the possibility and mystery of an existential, personal orientation in Christ. The fuller text is: "I have been crucified with Christ; it is no longer I who live, but Christ who lives in me; and the life I now live in the flesh I live by faith in the Son of God, who loved me and gave himself for me. I do not nullify the grace of God; for if justification were through the law, then Christ died to no purpose."

35. Luke 4:24.

36. *TD 1*, 128.

37. Balthasar, "The Fathers, the Scholastics, and Ourselves," originally published in 1939 as "Patristik, Scholastik und wir: *theologie der Zeit*" (Ensiedeln: Johannes Verlag, 1939), 42.

38. *TD 4*, 87.

39. Tobias Wolff, "In the Garden of the North American Martyrs" from *In the Garden of the North American Martyrs* (Hopewell, NJ: Ecco Press, 1981), 134.

40. Ibid., 135.

41. A further literary analogy surfaces here in the aesthetic differences in the relationship between the Anglican C. S. Lewis and the Catholic J. R. R. Tolkien. Lewis, like Barth, was disposed to straight allegory: Aslan in *The Chronicles of Narnia*, stands for the idea of God, a symbolic, one-to-one, even, relationship. Tolkien's aesthetic vision, like Balthasar's, looks for a groundedness in being. Gandalf, in *The Lord of the Rings* trilogy, doesn't stand in for the idea of Christ as much as he acts in the mode of Christ. His transfiguration, for example, in "The Two Towers" illustrates how we are called to be transfigured in Jesus in our own time, not only to dwell from a distance on the Transfiguration of Jesus depicted in Mark 8.

42. Luther's two kingdoms theory is faithful to the vision of Jesus as absolutely countercultural. But in its *contemptus mundi*, well beyond mere disinterestedness with the world, it provides very little relief for those looking for analogical linkage. Luther scholar Anders Nygren writes of the political character of the doctrine, which may offer analogical insight into the various other disciplines the doctrine influences:

> Luther, in issuing this solemn warning against confusing the two kingdoms or authorities, is setting his face against two different adversaries. On the one side, he opposes the Roman Catholic hierarchy, which in the name of the Gospel lays claim to worldly power, and thereby imperils the Gospel. But he is equally opposed to those whom he calls fanatics. They held that it is the Christian's task to seek to rule society by the principles of the Sermon on the Mount, and that evil should not be resisted, but all earthly law and power abolished. This view is, of course, found in various forms in our day, as it was then. We frequently encounter the statement that the great failure of our society has been that it has not the courage to apply the ethical principles of the Sermon on the Mount to our common life and our relations in the State. Such a view finds no support in Luther. He is against it: it is contrary to the will of God to try to rule the world through the Gospel. God has ordained an entirely different authority to rule the world. It is in accordance with His will that power and the sword are used to that end, and the world is under the sway of that authority, and not of the Gospel. (*Journal of Lutheran Ethics* 2, no. 8 [August 2002]: 26)

43. *TD* 1, 17.

44. See *GL* 1, 52–56. Balthasar pays tribute to Barth in almost everything he writes. Barth was one of Balthasar's most popular and revered conversation partners, and the two were good friends.

45. Gerhard Nebel, *The Event of the Beautiful* (Klett, 1953), 188. Cited in *GL* 1, 69.

46. *GL* 1, 63.

47. *A Conversation between Jan Kornum Larsen and Lars von Trier*, from *Kosmurama* 167 (April 1984), cited in *Lars von Trier*, 108.

48. Oakes, *Pattern of Redemption*, 230.

49. Ibid.

50. Ibid.

51. Aidan Nichols, *The Word Has Been Abroad: A Guide through Balthasar's Aesthetics.* (New York: Catholic University of America Press, 1998), 37.

52. Joseph Cardinal Ratzinger, "The Beauty and Truth of Christ," *L'Osservatore Romano* (6 November 2002), quoted in James Schall, "The Whole Risk for a Human Being: On the Insufficiency of Apollo," *Logos* 7, no. 2 (Spring 2004): 14.

53. When Bess acts out on her grief just before Jan is to return to his rig, her mother admonishes: "Endure or its back to the hospital again for you." Bess leaves the room in tears. Jan observes: "C'mon. She just wants it all." Later, in one of her dialogs with God, she states (in her own voice, as if uttering from an ingrained psychological script), "He'll be home in ten days. You must *endure*."

54. Trier, interview with Bjorkman: *Lars von Trier*, trans. Alexander Keillor, *Sight and Sound* 4, no. 11 (November 1996). Available: http://www.industrycentral.net/director_interviews/LVT01.HTM.

55. Christianity as the blend between realism and romanticism has inspired many to High Church Christianity. It seems to be the recipe particularly attractive to artists. In addition to Trier, some notable converts that have responded to this perspective are G. K. Chesterton, C. S. Lewis (indeed all of the *Inklings*, from Barfield to Tolkien, are keen on the mix), Dorothy Day, Christopher Dawson, Evelyn Waugh, Graham Greene, Marshall McCluhan, and Walker Percy. For a comprehensive discussion on twentieth-century converts, see Patrick Allitt, *Catholic Converts: British and American Intellectuals Turn to Rome* (Ithaca, NY: Cornell University Press, 1997).

56. Trier tells Bjorkman: "It is probably no coincidence that it largely takes place on the Isle of Skye, where many painters and writers moved during the English Romantic period of the nineteenth century" (Trier, interview with Bjorkman in *Lars von Trier*. Available: http://www.industrycentral.net/director_interviews/LVT01.HTM.

57. Bess's calendar is telling on this score. She crosses the days off in crayon, hoping that it will speed his return from the rig. Like a second grader, she draws a stick figure of a happy young girl with the caption "I Love Jan." Childish or childlike? A serious question and comment on the notion of theological innocence and Jesus' gospel exhortation to aspire to be Holy Innocents.

58. See *TD* 3, 233–59.

59. *TD* 4, 62.

60. Ibid.

61. Ibid., 481.

62. See Martin Heidegger, *Being and Time*, trans. John Macquarrie and Edward Robinson (New York: Harper & Row, 1962), 219–24.

63. *TD* 4, 63.

64. *TD* 3, 207.

65. See Michel Foucault, "The Eye of Power" in *Power/Knowledge: Selected Interviews and Other Writings, 1972–1977*, ed. and trans. Colin Gordon et al. (New York: Pantheon, 1980), 145–67.

66. Ed Block Jr., "Hans Urs von Balthasar's *Theodrama*: A Contribution to Dramatic Criticism," *Renascence* 48, no. 2 (Winter 1996): 163.

67. Ibid., 169.

68. Ibid.

69. Ibid., 165.

70. Nichols, *No Bloodless Myth*, 241.

71. Stuart Schwartz, *Implicit Understandings: Observing, Reporting, and Reflecting on the Encounters Between Europeans and Other Peoples in the Early Modern Era* (Cambridge: Cambridge University Press, 1994), 7. A comprehensive archive of Brebeuf's personal journal is available: http://puffin.creighton.edu/jesuit/relations/jesuit_bibliography.html.

72. Oakes, *Pattern of Redemption*, 237.

73. *TD 1*, 645–46. Balthasar cites Martin Buber, who is a key figure in chapter 5 of this study, as inspirational in this regard.

74. Eleanor Heartney, "Blood, Sex, and Blasphemy: The Catholic Imagination in Contemporary Art," *New Art Examiner* (November 1999). This lecture served as preparation for Heartney's recent work on the topic, *Postmodern Heretics: The Catholic Imagination in Contemporary Art* (New York: Middlemarch, 2004).

75. Nichols, *No Bloodless Myth*, 239.

76. Ibid. Italics added.

77. Ibid., 104–5.

78. *TD 4*, 494.

79. *TD 3*, 110.

80. William Everson, from "A Frost Lay White in California" in *The Dark God of Eros*, 71.

81. René Girard's work on the scapegoat mechanism is instructive here, clearly, but we will defer consideration of his insights until chapter 5.

82. Rowan Williams, "Balthasar and the Trinity," in *A Cambridge Companion to Hans Urs von Balthasar*, ed. Edward T. Oakes and David Moss (Cambridge: Cambridge University Press), 42.

83. *TD 4*, 499.

84. Joseph Ratzinger, *Eschatology: Death and Eternal Life*, trans. Michael Waldstein (Washington DC: Catholic University Press), 93.

85. Ibid., 97.

86. Oakes, *Pattern of Redemption*, 237–38.

87. See *TD 2*, 257.

88. See Nichols, introduction to *Mysterium Paschale: The Mystery of Easter*, trans. Aidan Nichols (Edinburgh: T & T Clark, 1990), 7. The Holy Spirit who "embodies the unity of the two is also the Guarantor for the unity of love that perdures even in this division" (*TD 4*, 232). There is no gap here, furthermore, in the triune Godhead. The Son never ceases to be God. As Balthasar writes of von Speyr's mystical insight in this regard: "It is fulfillment because God may expect everything from God" (*TD 2*, 257). Balthasar is quoting from von Speyr, *The World of Prayer* (San Francisco: Ignatius Press, 1985), 28.

89. Balthasar, *Mysterium Paschale*, 148–49. As a juxtaposition, Bess cries out from her own living hell just prior to her murder, "Father, are you here with me?" The

God voice had been nonrespondent for several scenes, but it answers now a definitive yes, which evokes the ineffable spiritual ecstasy of certitude in Bess.

90. Ratzinger, *Eschatology*, 217–18.

91. Ibid., 218.

92. Lumholdt, *Lars von Trier*, 110.

93. Ibid.

94. Ibid.

95. Colossians 1:17.

CHAPTER 5

1. *TL 1*, 52.

2. George Steiner, *Real Presences* (Chicago, University of Chicago Press, 1989), 229–30.

3. W. B. Yeats from "The Second Coming" in *The Collected Works of W. B. Yeats*, ed. Richard Finneran (New York: Scribner, 1996), 1:187.

4. The "vanished one" refers to Jesus. The term negotiates and honors the often-competing values of history and theology. Of the great postmodern critics, Michel de Certeau (1925–1986) has the most in common with Balthasar. Like Levinas and Kristeva, Certeau is a seminal figure in the pantheon of postmodern theorists; but Certeau was also a Jesuit priest, a fact underemphasized in the several general biographies of his life. Certeau entered the Jesuits in 1950 just as Balthasar was leaving, and there's no evidence that they ever met. Like Balthasar, Certeau was an interdisciplinary polymath, skilled in several disciplines. Like Balthasar, Certeau navigates the pesky problem of history that rightly preoccupies postmodern theory with creativity and credibility. Certeau, as one more explicitly ensconced in postmodernity, offers a host of philosophical options that validate the theological nature of art in the nomenclature of the age: Certeau's various discourses link the conventional language of Continental philosophy with the acrobatic neologisms of postmodern thinkers such as Derrida, Pierre Bourdieu, and Michel Foucault. For example (and, once again, from a trinitarian perspective), Certeau articulates, often in a manner more precise and more practical than Balthasar, the ways that God's various impressions "express" themselves upon the world. In his meditation on the death of God, Certeau offers theology that both complements Balthasar's perception of Holy Saturday (especially is Jesus' passivity) as well as asserts grounded pneumatology that follows God's kenotic act, the act that "makes room" for others. For Jesus to die is to "make room" for the Father; at the same time, it "makes room" for the polyglot and creative community of Pentecost, the plurality of authority in Scriptures, for the multiplicity of future Christian generations. Certeau then gives one very astute reading of how the "empty place"—Derrida's *Khora*—is actually the site for significant theological activity.

Certeau, like Balthasar, is focused on the community of God, for, in essence, the death of Jesus establishes the church. The empty space of death is revealed now as a site of wholeness and love, which is also the message that Trier presents in his depiction of Bess. The emptiness of the tomb on Easter Sunday, in a manner that is even more acute, incites not fear and trembling in those who peal back the rock but rather awe and wonder at how a hollow crypt engenders fulfillment in the founding of a unique community. The unique geometry of the event is further endorsed soon after in the dramatic interplay between revelation and concealment that attends the Resurrection narratives in the gospel, culminating with the Pentecost, during which concealment

is made iconographic for all ages in the person of the Holy Spirit. Certeau's distillation of the actions of the economic Trinity intersects fertilly with Balthasar's program,
especially in its transition from *Theo-Drama* to *Theo-Logic*. Both men draw from a variety
of disciplines, from sociology to psychology to anthropology, in the quest to understand theological phenomenon. All of this points to the need for a recovered epistemology, a realization that God's logic is "interdisciplinary" at the very least, interdisciplinary to the extreme point that it transcends the reductive and secularizing spirit of
many current philosophical systems. Certeau, then, and Levinas and Kristeva are excellent "parallel sources." As such, their work discloses several original ways in which
postmodernity aids the theological imagination in the common quest to address our
various crises in meaning. For further discussion on the matter, see Michel de Certeau,
"How Is Christianity Thinkable Today?" in *The Postmodern God*, ed. Graham Ward
(Oxford: Blackwell, 1997).

5. Steiner, *Real Presences*, 230.

6. See *LAC*, 150. Balthasar isquoting St. Anselm of Canterbury: "Reason comprehends rationally that He is incomprehensible" ("Consideratio rationabiliter com-
prehendt incomprehensibile esse").

7. See *TL 1*, 9. Also, Balthasar's concluding aria to the volume: "Eternity is a
circulation in which beginning and end join in unity" (272).

8. See John O'Donnell, "The Trinity as Divine Community," *Gregoranium* 69
(1988): 5–34. Balthasar's other influences on trinitarian theology are too numerous to
list here.

9. *TD 2*, 389.

10. *TL 1*, 272.

11. Aidan Nichols, *Say It Is Pentecost* (New York: Catholic University Press,
2001), 4.

12. Balthasar establishes this Christology convincingly in *A Theology of History*,
trans. Graham Harrison (San Francisco: Ignatius Press, 1994).

13. Nichols, *Say It Is Pentecost*, 4. Nichols is referring again to the debt Balthasar
pays to Maximus Confessor in figuring Christ as the key to the cosmos.

14. *TL 1*, 14.

15. Ibid.

16. Ibid., 15.

17. Ibid.

18. The Danish philosopher-theologian Soren Kierkegaard reacted vehemently to
Hegel's decisive vivisection of faith from reason, of mind from body, of essence
from existence, and so on down the line. According to Kierkegaard, the mystery of God
is not merely an objective exercise in which the logical faculties of human mind
work out problems in theology as people work out crossword puzzles on Sunday
afternoons. Mystery is lived out, by persons, as an existential participation in the real,
which, in turn, has a profoundly artistic and literary quality about it. In this specific
way, aesthetics in Kierkegaard is a handmaid to truth.

It's not so much a "what" when it comes to what we are after in our contemplation, but a "how." Ultimately, for Kierkegaard (and for Balthasar, who owes much to
Kierkegaard), truth is more likely a "who." Logic needs pragmatism; *doxa* (and *theoria*)
needs *praxis*; and according to most "trinitarianists," especially in Balthasar, God
negotiates these types of dichotomies in Jesus whose Incarnation provides the linking
form. Ideas in Kierkegaard depend precisely on the subjectivity that Hegel denies.
Ideas (while they may derive from objective spirit, as in Hegel) are only meaningful as
they relate to existence as such, especially reflected in the conduct of one's personal life

in the light of the ever-present existence of Christ. Truth, then, is found in radical inward experience in "subjects," an existential embrace of the real attained both by personal volition—by Kierkegaard's famous "leap of faith"—and, of course, by grace (which Kierkegaard, as a good Protestant, allows, but his explicit focus tends to be on the will of the subject). Like Aristotle, Kierkegaard also employs the narrative form of tragedy as a fulcrum that leverages the paradoxical drama of what faithful theism looks like in the modern world. He writes in *Fear and Trembling* (1843): "Let us consider in somewhat more detail the distress and anxiety in the paradox of faith. The tragic hero relinquishes himself in order to express the universal; the knight of faith relinquishes the universal in order to become the single individual. . . . Anyone who believes that it is fairly easy to be a single individual can always be sure that he is not a knight of faith. . . . On the contrary, this knight knows that it is glorious to belong to the universal. He knows that it is beautiful and beneficial to be the single individual who translates himself into the universal, the one who, so to speak, produces a trim, clean, and as far as possible, faultless edition of himself, readable by all" (Soren Kierkegaard, *Fear and Trembling*, trans. Howard V. Hong [Princeton: Princeton University Press, 1986], 75).

The temptation in Kierkegaard is to capitulate to modern Enlightenment culture, to those who "deafen one another with their noise and clamor and keep anxiety away with their screeching. A hooting carnival crowd like that thinks it's assaulting heaven, believes it's going along the same path as the night of faith" (ibid.). Enlightenment modernists, in his view, have lost an identity not only with Christ, the manifestation of God in culture, but also with the radical otherness that the life in faith implies precisely because God is countercultural. The sectarians have repeated a kind of Constantianism and updated it for their own purposes: God is assimilated into culture, as in Hegel; and the divine mysteries are normalized and subsumed by culture. In this configuration, there is no need for God, because nothing remains "hidden."

This one, grand conundrum requires some mode of reiteration because it touches the very heart of aesthetics. The Hegelian model of culture is one that is romanticized and abstracted. It does no service to the particular experience of the individual who trudges through history. The "corpse cold" (to invoke Emerson) predilections of modern rationalists, with their emphasis on remote ideas of the universal and the ideals of God, have explained away the need for subjective and individual intimacy. For Kierkegaard, the result is a new kind of dualism or at least one that is updated for the age. Kierkegaard's solution, though, lay in radical (Christian) inwardness: "Therefore, either there is an absolute duty to God—and if there is such a thing, it is the paradox just described, that the single individual is higher than the universal and as the single individual stands in an absolute relation to the absolute—or else faith has never existed because it has always existed, or else Abraham is lost, or else one must interpret the passage in Luke 14 as did that appealing exegete and explain the similar corresponding passages in the same way" (Kierkegaard, *Fear and Trembling*, 81).

Clearly Kierkegaard's critique of Hegel on the grounds of a "rationalistic romanticism" is just, but Kierkegaard himself is not off the hook. His theological emphasis illuminates another type of romanticism, the romanticism inherent in the art of tragedy. Tragedy fits the modus operandi and supplies a ripe structural environment for Kierkegaard's radical inwardness: whereas, in comedy, the resolution always establishes a reification and integration of community, that is, a reconciliation; tragedy resolves into the atomization of the community, in the alienation and isolation of the individual. At the end of the tragic play, protagonists are isolated, estranged, alone, or dead before their time. It's interesting to note that Kierkegaard, in his own life, achieved all of these states. In any event, Kierkegaard's aesthetic theory, with its high regard for tragic art as a manifestation of the great organizing pattern of existence, elucidates and reestablishes a sense of Christian eschatology in the form of theological aesthetics. In this vital sense, unique rapport exists between Balthasar and Kierkegaard.

19. It is doubtful that Descartes, in his famous truncation of essence and existence (the division of the whole person into smaller parts or functions being the ultimate product of *cogito ergo sum*), could imagine where such a vivisection of the person would end up: first with Nietzsche and then with the philosophical narcissism of Ayn Rand. Current supporters of the biological determinism camp, as one example, continue this line of thinking and siphon off, bit by bit, the inherent dignity of every human person in favor of the view that reduces human persons to the level of material functionalities.

20. The National Institute of Health reports that, for people born after 1945, the chances of being diagnosed with clinical depression are ten times greater than those born before 1945. Available: http://www.nimh.nih.gov/publicat/depresfact.cfm.

21. *TL* 1, 16.

22. Steiner, *Real Presences*, 4. Steiner continues: "The theological reach of the word is obvious, within language and form. . . . The conjecture is that 'God' is, not because our grammar is outworn; but that grammar lives and generates worlds because there is a wager on God" (p. 4).

23. *LAC*, 11.

24. Ibid.

25. *Dare*, 145. *Dare* is a footnote to Balthasar's entire theology. A deeply controversial work, it celebrates the possibility of Hope for even the most deplorable scoundrel; it also reiterates the gospel mandate that Love alone is credible and that God's grace is radical and implacable.

26. William Lynch, *Christ and Apollo: The Dimensions of the Literary Imagination* (New York: Sheed & Ward, 1960), 149.

27. David Lodge, *Therapy* (New York: Penguin, 1995).

28. Nichols, *Say It Is Pentecost*, 209. Nichols suggests Balthasar's affinity with Kierkegaard as opposed to the more obvious candidate Teilhard de Chardin. It's a keen observation, given the large scope of Teilhard's concern matches the breadth of Balthasar's project. But Nichols is astute to recognize that Balthasar, like Kierkegaard, is most concerned with "rubbing our noses in the hard particularity of Jesus' body."

29. Kierkegaard, of course, was a serious Lutheran. Yet, Daphne Hampson, in her *Christian Contradictions: The Structures of Lutheran and Catholic Thought* (Cambridge: Cambridge University Press, (2004), examines Kierkegaard against Catholicism, particularly in respect to the existential features of each tradition. Hampson suggests that Kierkegaard is very close to the Catholic approach, particularly in his sense of *via* that attends his stages of personal development. Balthasar, oddly, does not emphasize *via* as much as Kierkegaard does (again, he prefers the more circular *perichoresis*), but both are in alignment on the notion of *telos*, that is, the sense of mission and purpose. This, of course, is a distinguishing feature; and it separates both from the majority of postmodern thinkers. Furthermore, as far as subject formation goes, both Kierkegaard and Balthasar hold that a relationship with God is essential in developing an authentic concept of the self.

30. Buber, like Balthasar, ultimately defies labels. Certainly his most famous work, *I and Thou* (trans. W. Kaufman [New York, Scribner, 1970], 123), stakes its claim in the context of modernism; but there is enough cross-disciplinary and historical

breadth in his work that makes him especially relevant today. Perhaps this explains his popularity among scholars of interdisciplinary theological humanism.

31. Paul Elie attributes this quote to O'Connor in his *The Life You Save May Be Your Own* (New York: Farrar, Straus and Giroux, 2004), 42.

32. René Girard, "A Conversation with René Girard," *The Girard Reader*, ed. James G. Williams (New York: Crossroad, 1996), 290.

33. Ibid., 292. I'll note that Buber uses the term *interhuman* in much the same way, which illustrates a noteworthy distinction. Balthasar also tends to prefer words such as *creature* and *person* as opposed to the more mechanistic terms *subject* and *individual*.

34. René Girard, "Eating Disorders and Mimetic Desire," *Contagion: Journal of Violence, Mimesis, and Culture* 3 (Spring 1996), 4.

35. The notion of scapegoat is the key component of Girardian theory. It appears originally in Leviticus when two goats are brought to the temple. The Israelites place their sins on the back of one before sending the goat, laden with their sins, into the desert to die. Girard believes the scapegoat (i.e., human sacrifices) functions to remove accumulated violence from the core of a community. He bases this belief on his theory of mimetic desire and extends the dynamic from individuals to communities. Briefly, the theory states that when two groups begin to compete for the same third object, they initiate a series of escalating and reciprocal violent actions against one another, which would ultimately result in their mutual annihilation would they not be able to jointly focus the cause and dynamism of their hostilities on an arbitrarily designated "other." Sacrificing the scapegoat thereby functions to rid the community of its own destructive impulses. The scapegoat is generally selected because in appearance it is similar enough to the original two competing groups to enable their identification with the scapegoat. But the scapegoat is different enough to justify its killing.

In proper scapegoating circles, all community members must in some manner (whether symbolically or actually) touch or whip the scapegoat, signifying their unanimity in its sacrifice. It is this sense of resolution and closure that the scapegoat's death brings to the community. The crux, though, is that this "closure" is illusory and therefore temporary in any "sacrifice" that does not involve Jesus. The sacrifice provides only a whiff of relief and creates only a false sense of community. Girard terms this scapegoat process the "victimage mechanism" and argues that, in order for it to be effective, the community must remain unconscious of its workings. He further asserts that the ritual and sacrificial killing of the scapegoat is an unconscious reenactment of what he believes to be a founding or originary murder (which has been intentionally obscured by mythology). Indeed, the function of mythology for Girard is to hide the founding sacrifice by transforming the act into some other ritual action. Finally, Girard believes, as I am presently disclosing, this victimage mechanism has been revealed in the crucifixion of Jesus, who, innocent and nonviolent, went to the cross willingly to protest sinful humanity's "kingdom of violence" (see Girard, *Things Hidden Since the Foundation of the World* [Stanford: Stanford University Press, 1987], 219). Girard asserts that his conclusion renders ineffective, once and for all, a non-sacrificial reading of the gospel texts. In this reading, human beings (not deities) are responsible for their violent condition. Oddly, Girard has since waffled on this point and can conceive of a sacrificial reading of the gospel after all, which implies a new appreciation for "top-down" theology and transcendence as well as a more developed anthropology of the cross, concepts that, while very appealing, are well beyond the scope of my concern here.

36. See Girard, *Things Hidden Since the Foundation of the World*, 192–93.

37. Ibid., 219.

38. Ibid.

39. Flannery O'Connor, "A Good Man Is Hard to Find" in *Collected Works* (New York: Library of America, 1988), 151.

40. René Girard, "The Anthropology of the Cross," in *The Girard Reader*, 269.

41. Ibid.

42. The Latin root of *conversion* is "convertere": "to turn with." The structural dynamic of conversion is entirely correspondent with trinitarian *perichoresis*: the Divine dance of God. All persons are invited to turn in this way.

43. Girard, "Anthropology of the Cross," 290.

44. Lodge builds a playful intertextual pun from Shakespeare's *King Lear*. Tubby quips in his journal on the tragic metonymy that has blossomed from his injured knee: "reason not the knee." Lear, in passionately addressing his sorrow to Regan and Goneril, bursts "O, Reason not the need" (2.4.263)

45. Lodge, *Therapy*, 23.

46. Ibid.

47. Ibid., 34.

48. Ibid., 36–37.

49. Another well-known Kierkegaardian state. See Lodge, "Kierkegaard for Special Purposes," in *Consciousness and the Novel: Connected Essays* (Cambridge: Harvard University Press, 2002). The idea of "coinciding with oneself," in this case, is a quality associated with Tubby's wife, Sally, who "takes herself for granted." The concept is clear—to be totally present to one's self in space and in time. It reminds me of the Greek idea of being *in kairo*, which is the attainment of the temporal virtue of "hitting on all cylinders."

50. *TD* 4, 299.

51. Ibid.

52. See ibid., 299–313.

53. Ibid., 310.

54. Judith Butler, *The Psychic Life of Power: Theories in Subjection* (Stanford, CA: Stanford University Press, 1997), 80–81

55. Ibid., 2.

56. Ibid., 3.

57. A *gyre*, quite literally, is an ever-widening spiral. The figure is meaningful, for Butler, in its inverse: an ever-widening spiral confined to the parameters of a subject's internal psychic terrain.

58. Butler, *Psychic Life of Power*, 168.

59. Butler terms this critical stage in the process as "an iterability of the subject that shows how agency may well consist in opposing and transforming the social terms by which it is spawned" (ibid., 29).

60. *TL* 1, 109. Balthasar's theories on personalism, of course, are basic in his theology.

61. Ibid., 71, 76, 78.

62. Lodge spells out the relevance of the Kierkegaardian "stages of personal development" to Tubby's personal journey when he has Tubby explain it to an English news crew. Pilgrims all, they make their way from Le Puy to Santiago de Compostela (Lodge, *Therapy*, 304 304–5).

63. Soren Kierkegaard, *Concluding Unscientific Postscript*, trans. David F. Swenson and Walter Lowrie (Princeton: Princeton University Press, 1941), 232.

64. Lodge, *Therapy*, 203.

65. Ibid., 304.

66. Ibid., 209.

67. Ibid., 210.

68. Ibid.

69. Ibid., 209.

70. Martin Buber, *On Judaism*, ed. Nahum Glatzer (New York: Schocken, 1967), 82.

71. Ibid., 84.

72. *LAC*, 102.

73. See *TL 1*, 143. Balthasar returns to this idea often in his *Theo-Logic* and refers to it in a variety of ways. The "Something More" Balthasar posits is critical to knowing: "It is this never-failing 'something more' than what we already know, without which there would be neither knowing nor anything to be known" (*TL 1*, 111). Of course, the mysterious "more" points to the ineffable and inexhaustible nature of God. In postmodern parlance, the term has been transmuted into such terms as *excess* and *surplus*.

74. *TL 1*, 173–76.

75. Ibid., 238.

76. Julia Kristeva, "In the Beginning Was Love," cited in *The Postmodern God*, ed. Graham Ward (Oxford: Blackwell, 1997), 232. The work of Julia Kristeva (b. 1941) shows us how psychoanalytical theory, as a fully refined critical option for postmodern theory, can also aid discourses in theology. Kristeva, whose education is decidedly bipolar (in convent schools and then in the exciting welter of communist groups of the late sixties), is a recent "revert" to Catholicism.

77. Buber, *I and Thou*, 123.

78. Ibid., 165.

79. Ibid.

80. See Curtis Bradford, "Yeats's Byzantium Poems: A Study of Their Development," *PMLA* 75 (March 1960): 111.

81. Buber, *I and Thou*, 141.

82. Kierkegaard, *Concluding Unscientific Postscript*, 162.

83. The pilgrimage heart of *Therapy* supports the idea that, in the novel, the language of the return is clearly Catholic. In Catholicism, as we have shown, community is particularly important. In this sense, the clearest difference is articulated in the creeds: in the Apostle's Creed ("I believe...") and in the Nicene Creed ("We believe..."). Lodge concludes: "The three of us are best friends. We're going off together for a little autumn break, actually. To Copenhagen. It was my idea. You could call it a pilgrimage" (Lodge, *Therapy*, 321).

84. *TL 1*, 112.

85. Ibid., 109.

86. Another well-known Kierkegaardian state. See also Lodge, "Kierkegaard for Special Purposes," in *Consciousness and the Novel*, 274.

87. Lodge, *Therapy*, 221.

88. Ibid., 247.

89. Ibid., 307.

90 Buber, *I and Thou*, 109.

91. Lodge, *Therapy*, 305.

92. Ibid., 321.

93. William James, *The Varieties of Religious Experience* (New York: Modern Library, 1902), 47, cited in Edwin Block, "Why the Theater Still Matters," *Logos* 8, no. 1 (Winter 2005): 71.

94. *TL 1*, 174.

95. Ibid.

96. Ibid., 272.

97. Ibid., 175. Balthasar discusses Buber's contribution to discourses in Personalism comprehensively in his *Martin Buber and Christianity* (London: Harvill Press, 1961).

98. Catherine Mowry LaCugna, *God for Us: The Trinity and the Christian Life* (New York: HarperCollins, 1991), 292.

99. Ibid., 303.

100. Joel 2:12–18.

101. LaCugna, *God for Us*, 303.

102. *TL 1*, 272.

103. Paul Fiddes, *The Promised End: Eschatology in Theology and Literature* (London: Blackwell, 2000), 263.

104. Ibid., 273.

105. *TD 2*, 178.

106. *TD 5*, 485–86, cited in Aidan Nichols, *No Bloodless Myth: A Guide through Balthasar's Dramatics* (Washington, DC: Catholic University of America Press, 2000), 239.

CHAPTER 6

1. See Donald MacKinnon, "Some Reflections on Hans Urs von Balthasar's Christology with Special Reference to Theodranatik II/2 and III," in *The Analogy of Beauty: The Theology of Hans Urs von Balthasar*, ed. John Riches (Edinburgh: T & T Clark, 1986), 167.

2. "If Christ is to be *the* Unique One, then, when we look at his form, what must happen is that all other forms, in spite of their qualitative difference and even opposition, come more and more to exhibit related characteristics, while he, who had seemed to be related to them and capable of being classified under the same general categories, now appears in greater isolation, incapable of being reduced to anything whatever" (*GL 1*, 502).

3. *TL 1*, 112. Again, Balthasar returns to the "mysterious more" idea often. It is the concept that, after all is said, is always the great remainder, the vastness (or "excess") that is God. In the following passage, Balthasar offers gratitude that the God he imagines alone saves the world not from death and isolation but from boredom. Now this is a theology for aesthetes: "This excess transcending all that we can grasp by conceptual analysis, delimitation, and cataloging, this eternal 'more' belonging to every being, saves the revelation of things and the knowledge of them from immediately becoming insuperably boring" (*TL 1*, 142).

4. *TL 1*, 143.

5. Gerald Bednar, *Faith as Imagination: The Contribution of William Lynch SJ* (New York: Sheed & Ward, 1996), 166.

6. Postmodernist philosopher Emmanual Levinas follows this strand of thinking in his emphasis that we risk participation (over observation) when we encounter our neighbor. Only in true encounter can we find *"the trace of God,"* and this encounter originates in the spirit of love (see Emmanuel Levinas, "Meaning and Sense" in *Emmanuel Levinas, Basic Philosophical Writings*, ed. Adriaan T. Peperzak, Simon Critchley, Robert Bernasconi (Bloomington: Indiana University Press, 1996), 64.

7. Ibid., 169.

8. *TL* 1, 111.

9. Denise Levertov, "On Belief in the Physical Resurrection of Jesus," in *The Stream and the Sapphire: Selected Poems on Religious Themes* (New York: New Directions, 1997), 79–80.

Bibliography

BALTHASAR—PRIMARY SOURCES

Balthasar, Hans Urs von. *Patristik, Scholastik und wir: theologie der Zeit*. Ensiedeln: Johannes Verlag, 1939.
Martin Buber and Christianity: A Dialogue Between Israel and the Church. Translated by Alexander Dru. London: Harvill Press, 1961.
A Theological Anthropology. Translated by Franz Benziger. New York: Sheed & Ward, 1963.
"Conversion in the New Testament." *Communio* 1 (September 1974): 54–87.
Seeing the Form. Vol. 1, *The Glory of the Lord*. Edited by Joseph Fessio. Translated by Erasmo Leiva-Merikakis. San Francisco: Ignatius Press, 1983.
Studies in Theological Style: Lay Styles. Vol. 3, *The Glory of the Lord: A Theological Aesthetics*. Edited by John Riches. Translated by Andrew Louth, John Saward, Martin Simon, and Rowan Williams. San Francisco: Ignatius Press, 1984.
Studies in Theological Style: Clerical Styles. Vol. 2, *The Glory of the Lord: A Theological Aesthetics*. Edited by John Riches. Translated by Andrew Louth, Francis McDonough, and Brian McNeil. San Francisco: Ignatius Press, 1984.
"On the Concept of the Person." *Communio* 13 (Spring, 1986): 18–26.
Prayer. Translated by Graham Harrison. San Francisco: Ignatius Press, 1987.
Dare We Hope That All Men Might Be Saved? Translated by David Kipp and Lothar Krauth. San Francisco: Ignatius Press, 1988.
My Work: A Retrospective. San Francisco: Ignatius Press, 1988.
Presence and Thought. Translated by Marc Sebanc. San Francisco: Ignatius Press, 1988.
Prolegomena. Vol. 1, *Theo-Drama, Theological Dramatic Theory*. Translated by Graham Harrison. San Francisco: Ignatius Press, 1988.
Test Everything. Hold Fast to Everything That Is Good. Translated by Maria Shrady. San Francisco: Ignatius Press, 1989.

The Dramatis Personae: Man in God. Vol. 2, *Theo-Drama, Theological Dramatic Theory.* Translated by Graham Harrison. San Francisco: Ignatius Press, 1990.

Mysterium Paschale: The Mystery of Easter. Translated by Aidan Nichols. Edinburgh: T & T Clark, 1990.

Truth Is Symphonic: Aspects of Christian Pluralism. Translated by Graham Harrison. San Francisco: Ignatius Press, 1990.

The Dramatis Personae: The Person in Christ. Vol. 3, *Theo-Drama, Theological Dramatic Theory.* Translated by Graham Harrison. San Francisco: Ignatius Press, 1992.

The Action. Vol. 4, *Theo-Drama, Theological Dramatic Theory.* Translated by Graham Harrison. San Francisco: Ignatius Press, 1994.

A Theology of History. Translated by Graham Harrison. San Francisco: Ignatius Press, 1994.

Bernanos: An Ecclesial Existence. Translated by Erasmo Leiva-Merikakis. San Francisco: Ignatius Press, 1996.

The Last Act. Vol. 5, *Theo-Drama, Theological Dramatic Theory.* Translated by Graham Harrison. San Francisco: Ignatius Press, 1998.

The Truth of the World. Vol. 1, *Theo-logic.* Translated by Adrian J. Walker. San Francisco, Ignatius Press, 2002.

Cosmic Liturgy: The Universe According to Maximus the Confessor. Translated by Brian E. Daley. San Francisco: Ignatius Press, 2003.

Love Alone Is Credible: The Way of Revelation. Translated by D. C. Schindler. San Francisco: Ignatius Press, 2004.

BALTHASAR—SECONDARY SOURCES

Dalzell, Thomas. *The Dramatic Encounter of Divine and Human Freedom in the Theology of Hans Urs von Balthasar.* Berlin: Peter Lang, 1997.

————. "The Lack of Social Drama in Balthasar's Theological Dramatics." *Theological Studies* 60 (September 1999): 3–27.

Dupre, Louis. "Hans Urs von Balthasar's Theology of Aesthetic Form." *Theological Studies* 49 (June 1988): 299–318.

Field, Stephen. "Balthasar and Rahner on the Spiritual Senses." *Theological Studies* 57 (June 1996): 224–41.

Gardner, Lucy, ed. *Balthasar at the End of Modernity.* Edinburgh: T & T Clark, 1999.

Gawronski, Raymond. *Word and Silence: Hans Urs von Balthasar and the Spiritual Encounter Between East and West.* Grand Rapids, MI: Wm. Eerdmans, 1995.

Laak, Walter vaan. *Allversöhnung: Die Lehre von der Apoksatasis. Ihre Grundlegung durch Origenes und ihre Bewertung in der gegenwärtigenTheologie bei Karl Barth und Hans Urs von Balthasar.* Sinzig, 1990.

Nichols, Aidan. *No Bloodless Myth: A Guide through Balthasar's Dramatics.* New York: Catholic University of America Press, 2000.

————. *Say It Is Pentecost: A Guide through Balthasar's Logic.* New York: Catholic University of America Press, 2001.

————. *The Word Has Been Abroad: A Guide through Balthsar's Aesthetics.* New York: Catholic University of America Press, 1998.

O'Donnell, John. *Hans Urs von Balthasar.* Collegeville, MN: Liturgical Press, 1992.

O'Hanlon, Gerald. *The Immutability of God in the Theology of Hans Urs von Balthasar.* Cambridge: Cambridge University Press, 1990.

Oakes, Edward. *Pattern of Redemption: The Theology of Hans Urs von Balthasar.* New York: Continuum, 1994, 1997.

Scheck, Christopher. *The Ethical Thought of Hans Urs von Balthasar*. New York: Crossroads, 2001.

Schindler, David (ed.) *Hans Urs von Balthasar: His Life and Work*, David Schindler (ed), (San Francisco: Ignatius Press, 1991.

———. *Heart of the World, Center of the Church*: Communio, *Ecclesiology, Liberalism, and Liberation*. Edinburgh: T & T Clark, 1996.

Stinglehammer, Hermann. *Freiheit in der Hingabe. Trinitarische Freiheitslehre bei Hans Urs von Balthasar. Ein Beitrag zur Rezeption der Theodramatik*. Dissertation, Passau: Theologische Fakultat, 1995.

Williams, Rowan. "Balthasar and Rahner." In *The Analogy of Beauty*, edited by John Riches, 93–115. Edinburgh: T & T Clark, 1986:

———. "Balthasar and the Trinity." In *A Cambridge Companion to Hans Urs von Balthasar*, edited by Edward T. Oakes and David Moss, 42–50. Cambridge: Cambridge University Press, 2004.

THEOLOGICAL AND RELIGIOUS AESTHETICS

Bednar, Gerald. *Faith as Imagination: The Contribution of William F. Lynch S.J.* Kansas City: Sheed & Ward, 1996.

Begbie, Jeremy. *Voicing Creation's Praise: Towards a Theology of the Arts*. Edinburgh: T & T Clark, 1991.

Benjamin, Walter. *Illuminations*. Edited and introduced by Hannah Arendt. New York: Schocken, 1969.

Brown, Frank Burch. *Religious Aesthetics: A Theological Study of Making and Meaning*. Princeton: Princeton University Press, 1989.

———. *Transfiguration: Poetic Metaphor and the Languages of Religious Belief*. Chapel Hill: University of North Carolina Press, 1983.

Dillenberger, John. *A Theology of Artistic Sensibilities: Visual Arts and the Church*. New York: Crossroad, 1986.

Dupre, Louis. *Symbols of the Sacred*. New York: Eerdmans, 1999.

Eco, Umberto. *Art and Beauty in the Middle Ages*. Translated by Hugh Bredin. New Haven, CT: Yale University Press, 1986.

Ferretter, Luke. *Towards a Christian Literary Theory*. New York: Palgrave McMillan, 2003.

Garcia-Rivera, Alejandro. *The Community of the Beautiful*. Collegeville, MN: The Liturgical Press, 1999.

———. *A Wounded Innocence: Sketches for a Theology of Art*. Collegeville, MN: The Liturgical Press, 2003.

Gilson, Etienne. *The Arts of the Beautiful*. New York: Scribner's, 1965.

———. *Forms and Substances in the Arts*. Translated by Salvator Attanasio. New York: Scribner's, 1964.

Gunn, Giles. *The Interpretation of Otherness: Literature, Religion, and the American Imagination*. New York: Oxford University Press, 1979.

Hofstadter, Albert, and Richard Kuhns, eds. *Philosophies of Art and Beauty*. Chicago: University of Chicago Press, 1964.

Ingarden, Roman. *Selected Papers in Aesthetics*. Edited by Peter J. McCormick. Munich: Philosophia Verlag; Washington, DC: Catholic University Press, 1985.

John Paul II. "Letter to Artists." *Origins* 28, no. 49 (1999): 786–93.

Levine, George, ed. *Aesthetics and Ideology*. New Brunswick, NJ: Rutgers University Press, 1994.

Maritain, Jacques. *Approaches to God.* Translated by Peter O'Reilly. New York: Collier, 1954.
———. *Art and Scholasticism and Other Essays.* Translated by J. F. Scanlon. New York: Sheed & Ward, 1943.
———. *Creative Intuition in Art and Poetry.* Bollingen Series 35. New York: Sheed & Ward, 1960.
———. *A Preface to Metaphysics.* New York: New American Library, 1962 (chapters 1–3).
———. *The Range of Reason.* New York: Charles Scribner, 1942, 1952.
Nichols, Aidan. *The Art of God Incarnate: Theology and Image in the Christian Tradition.* London: Darton, Longman, and Todd, 1980.
Santayana, George. *The Sense of Beauty: Being the Outline of Aesthetic Theory.* New York: Dover, 1955.
Scarry, Elaine. *On Beauty and Being Just.* Princeton: Princeton University Press, 1999.
Tillich, Paul. *On Art and Architecture.* Edited by John Dillenberger and Jane Dillenberger. New York: Crossroad, 1987.
———. *Theology of Culture.* New York: Oxford University Press, 1959.
Viladesau, Richard. *Theological Aesthetics: God in Imagination, Beauty, and Art.* New York: Oxford University Press, 1999.
———. *Theology and the Arts: Encountering God through Music, Art, and Rhetoric.* New York: Paulist Press, 2000.

THEOLOGY AND LITERATURE

Daly, Gabriel. *Transcendence and Immanence: A Study of Catholic Modernism and Integralism.* Oxford: Oxford University Press, 1980.
Donoghue, Denis, *Adam's Curse: Reflections on Religion and Literature.* Notre Dame: University of Notre Dame Press, 2001.
———. "The Analogical Imagination after *Christ and Apollo.*" *Religion and Literature* 32 (Autumn 2000): 1–22.
Fiddes, Paul. *Freedom and Limit: The Dialogue between Literature and Christian Doctrine.* Macon: Mercer University Press, 1999.
———. *The Promised End: Eschatology in Theology and Literature.* London: Blackwell, 2000.
Lodge, David. *Consciousness and the Novel: Connected Essays.* Cambridge: Harvard University Press, 2002.
Lynch, William. *Christ and Apollo: The Dimensions of the Literary Imagination.* New York: Mentor-Omega, 1963.
———. *Christ and Prometheus: A New Image of the Secular.* Notre Dame: University of Notre Dame Press, 1970.
———. *Images of Faith: An Exploration of the Ironic Imagination.* Notre Dame: University of Notre Dame Press, 1973.
———. "Theology and the Imagination." *Thought* 29 (Spring 1954): 61–86.
———. "Theology and the Imagination III: The Problem of Comedy." *Thought* 30 (Spring 1955): 24–44.
Mallard, William. *The Reflection of Theology in Literature: A Case Study in Theology and Culture.* San Antonio: Trinity University Press, 1977.
Marcel, Gabriel. "On the Ontological Mystery." In *The Philosophy of Existentialism.* Translated by Manya Harari, 9–56. New York: Citadel Press, 1956.
Murphy, Francesca Aran. *Christ, the Form of Beauty: A Study of Theology and Literature.* Edinburgh: T & T Clark, 1995.

Nussbaum, Martha. *Love's Knowledge: Essays on Philosophy and Literature*. New York: Oxford University Press, 1990.

Percy, Walker. *The Message in the Bottle: How Queer Man Is, How Queer Language Is, and What One Has to Do with the Other*. New York: Farrar, Straus, and Giroux, 1975.

———. *Signposts in a Strange Land*. New York: Picador, 2000.

Scott, Nathan. *The New Orpheus: Essays toward a Christian Poetic*. New York: Sheed & Ward, 1964.

Tate, Allen. *A Man of Letters in the Modern World*. New York: Meridian, 1955.

NARRATIVE ART—PRIMARY: LITERATURE AND POETRY

Dillard, Annie. "Holy the Firm." In *The Annie Dillard Reader*, 425–54. New York: HarperCollins, 1994.

———. "A Pilgrim at Tinker Creek." In *The Annie Dillard Reader*, 279–323. New York: HarperCollins, 1994.

———. *For the Time Being*. New York: Vintage, 1999.

Dubus, Andre. *Meditations from a Moveable Chair*. New York: Vintage, 1998.

———. "Sacraments." In *Signatures of Grace*, edited by Thomas Grady and Paula Huston. New York: Plume, 2001.

Everson, William (Brother Antoninus). *Dark God of Eros: A William Everson Reader*. Introduced and edited by Albert Gelpi. Santa Clara/Berkeley: SCU Press/Heyday Books, 2003.

———. *The Excesses of God*. Stanford, CA: Stanford University Press, 1988.

———. *The Veritable Years, 1949–1966*. Santa Rosa, CA: Black Sparrow Press, 1978.

Hansen, Ron. *Atticus*. New York: HarperCollins, 1996.

———. *Mariette in Ecstasy*. New York: HarperCollins, 1991.

Kerouac, Jack. *Dr. Sax*. New York: Grove Press, 1959.

———. *Visions of Gerard*. New York: Farrar, Straus, and Giroux, 1963.

L'Heureux, John. "The Anatomy of Desire." In *Fiction and Horizon*, edited by John May, 784–89. New York: Houghton and Mifflin, 1991.

———. *The Shrine at Altamira*. New York: Grove Press, 1992.

Levertov, Denise. "Dying and Living." In *Light Up the Cave*, 98–114. New York: New Directions, 1981.

———. "Rilke as Mentor." In *Light Up the Cav*, 283–90. New York: New Directions, 1981.

———. *The Stream and the Sapphire: Selected Poems on Religious Themes*. New York: New Directions, 1981.

Lodge, David. *Paradise News*. New York: Penguin, 1993.

———. *Souls and Bodies*. New York: Penguin, 1990.

———. *Therapy*. New York: Penguin, 1995.

———. *Thinks*. New York: Penguin, 2002

McCarthy, Cormac. *Blood Meridian*. New York: Vintage, 1992.

———. *The Crossing*. New York: Knopf, 1994.

O'Connor, Flannery. *Collected Works*. New York: Library of America, 1988.

———. *The Habit of Being*. New York: Farrar, Straus, and Giroux, 1978.

———. *Mystery and Manners: Occasional Prose*. Edited by Sally Fitzgerald. London: Faber and Faber, 1972.

Percy, Walker. *Lancelot*. New York: Farrar, Straus and Giroux, 1977.

———. *Lost in the Cosmos: The Last Self-Help Book*. New York: Farrar, Straus and Giroux, 1983.

———. *Love in the Ruins: The Adventures of a Bad Catholic at a Time Near the End of the World*. New York: Farrar, Straus and Giroux, 1971.

———. *The Moviegoer*. New York: Knopf, 1961.

———. *The Thanatos Syndrome*. New York: FSG, 1987.

Powers, J. F. *Morte D'Urban*. Garden City, NY: Doubleday, 1962.

———. *The Prince of Darkness and Other Stories*. Garden City, NY: Doubleday, 1951.

Tate, Allen. *Collected Poems*. New York: Farrar, Straus and Giroux, 1977.

Toole, John Kennedy. *A Confederacy of Dunces*. New York: Wings Books, 1980.

Wolff, Tobias. "In the Garden of the North American Martyrs." In *In the Garden of the North American Martyrs*, 123–35. Hopewell, NJ: Ecco Press, 1981.

Wolff, Tobias. "The Liar." In *In the Garden of the North American Martyrs*, 155–75. Hopewell, NJ: Ecco Press, 1981.

Wolff, Tobias. "Worldly Goods." In *In the Garden of the North American Martyrs*, 101–16. Hopewell, NJ: Ecco Press, 1981.

NARRATIVE ART—PRIMARY: FILM

Anderson, Wes. *Rushmore* (USA). 1998.

Kieslowski, Krzysztof. *Decalogue: One* (TV) (USA). 1988.

Trier, Lars von. *Breaking the Waves* (Denmark/Sweden/France/Holland/Norway). 1996.

———. *Dancer in the Dark* (Denmark/France/USA). 2000.

———. *The Idiots* (Denmark). 1998.

NARRATIVE ART—SECONDARY: SELECTED LITERARY
CRITICISM AND COMMENTARY

Asals, Frederick. *Flannery O'Connor: The Imagination of Extremity*. Athens: University of Georgia Press, 1982.

Baumgaertner, Jill P. *Flannery O'Connor: A Proper Scaring*. Wheaton, IL: Harold Shaw Publishers, 1988.

Broughton, Panthea. *The Art of Walker Percy: Strategems of Being*. New Orleans, LA: Louisiana State University Press, 1979.

Davidson, Donald, and Allen Tate. *The Literary Correspondence of Donald Davidson and Allen Tate*. Edited by John Tyree Fain and Thomas Daniel Young. Athens: University of Georgia Press, 1974.

Desmond, John. *Risen Sons: Flannery O'Connor's Vision of History*. Athens: University of Georgia Press, 1987.

Foote, Shelby and Walker Percy. *The Correspondence of Shelby Foote and Walker Percy*. New York: W. W. Norton and Co., 1998.

Frye, Northrop. *Anatomy of Criticism*. Princeton: Princeton University Press, 1971.

Giannone, Richard. *Flannery O'Connor and the Mystery of Love*. Urbana: University of Illinois Press, 1989.

Gordon, Sarah. *Flannery O'Connor: The Obedient Imagination*. Athens: University of Georgia Press, 2000.

Kilcourse, George. *Flannery O'Connor's Religious Imagination: A World with Everything off Balance*. New York: Paulist Press, 2001.

Kinney, Arthur. *Flannery O'Connor's Library: Resources of Being*. Athens: University of Georgia Press, 1985.

Kobre, Michael. *Walker Percy's Voices*. Athens: University of Georgia Press, 2000.

Lawson, Lewis et al., eds. *Conversations with Walker Percy*. Jackson: University of Mississippi Press, 1985.

Lodge, David. *Consciousness and the Novel: Connected Essays*. Cambridge, MA: Harvard University Press, 2002.

Mayer, David. *Drooping Sun, Coy Moon: Essays on Flannery O'Connor*. Kyoto: Yamaguchi Publishing House, 1995.

McMullen, Joanne Halleran. *Writing against God: Language as Message in the Literature of Flannery O'Connor*. Macon, GA: Mercer University Press, 1996.

Muller, Gilbert H. *Nightmares and Visions: Flannery O'Connor and the Catholic Grotesque*. Athens: University of Georgia Press, 1972.

Pridgen, Allen. *Walker Percy's Sacramental Landscapes: A Search in the Desert*. New York: Susquehanna University Press, 2000.

Quinlan, Kieran. *Walker Percy: The Last Catholic*. New Orleans: Louisiana State University Press, 1998.

Ragen, Brian Abel. *A Wreck on the Road to Damascus: Innocence, Guilt, and Conversion in Flannery O'Connor*. Chicago: Loyola University Press, 1989.

Rath, Sura. "Ruby Turpin's Redemption: Thomistic Resolution in Flannery O'Connor's *Revelation*." *Flannery O'Connor Bulletin* 19 (1990): 1–8.

Tolson, Jay. *A Pilgrim in the Ruins*. Chapel Hill: University of North Carolina Press, 2000.

NARRATIVE ART—SECONDARY: FILM STUDIES

Blake, Richard A. *Afterimage: The Indelible Catholic Imagination of Six American Filmmakers*. Chicago: Loyola University Press, 2000.

Chattaway, Peter. "Jesus in the Movies." *Bible Review* (February 1998): 29–46.

Cunningham, David S. *Reading Is Believing: The Christian Faith through Literature and Film*. Grand Rapids, MI: Brazos, 2002.

Fraser, Peter. *Images of the Passion: The Sacramental Mode in Film*. Westport, CT: Praeger Publishers, 1998.

Johnston, Robert K. *Reel Spirituality: Theology and Film in Dialogue*. Grand Rapids, MI: Baker Book House, 2000.

Loughlin, Gerald. "Seeing in the Dark: Plato's Cinema and Christ's Cave." *Studies in Christian Ethics* 13, no. 1 (2000): 33–48.

Lumholdt, Jan, ed. *Lars von Trier*. Biloxi: University of Mississippi Press, 2003.

Martin, Thomas M. *Images and the Imageless: A Study in Religious Consciousness and Film*. Lewisburg, PA: Bucknell University Press; London: Associated University Presses, 1981.

May, John R., ed. *New Image of Religious Film*. Kansas City, MO: Sheed & Ward, 1997.

———. *Nourishing Faith through Fiction: Reflections of the Apostles' Creed in Literature and Film*. Kansas City, MO: Sheed & Ward, 2002.

Miles, Margaret R. *Seeing and Believing: Religion and Values in the Movies*. Beacon Press, 1996.

Stone, Bryan P. *Faith and Film: Theological Themes at the Cinema*. St. Louis, MO: Chalice Press, 2000.

Tatum, W. Barnes. *Jesus at the Movies: A Guide to the First Hundred Years*. Santa Rosa, CA: Polebridge Press, 1997.

Trier, Lars von. *Breaking the Waves*. London: Faber, 1996.

NARRATIVE ART—SECONDARY: THE CATHOLIC IMAGINATION

Allitt, Patrick. *Catholic Converts: British and American Intellectuals Turn to Rome*. Ithaca, NY: Cornell University Press, 1997.

Gandolfo, Anita. *Testing the Faith: The New Catholic Fiction in America*. New York: Greenwood Press, 1992.

Giles, Paul. *American Catholic Arts and Fictions: Culture, Ideology, and Aesthetics*. Cambridge: Cambridge University Press, 1992.

Greeley, Andrew. *The Catholic Imagination*. Berkeley: University of California Press, 2000.

Green, Garret. *Imagining God: Theology and the Religious Imagination*. San Francisco: Harper & Row, 1989.

Groome, Thomas. *The Catholic Imagination: Eight Gifts for Life*. San Francisco: Harper, 2002.

Hanson, Ellis. *Decadence and Catholicism*. Cambridge: Harvard University Press, 1997.

Heartney, Eleanor. *Postmodern Heretics: The Catholic Imagination in Contemporary Art*. New York: Middlemarch, 2004.

Labrie, Ross. *The Catholic Imagination in American Literature*. Columbia: University of Missouri Press, 1997.

Sparr, Arnold. *To Promote, Defend, and Redeem: The Catholic Literary Revival and the Cultural Transformation of American Catholicism*. Westport, CT: Greenwood Press, 1990.

Wood, Ralph. *The Comedy of Redemption: Christian Faith and Four American Novelists*. Notre Dame: University of Notre Dame Press, 1988.

OTHER SOURCES

Baudrillard, Jean, *The Transparency of Evil: Essays on Extreme Phenomena*. Translated by James Benedict. London: Verso, 1992.

Bernanos, Georges. *The Heroic Face of Innocence*. Edinburgh: T & T Clark, 1999.

Blondel, Maurice. *Letter on Aplogetics and History and Dogma*. Translated by Alexander Dru. London: Harvill Press, 1964.

Buber, Martin. *I and Thou*. Translated by W. Kaufman. New York: Scribner, 1970.

———. *On Judaism*. Edited by Nahom Glatzer. New York: Schocken, 1967.

Bull, Malcolm, ed. *Apocalypse Theory and the Ends of the World*. Oxford: Blackwell, 1995.

Butler, Judith. *The Psychic Life of Power*. Stanford: Stanford University Press, 1997.

Caputo, John. *The Prayers and Tears of Jacques Derrida: Religion without Religion*. Bloomington: Indiana University Press, 1997.

Certeau, Michel de. "The Gaze: Nicholas of Cusa." Translated by Catherine Porter. *Diacritics* (Fall 1987): 2–38.

———. "How Is Christianity Thinkable Today?" In *The Postmodern God*, edited by Graham Ward. Oxford: Blackwell, 1997.

———. *The Practice of Everyday Life*. Translated by Steven Rendall. Berkeley: University of California Press, 1984.

Chesterton, Gilbert Keith. *The Everlasting Man*. San Francisco: Ignatius Press, 1993.

———. *Orthodoxy*. San Francisco: Ignatius Press, 1995.

Congar, Yves. *I Believe in the Holy Spirit III: The River of Life Flows in the East and the West*. Translated by David Smith. Londin: Geoffrey Chapman, 1983.

Danielou, Jean. *L'Etre et le Temps Chez Gregoire de Nyse*. Leiden: Brill, 1970.

Delp, Mark. *On the Concept of Motion According to Pseudo-Dionysius.* Master's thesis, Graduate Theological Union, 1989.

Deleuze, Gilles. *Difference et Repetition.* Paris: Presses Universitaires de France, 1972.

Derrida, Jacques. *The Gift of Death.* Translated by David Wills. Chicago: University of Chicago Press, 1995.

————. *Of Grammatology.* Translated by C. G. Spivak. Baltimore, MD: Johns Hopkins University Press, 1982.

————. *On the Name.* Edited by Thomas Dutoit. Stanford: Stanford University Press, 1995.

————. "Violence and Metaphysics: An Essay on the Thought of Emmanuel Levinas." In *Writing and Difference,* translated and introduction by Alan Bass. London: Routledge and Kegan Paul, 1978.

————. *Writing and Difference.* Translated by Alan Bass. Chicago: University of Chicago Press, 1978.

Fiddes, Paul. *The Creative Suffering of God.* Oxford: Clarendon Press, 1992.

Foucault, Michel. *Power/Knowledge: Selected Interviews and Other Writings, 1972–1977.* Edited by Colin Gordon. New York: Pantheon Books, 1980.

Garcia-Rivera, Alejandro. "Creator of the Visible and Invisible: Liberation Theology, Postmodernism, and the Spiritual." *JHLT* 3, no. 4 (1996): 33–48.

Gelpi, Donald. *Peirce and Theology, Essays on the Authentication of Doctrine.* Lanham, MD: University Press of America, 2001.

Girard, René. "Eating Disorders and Mimetic Desire." *Contagion: Journal of Violence, Mimesis, and Culture* 3 (Spring 1996): 1–17.

————. *I See Satan Fall Like Lightening.* Maryknoll, NY: Orbis Press, 2001.

————. *Things Hidden Since the Foundation of the World.* Stanford: Stanford University Press, 1987.

Guardini, Romano. *The World and the Person.* Translated by Stella Lange. Chicago: Henry Regnery, 1965.

Heidegger Martin. *Being and Time.* Translated by John Macquarrie and Edward Robinson. New York: Harper & Row, 1962.

Herberg, Will. *Four Existentialist Theologians. A Reader from the Works of Jacques Maritain, Nicolas Berdyaev, Martin Buber and Paul Tillich.* Garden City, NY: Doubleday, 1958.

Ignatius of Loyola. *The Spiritual Exercises of Ignatius of Loyola.* Translated by Louis Puhl. Chicago: Loyola University Press, 1993.

Kant, Immanuel. *The Critique of Judgment.* Translated by J. C. Meredith. Oxford: Clarendon Press, 1928, 1988.

————. *The Critique of Pure Reason.* Translated by J. Meiklejohn. London: Dent, 1934, 1988.

————. *Religion within the Limits of Reason Alone.* Translated by Theodore M. Green and Hoyt H. Hudson. New York: Harper, 1934, 1960.

Kierkegaard, Soren. *Concluding Unscientific Postscript.* Translated by David F. Swenson and Walter Lowrie. Princeton, NJ: Princeton University Press, 1941.

————. *Either/Or.* Translated by Howard V. Hong. Princeton: Princeton University Press, 1988.

————. *Fear and Trembling/Repetition.* Translated by Howard V. Hong. Princeton: Princeton University Press, 1986.

Knox, John. "A Vindication of the Doctrine That the Sacrifice of the Mass Is Idolatry" (1550). Available: http://www.swrb.com/newslett/actualNLs/vindicat.htm.

Kristeva, Julia. "In the Beginning Was Love." In *The Postmodern God*, edited by Graham Ward, 223–232. Oxford: Blackwell, 1997.

———. "Reading the Bible." In *New Maladies of the Soul*, translated by Ross Guberman. New York: Columbia University Press, 1995.

Lash, Nicholas. *Easter in Ordinary: Reflections on Human Experience and the Knowledge of God*. London: SCM, 1988.

Leiva-Merikakis, Erasmo. *Love's Sacred Order*. San Francisco: Ignatius Press, 2000.

Levinas, Emmanuel. *Autrement qe'etre ou au del'essence*. The Hague: Martinis Niijhoff, 1974.

———. "The Trace of the Other." In *Deconstruction in Context*, edited by Mark C. Taylor, translated by Alphonso Lingis. Chicago: University of Chicago Press, 1986.

Lubac, Henri de. *Catholicism: A Study in Dogma in Relation to the Corporate Destiny of Mankind*. New York: Sheed & Ward, 1964.

———. *The Drama of Atheist Humanism*. San Francisco: Ignatius Press, 1995.

———. "Duplex hominis beatitude." *Recherches de science religieuse* 35 (1948): 290–99.

———. *The Motherhood of the Church*. San Francisco: Ignatius Press, 1986.

Lundin, Roger, et al. *The Promise of Hermeneutics*. New York: Eerdmans, 1999.

Lyotard, Jean-Francois. *The Post-Modern Condition: A Report on Knowledge*. Translated by Geoff Bennington and Brian Massumi. Manchester: Manchester University Press, 1989.

Milbank, John. *Theology and Social Theory: Beyond Secular Reason*. Oxford: Blackwell, 1998.

Milosz, Czeslaw. *To Begin Where I Am*. New York: Farrar, Straus and Giroux. 2001.

———. *The New American Bible*. New York: The Confraternity of Christian Doctrine, 1986.

Pickstock, Catherine. *After Writing: On the Liturgical Consummation of Philosophy*. Oxford: Blackwell, 1998.

Psuedo-Dionysius (Denys). *The Divine Names, the Mystical, Ecclesiastical, and Celestial Hierarchies* in *Pseudo-Dionysius: The Complete Works*, Edited by John Farina. Translated by Colm Lubheid. Classics of Western Spirituality. New York: Paulist Press, 1987.

Rahner, Karl. "Experience of Self and Experience of God." In *Karl Rahner: Theologian of the Graced Search for Meaning*, 172–83. Edited by Geffrey Kelly. Minneapolis: Augsburg Press: 1997.

———. "Nature and Grace". In *Karl Rahner: Theologian of the Graced Search for Meaning*, 96–110. Edited by Geffrey Kelly. Minneapolis: Augsburg Press: 1997.

Rousselot, Pierre. *The Intellctualism of St. Thomas*. Translated by James O'Mahoney. New York: Sheed & Ward, 1935.

Schwartz, Stuart. *Implicit Understandings: Observing, Reporting, and Reflecting on the Encounters between Europeans and Other Peoples in the Early Modern Era*. Cambridge: Cambridge University Press, 1994.

Spohn, William. *Go and Do Likewise: Jesus and Ethics*. New York: Continuum, 1999.

Steiner, George. *Language and Silence*. New York: Atheneum. 1967.

———. *Real Presences*. Chicago: The University of Chicago Press, 1989.

Stiver, Dan. *The Philosophy of Religious Language*. Oxford, Blackwell, 1996.

Tracy, David. *The Analogical Imagination: Christian Theology and the Culture of Pluralism*. New York: Crossroad, 1981.

———. *Plurality and Ambiguity: Hermeneutics, Religion, Hope*. Chicago: University of Chicago Press, 1994.

Ward, Graham. *Barth, Derrida, and the Language of Theology*. Cambridge: Cambridge University Press, 1995.

————, ed. *Michel de Certeau S.J. New Blackfriars* 77, no. 909 (1996): 518–28.

————, ed. *The Postmodern God*. Oxford: Blackwell, 1997.

————. *Theology and Contemporary Critical Theory*. New York: St. Martin's Press, 1996.

Watt, Ian. *The Rise of the Novel*. Berkeley: University of California Press, 1957.

Wyschograd, Edith. *Saints and Postmodernism: Revisioning Moral Philosophy*. Chicago: University of Chicago Press. 1990.

Index